SMALL SPACE, BIG HARVEST

Turn Your Small Garden into a Vegetable Garden—Naturally!

Duane Newcomb

Prima Publishing
P.O. Box 1260BK
Rocklin, CA 95677
(916) 786-0426

Book design by Patricia Pennington
Illustrations by John Carlance
Cover design by The Dunlavey Studio, Sacramento
Cover illustration by Zhee Singer

This edition is reprinted by permission of Rodale Press.

Library of Congress Cataloging-in-Publication Data
Newcomb, Duane G.
   Small space, big harvest : turn your small garden into a
vegetable factory—naturally! / Duane Newcomb.
     p. cm.
   Includes index.
   ISBN 1-55958-289-8 : $14.95
   1. Vegetable gardening. 2. Organic gardening. I. Title.
SB324.3.N495 1993
635′.0484—dc20   92-39921
                                 CIP

93 94 95 96 97 RRD 10 9 8 7 6 5 4 3 2 1
Printed in the United States of America

How to Order:
Quantity discounts are available from Prima Publishing, P.O. Box
1260BK, Rocklin, CA 95677; telephone (916) 786-0426. On your letter-
head include information concerning the intended use of the books and
the number of books you wish to purchase.

CONTENTS

INTRODUCTION

WELCOME TO THE VEGETABLE FACTORY

GARDENING IS IN FASHION. More than 40 million households have vegetable gardens, producing over $18 billion worth of food a year. Somewhere in those figures is a new and different type of gardener, a different type of garden, and a taste for a different kind of vegetable.

Baby and gourmet vegetables are a new wrinkle. Both have begun to appear in such innovative restaurants as Alice Water's Chez Panisse in Berkeley and Lawrence Forgione's An American Place in New York. The craze has spread to specialty food markets, and now a number of seed companies offer good selections of both baby and gourmet crops.

There has also been a change in the vegetable garden itself. In some newer neighborhoods, gardens are so small that just ten years ago they wouldn't have been taken seriously. Gardeners then thought in terms of plots measuring 20 by 50 feet or larger, with vegetables planted single file in long rows. Now many of us live in attached houses and apartments, and tiny lots have become the norm. There also just may not be enough room—or time, in a double-income family— for a larger garden.

Luckily, today's gardens make more efficient use of space and time. Intensive gardening techniques, introduced in the 1960s, arrange vegetables across the beds, cutting the space needed. Properly handled, a 25-square-foot garden (only 5 feet by 5 feet) will produce a minimum of 200 pounds of vegetables. A 100-square-foot (10 by 10) garden can yield 1,000 pounds, or enough fresh vegetables during the growing season for a family of four.

And that's what this book is all about. It is a book for people who are short on time and space but still want to have a vegetable garden. It combines intensive gardening with some rather unconventional techniques to create a Vegetable Factory. One of these techniques is the use of dynamic plant groupings, which consist of key producer plants surrounded by secondary plantings. Planted together, these groupings create a postage-stamp–size, interactive vegetable community that outproduces most traditional gardens.

The Vegetable Factory concept uses "super soil" and spacing designed to allow the leaves to overlap at maturity. Constructed this way, a small garden grows fast, requires very little weeding, and is a lot less work than a conventional garden. And best of all, the backyard Vegetable Factory is fun.

Give it a try. I'm sure you'll be surprised at what you can produce. Welcome to the world of the backyard Vegetable Factory.

CHAPTER 1

PLANNING THE VEGETABLE FACTORY

IS IT POSSIBLE TO GROW ENOUGH vegetables in a small space to make the effort worthwhile? Yes—even the tiniest of urban backyards can produce significant crops of every vegetable.

The reason? Over the past several years, urban horticulturists and innovative home gardeners have come up with a number of techniques that double and triple the quantities of vegetables you can grow in a given space. As a result, we are in the midst of what might be called a garden revolution. A 5-by-5-foot garden can yield a couple of hundred tomatoes, 100 or so carrots, 40 or 50 beets, all the leaf lettuce you can eat, and a lot more.

VEGETABLE FACTORY PRINCIPLES

Before we go any further, let's look at just what makes a Vegetable Factory garden special. These features are covered in depth in Chapters 2 through 7.

Planting in intensive growing beds: Vegetable Factory growing beds are simply small areas in which to grow vegetables. The size of these beds allows you to use all available garden space by growing plants a few inches apart across the entire bed (intensive planting), using every inch of soil.

Depending on the crop, these beds can produce up to 30 times as many vegetables as a conventional garden. In addition, if you keep the beds the same size every year, they become easier to plan and plant each season.

Less initial preparation: The small size of these gardens makes soil preparation relatively easy. You can dig almost any Vegetable Factory garden by hand in 45 minutes or roto-till it in less than 10 minutes.

Less watering and weeding: When plants are mature, the leaves of the vegetables in Vegetable Factory gardens will overlap. This creates a microclimate below, shading the ground so that water does not evaporate as quickly as it does in a conventional garden. The water is held under the leaves in the form of humid air, and as a result, a Vegetable Factory bed needs only half the water more conventional gardens require. In addition, the overlapping leaves shade out most weeds.

Super soil: Vegetable Factory gardens use a special soil formula that incorporates massive amounts of organic materials and nutrients. This "super soil" will support tremendous growth.

Dynamic plant groupings: In a Vegetable Factory, key producer plants are surrounded by secondary and tertiary plantings. For example, a grouping could consist of one tomato combined with bush beans, peppers, onions, radishes, and carrots. Planted together, these groupings create a tiny vegetable community that outproduces most other gardens.

Season extension: You can more than double your production by extending the season a month or two in both spring and fall. The Vegetable Factory employs protective devices ranging from inexpensive plastic jugs to elaborate bed-wide greenhouses. In some areas, you can grow crops under cover all year long.

Full use of vertical space: Innovative supports allow you to take advantage of the unused space above the garden, to double or triple production of vine crops. On a per-foot basis, a plant growing upward greatly outyields one allowed to sprawl. Vegetable Factory gardeners think of their gardens in terms of three dimensions.

Container gardening: With a container, you can grow plants anywhere: Eggplant, Swiss chard, or tomatoes, in half whiskey barrels on a patio; cucumbers, lettuce, or tomatoes in wire baskets under the eaves; or an entire salad garden in paper-pulp pots on the steps. Container gardening is especially suited to apartment dwellers who don't have room for an in-ground garden. It also works well in combination with a conventional Vegetable Factory garden. A small bed of greens can be supplemented by a couple of containers of tomatoes on a patio, or you can grow vegetables in-ground and hang baskets of herbs from posts around the garden.

WHAT SHOULD YOU GROW?

What vegetables do you and your family like? It doesn't make any sense to plant Brussels sprouts if your family won't eat them. Pick varieties from the selection chart in Appendix D. Then make a list of those you intend to plant. You also might try growing your own gourmet and baby vegetables: baby beets, baby bok choy, baby corn, courgettes, haricots verts, and more. Make your selection from the checklists in Vegetable Wizardry and Special Gardens.

Consider growing a specialty garden. Salad-loving gardeners with limited space can concentrate on greens such as Bibb lettuce, pungent radicchio, French endive, spinach, the cresses, and red, green and Chinese cabbage. You might try baby lettuces, including 'Red Grenoblois', 'Lolo Rjosso', 'Little Gem', and 'Lolo Bianco'. Other specialties to consider are an oriental vegetable garden and an herb garden.

One Vegetable Factory rule is: Think small. Plan in terms of one or two of the larger plants: one cucumber, one tomato, one zucchini, and so forth: or 20 to 30 root and leafy plants such as beets, carrots, and spinach. The reason is that Vegetable Factory gardens are several times more productive per plant than conventional gardens. In addition, you should try to plant only the quantities you intend to use. See the table, How Much to Plant?, for recommended quantities to plant per person. Multiply these quantities by the number of people you intend to feed.

WHERE SHOULD YOUR GARDEN GROW?

Today, smaller lots can make it difficult to find a place for the garden. The house may take up most of the land, leaving only a shaded strip along the side and tiny

How Much to Plant?

Vegetable	Plants Per Person	Vegetable	Plants Per Person
Asparagus	20	Muskmelon	2
Bean, lima (bush)	1 or 2	Mustard	4 to 6
Bean, lima (pole)	1 or 2	Okra	1 or 2
Bean, snap (bush)	2 or 3	Onion	20 to 30
Bean, snap (pole)	1 or 2	Parsnip	15
Beet	10 to 20	Pea,	
Brussels sprouts	1	edible-podded	3 or 4
Cabbage	2	Pepper	1 or 2
Cabbage, Chinese	2 or 3	Potato	1 or 2
Cardoon	1	Pumpkin	1
Carrot	40 to 60	Radish	30 to 60
Cauliflower	8 to 12	Rutabaga	5 to 10
Celeriac	1	Salsify	3 to 10
Celery	2 or 3	Shallot	4 to 10
Collards	3 to 5	Spinach	3 to 6
Corn, sweet	4	Spinach, Malibar	5 to 10
Cucumber	1 or 2	Spinach,	5
Eggplant	1	New Zealand	
Florence fennel	1	Squash, summer	1
Garlic	3	Squash, winter	1 or 2
Horseradish	1 or 2	Sweet potato	2 or 3
Kale	2 to 4	Swiss chard	2
Kohlrabi	5 or 6	Tomato	1 or 2
Leek	6 to 10	Turnip	8 to 15
Lettuce, head	3 or 4	Watermelon	1
Lettuce, leaf	4		

patches of lawn and flowerbeds in the front and backyards. To grow a Vegetable Factory garden, you will need a 25-square-foot space (5 by 5 feet), *or* its equivalent scattered around a flowerbed, *or* enough room on a patio for at least three containers measuring 2 feet in diameter.

Look first at the backyard. Is there a spot in either corner against the fence? What about the side yards and the front yard? If you have a flowerbed, consider devoting a 5-foot section of it to vegetables, or even scattering the crops among the flowers. Make a sketch of your overall lot, and mark potential locations.

Here are other tips for locating your Vegetable Factory:

Consider planting several Vegetable Factory gardens instead of just one. Many gardeners find that although they lack the room for a regular garden, they have enough odd-shaped spaces around the yard to allow them to tuck in a few small gardens. You can plant all of these in mixed vegetables, or use one for a salad garden, one for gourmet vegetables, and so forth.

Locate your Vegetable Factory plots where they will not be shaded by buildings or trees if at all possible. Vegetables that produce "fruit," such as cucumbers, corn, eggplant, peppers, squash, and tomatoes, do best if they receive full sun for at least six to eight hours a day. The cool-season vegetables like beets, cabbage, carrots, chives, green onions, kale, leeks, lettuce, mustard, parsley, radishes, Swiss chard, and turnips, however, will perform nicely and even flourish in a location with some shade. (See the table on page 62).

If you do not have a space that receives even this much sun, you may be able to satisfy light requirements by reflecting light and heat into the garden. See Chapter 4, Protection from the Elements.

Keep your garden away from trees. They cast unwanted shade and compete for nutrients. Tree roots may take food from the soil in a circle as far out as the tree's branches, and plants within this circle often do poorly.

Avoid low wet areas. This applies to areas that are slow to dry in the spring, areas that have a serious weed problem (such as a heavy infestation of crabgrass), and steep slopes. If you garden on a slope, terrace the slope so that you are gardening on a flat surface.

Place your garden as close to a water supply as possible. This will save you a lot of time and trips back and forth during the gardening season.

Garden along a fence or against the side of a building when possible. Vine crops will then have a ready-made vertical support, which can double or triple your harvest.

SELECTING THE SHAPE

The best shape for a Vegetable Factory bed is square, since that shape can be fitted easily into the corner of a small yard or snugly up against a fence. Some irregularly shaped lots, however, may be better suited to a triangular bed. The size depends on how much you decide to grow and the available space. Consider beds between

5 and 10 feet square. Anything over 10 feet becomes difficult to squeeze into many of today's small yards.

Even at 5 or 10 feet square, you won't be able to reach all of the bed from the outside. Consider putting one or two stepping stones in the middle of the bed for easy access without taking up much space.

If you do not have at least 25 square feet of space, consider mixing vegetables in dynamic plant groupings in a flower bed. See Chapter 3, Planting the Vegetable Factory.

GARDENING ON PAPER

Always begin by putting your garden plan on paper. Some gardeners draw this plan to scale (for example, making ¼ inch equal 1 foot), which allows them to allocate space accurately. Others simply draw a rough sketch and go from there. I like to use graph paper, because it enables me to see at a glance how much space I have. With a 5-foot bed, I let each square equal 2 inches, and with 10-foot beds, 4 inches. Graphing allows you to easily plant in small groups; you can count the number of plants, or even seeds, that you are going to use. I have used a compass when planting in circles and also have drawn in irregular shapes.

Here are a few tips.

● Plant in dynamic plant groupings as explained in Chapter 3 (see the table on page 60). In general, major vegetables should be surrounded by secondary vegetables and intercropped plantings. Intercropping (or interplanting) consists of planting quick-maturing vegetables between those that mature more slowly. For instance, plant radishes in the same space in which you have transplanted tomatoes. Harvest the radishes four to five weeks before the tomato vines take over the space.

● Plant vines (cucumbers, melons, peas, squash) against a fence or support at the north end of your garden. This ensures that the smaller plants get enough sun each day and keeps them from being shaded out by the taller plants. Use smaller vertical supports within the interior of the garden. These can be planted with bush varieties of cucumbers, melons, and winter squash.

● Include herbs and flowers in every garden. These have been found by many gardeners to protect vegetables from a number of insect pests. Many gardeners believe, for instance, that borage attracts bees and repels tomato hornworms, that marigolds keep bean beetles away from snap beans and repel nematodes, and that garlic and chives repel aphids. Spot herbs and flowers among the vegetables where you have space.

● Plan several successive plantings of such vegetables as beans, lettuce, and radishes. This ensures a continued supply of these vegetables throughout the season.

● Don't place plants in a square grid pattern, but in semicircles, and tuck plants in here and there. Grid planting wastes space, as we'll see in Chapter 3.

● Put your major plants on paper first, using the garden zones discussed in Chapter 3. Start with the vine crops, which will grow up your major supports at one end (zone A). Place key producer plants such as cabbage, eggplant, and tomatoes in zone B. Follow up with the leaf and root crops in the remainder of zone B and in zone C.

● Make sure you space all major plants properly on your plan. Winter squash, for instance, requires 12 inches between plant centers. This means if you have a 5-by-5-foot garden, you can plant six squash across the north end to grow up the vertical support frame. Use a compass to draw a 12-inch circle around each plant. This defines the growing space needed for the squash (see the table on page 66). Do the same thing for the key producer plants. Finally, indicate on your plan where the secondary and tertiary vegetables will be located.

GARDEN PLAN 1

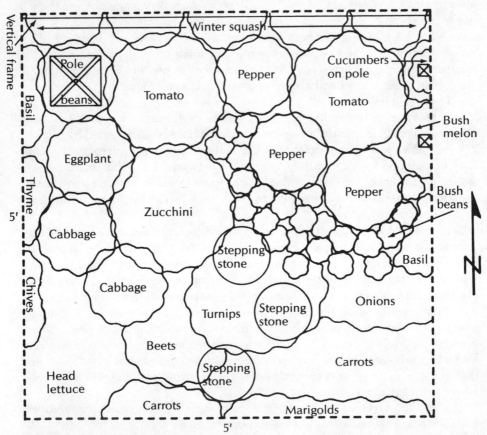

Plant peas before winter squash
Interplant radishes, green onions, leaf lettuce, fast-maturing turnips with the larger plants

Before planning your garden on paper, read the complete explanation of dynamic plant groupings and Vegetable Factory zones in Chapter 3, Planting the Vegetable Factory.

The garden plans on these and the following pages will help you get started.

What you now have is a sense of the basics. Some of these are age-old approaches. Others, such as intensive planting, vertical gardening, and season extending, are just beginning to come into popular use.

In the succeeding chapters, you will find detailed instructions and suggestions about each of these topics. All are meant to give you the greatest enjoyment— *and* the greatest harvest—from your Vegetable Factory garden.

GARDEN PLAN 2

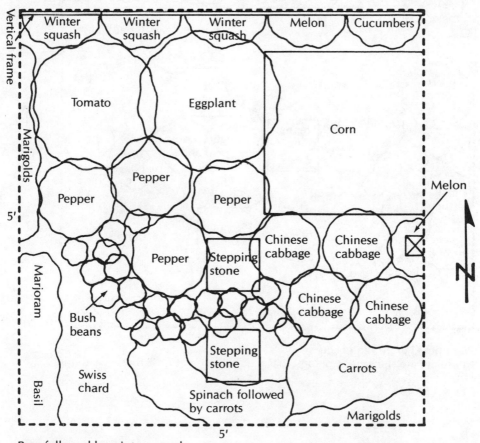

Peas followed by winter squash
Intercrop radishes, green onions, leaf lettuce, fast-maturing turnips with larger crops

GARDEN PLAN 3

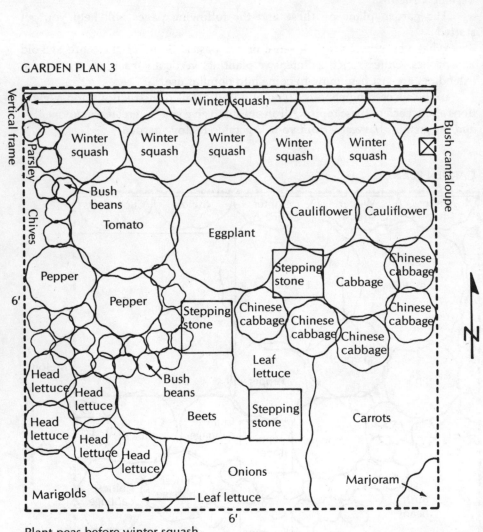

Plant peas before winter squash
Interplant radishes, green onions, leaf lettuce, fast-maturing turnips with the larger plants

GARDEN PLAN 4

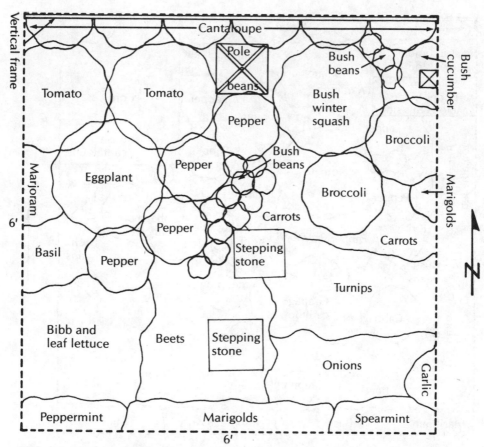

Plant peas before cantaloupe
Interplant radishes, green onions, leaf lettuce, fast-maturing turnips with the larger plants

GARDEN PLAN 5

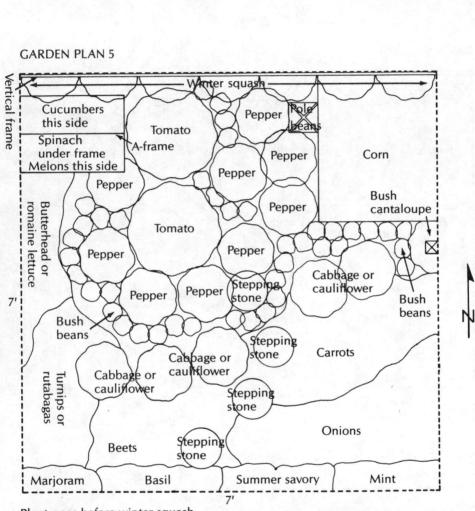

Plant peas before winter squash
Intercrop radishes, green onions, leaf lettuce, fast-maturing turnips with the larger plants

GARDEN PLAN 6

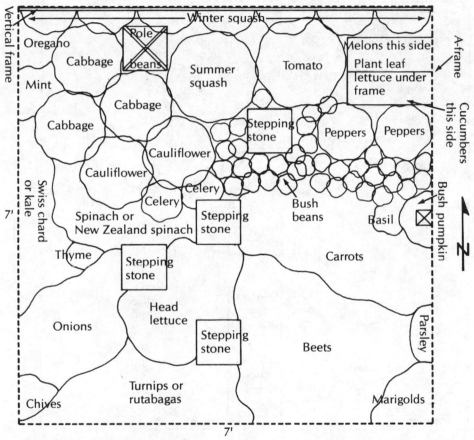

Plant peas before winter squash
Intercrop radishes, green onions, leaf lettuce, fast-maturing turnips with the larger plants

GARDEN PLAN 7

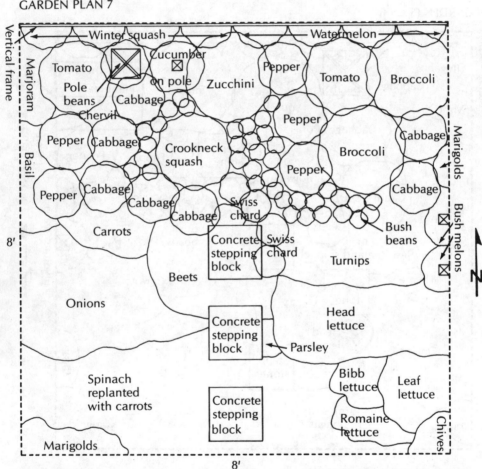

Plant peas before winter squash and watermelons
Intercrop radishes, green onions, leaf lettuce, fast-maturing turnips with the larger plants

GARDEN PLAN 8

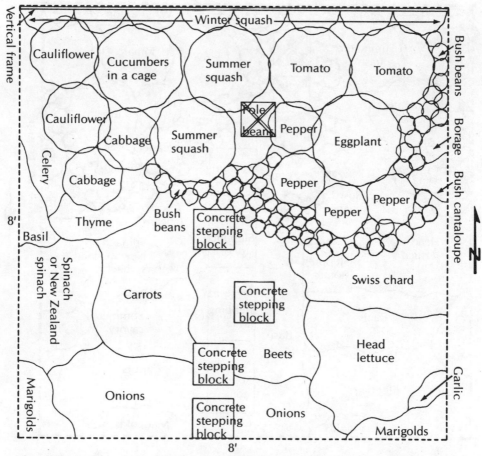

Plant peas before winter squash
Intercrop radishes, green onions, leaf lettuce, fast-maturing turnips with the larger plants

GARDEN PLAN 9

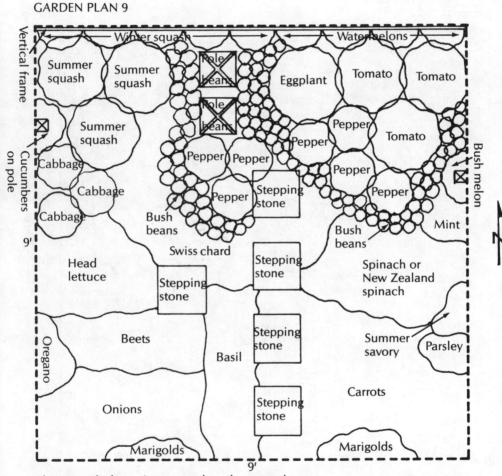

Winter squash — Watermelons

Vertical frame

Cucumbers on pole

Summer squash | Summer squash

Pole beans

Eggplant | Tomato | Tomato

Pole beans

Summer squash

Pepper

Cabbage

Pepper | Pepper

Tomato

Cabbage

Pepper | Pepper

Pepper

Bush melon

Cabbage

Pepper | Stepping stone

Pepper

Bush beans

Swiss chard

Mint

9'

Stepping stone

Bush beans

Head lettuce

Stepping stone

Spinach or New Zealand spinach

N

Oregano

Stepping stone

Stepping stone

Beets

Basil

Summer savory | Parsley

Onions

Stepping stone

Carrots

Marigolds

Marigolds

9'

Plant peas before winter squash and watermelons
Intercrop radishes, green onions, leaf lettuce, fast-maturing turnips with the larger plants

GARDEN PLAN 10

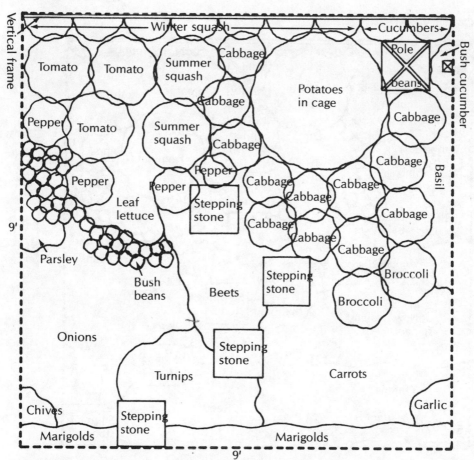

Plant peas before winter squash and cucumbers
Intercrop radishes, green onions, leaf lettuce, fast-maturing turnips with the larger plants

GARDEN PLAN 11

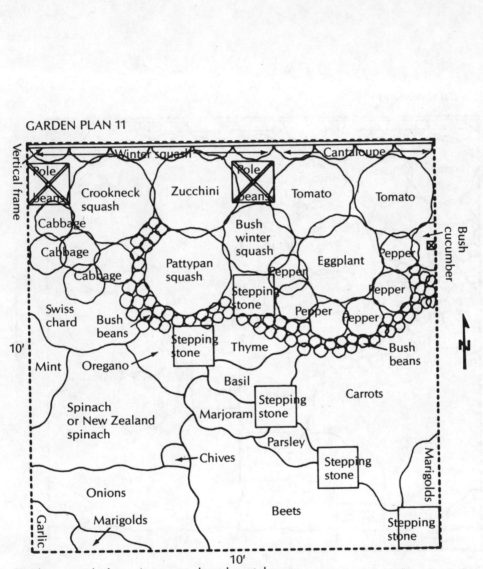

Plant peas before winter squash and cantaloupe
Intercrop radishes, green onions, leaf lettuce, fast-maturing turnips with the
larger plants

GARDEN PLAN 12

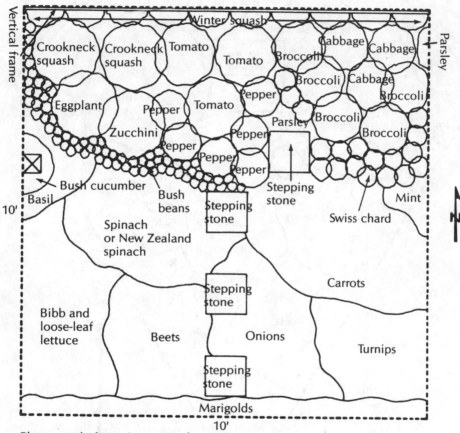

Plant peas before winter squash
Intercrop radishes, green onions, leaf lettuce, fast-maturing turnips with the larger plants

GARDEN PLAN 13

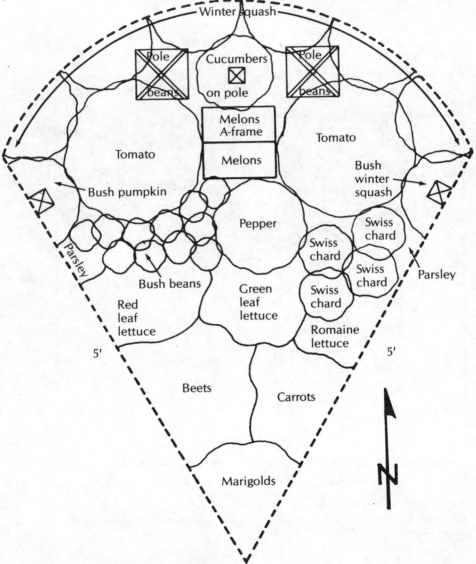

Winter squash

Pole beans

Cucumbers on pole

Pole beans

Melons A-frame

Melons

Tomato

Tomato

Bush winter squash

Bush pumpkin

Pepper

Swiss chard

Swiss chard

Parsley

Swiss chard

Swiss chard

Parsley

Bush beans

Red leaf lettuce

Green leaf lettuce

Romaine lettuce

5'

5'

Beets

Carrots

N

Marigolds

Plant peas before winter squash
Intercrop radishes, green onions, leaf lettuce, fast-maturing turnips with the larger plants

CHAPTER 2

VEGETABLE FACTORY SOIL

THE ODDS ARE THAT your soil is far from perfect. Perhaps it has too much clay, contains too many rocks and pebbles, or is too sandy. Whatever the problem, there's a way to overcome it. In this chapter I'll describe how to build "super soil" in your Vegetable Factory garden with the least amount of work.

SOIL COMPONENTS

Soil has four main components—minerals, organic matter, water, and air. In average soil, the mineral component is about 50 percent of the total volume. Air and water make up 20 to 25 percent each and organic content accounts for about 5 percent.

There are three kinds of mineral particles in the soil, classified by size: clay, sand, and silt. **Clay** particles are so small that you can't see them without magnification. They lie extremely close together and absorb water slowly. But once these particles absorb water, they hold it so tightly that plants have trouble using it, and air can't get in. Visualize clay soil as a number of flat plates piled one on top of the other in such a way that there is little space between the plates to hold water.

When clay dries, it's even worse. Plant roots have difficulty penetrating the soil, which contains little air and water. On my own property, I have soil that is at least 65 percent clay. Once this soil dries out in summer, I find it impossible to dig unless I first soak it with a hose.

Silt particles are larger than clay but are still about as fine as white flour. They are powdery when dry and greasy when wet.

Sand, on the other hand, has round or angular particles many times larger than clay. Think of these particles as marbles in a container. There are lots of open spaces between the particles of soil, with plenty of room for roots. But since the particles do not hold moisture, water runs through rapidly and leaches (dissolves) away many of the nutrients.

DETERMINING YOUR SOIL TYPE

Most of us have soil that is a combination of the three kinds of particles. Before you start to prepare your yard for a Vegetable Factory bed, find out what the soil is made of. Here's a simple way to evaluate soil structure:

1. Put about three tablespoons of your soil into a container, and add just enough water to thoroughly wet the particles, but not enough to make the soil runny.

2. Pick up the wet soil and roll it into a ball. Next, place the ball in the palm of your hand and roll it out into a long, thin cylinder. The sandier the soil, the harder it will be to roll into a ball and hold together as a cylinder. With a clay content of at least 35 to 40 percent, you can pick up the cylinder and bend the ends until they touch without breaking it. This gives you a pretty good idea of the sand/clay content of your soil.

3. Finally, rub the mixture against your palm. Clay gives the soil a shine when you press down. Sand feels gritty. Silt gives the soil a greasy quality but will not make soil as plastic as clay does.

Loam is a term used to describe any good soil. It refers to a mixture of silt, sand, and clay (the U.S. Department of Agriculture considers loam to consist of 7 to 27 percent clay, 28 to 50 percent silt, and 20 to 45 percent sand), plus a good supply of decomposed organic material called humus. A loam soil drains well, yet retains enough water for plant growth. Air can circulate, and the soil provides plenty of room for roots to grow easily. Our goal is to create a good loam for your Vegetable Factory garden.

MAKING A BETTER SOIL

Most problem soils can be improved by adding organic material. This reduces soil compaction and supplies vegetables with more nutrients.

If your soil has a high clay content, you can work in organic matter to improve the drainage. The organic particles will allow air and water to circulate between the tight clay plates. If your soil is sandy, drains rapidly, and dries out too quickly, organic matter will act like a sponge to build up its water-holding capacity.

Organic matter, or humus, is simply the decayed remains of plant and animal matter. To change the physical structure of your soil, you need to add massive amounts. In a Vegetable Factory garden, this means at least one-third of the final soil mix must be organic matter.

Once you add organic matter, the microorganisms in the soil start to decompose it, using the carbon and nitrogen available in the organic material as food. This decomposition takes place rapidly when the carbon-to-nitrogen ratio is about 10 parts carbon to 1 part nitrogen. If you upset this ratio by adding organic material high in carbon and low in nitrogen, such as straw, without compensating with a high-nitrogen material such as bloodmeal, decomposition slows down. As the decomposer organisms in the soil use up the available carbon and increase in numbers, they also need nitrogen to keep the action going.

If the amount of nitrogen in the organic material is insufficient to take care of their needs, the microorganisms borrow nitrogen from the soil. This puts them in direct competition with the plants in your garden, slowing plant growth. To prevent a temporary depletion of nitrogen when undecomposed organic material is added, you must add additional nitrogen in the form of organic nutrients. See the table, Natural Plant Foods, on page 26 for a list of nutrient sources that have a high nitrogen content.

Organic matter continually breaks down and decomposes, so you must periodically add more to your soil. Most gardeners do this once a year, but a Vegetable Factory garden will benefit from additional material each time you take out one crop and plant another.

ADDING ORGANIC MATTER

Compost is the best form of organic matter for your garden. It is simply a mixture of decomposed organic material. Compost is a form of humus, but the decomposition takes place outside of the soil in a compost pile. When compost is placed in the garden, all its nutrients are available to the plants. Instructions for making your own compost are covered later in this chapter.

Leaf mold, another fine soil amendment, is made of decomposed leaves. Since it has already been decomposed, its nutrients are ready to use. A recent study by the University of Arkansas found that 3 inches of well-decomposed leaf mold tilled into the upper 6 inches of soil can increase the production of most vegetables by 35 to 150 percent. This study was conducted in standard Experiment Station beds. You can put leaves in your compost pile, shred them with a leaf shredder or lawn mower, or buy leaf mold from a nursery.

Sawdust is an excellent soil conditioner. It is easy to use, costs very little, and aerates the soil well. However, unless you use thoroughly composted or decomposed sawdust, you must add additional nitrogen, as fresh sawdust will rob the soil of nitrogen during decomposition.

Peat moss consists of the decomposed remains of prehistoric plants that have been compressed for thousands of years at the bottoms of bogs and swamps. Peat moss has good aeration and the highest water retention of all soil conditioners. You do not need to add nitrogen.

Animal manures are vital to a garden, for they are good soil builders and also add many nutrients, especially nitrogen. But just to make the choice a little harder for us, each type of manure has different properties and varying amounts of nitrogen, phosphorus, and potassium.

Hen, horse, sheep, and rabbit manures are known as "hot" manures because of their high nitrogen content. Cow and swine manures are called "cold" manures because they are low in nitrogen and break down fairly slowly. I prefer using horse manure, as I have found that it gives me the best results.

Use rotted manure, not fresh. The bacteria in your soil will need extra nitrogen to break down fresh manure, and this can divert nitrogen from your plants. And manure that has already rotted or decomposed is in a form your plants can use immediately.

Practically every city and suburban area has a stable where you can pick up rotted manure. I pick mine up in March, when it is completely rotted. You can buy dried manure in sacks at a nursery. Work it into your garden soil directly from the sack.

Do not buy steer manure, because its high salt content offsets any benefit that manure might have. Although these salts can be leached out by watering the steer manure, this leaching also washes out the nitrogen.

Vermiculite is a marvelous material, made by heating mica rock until it explodes like popcorn. It is lightweight, holds water better than a sponge, and works wonders when mixed with soil. Vermiculite will help improve the friability (the ability to crumble) and water-holding capacity of both sandy and clay soils. For best results, mix vermiculite into your garden soil at a rate of 10 to 20 percent of soil volume. Vermiculite lasts forever, and may be one of the best investments you make for your garden.

All of these organic materials, except sawdust, can be purchased from a nursery or garden center. You will often find sawdust advertised for sale in the classified section of local newspapers.

CREATING VEGETABLE FACTORY COMPOST

Start creating compost for your Vegetable Factory garden now, if you don't already compost. A lot of city and suburban gardeners don't compost because they are afraid that it will be messy and will smell. Since most Vegetable Factory gardens are small, compost can be made inside containers, eliminating both any offensive smell and the difficulty of handling large amounts of material.

Compost is simply a decayed mixture of table scraps, grass clippings, leaves, and other organic materials. What you compost depends on your lifestyle. However, everybody eats, so start to collect kitchen scraps in a closed container. Separate fats, meat scraps, paper products, and of course cans and other inorganic materials. If you mow a lawn, you may want to use clippings in your compost. Add leaves in the fall.

Compost Basics

Good composting depends on particle size, the amount of nitrogen available, the heat produced, moisture in the pile, and how often the pile is turned.

The smaller the particle size, the faster the decomposition, because decomposer bacteria have more surface area to work on. If the leaves, stems, and other materials are shredded before being added to the compost pile, they'll decay faster and be ready sooner. I suggest getting a good chipper/shredder for your Vegetable Factory garden to reduce bulky materials to quick-composting size. There are several small ones on the market that can be stored easily in the garage. See Sources of Seeds and Supplies for suppliers of chipper/shredders.

The bacteria in the pile need nitrogen. If there is too much carbon-rich organic material in proportion to the available nitrogen, the bacteria will not work as fast, and the decomposition will go slowly. You will notice low heat production in the compost pile.

While leaves make one of the best organic conditioners they are sometimes hard to compost, because they consist primarily of carbon, with little nitrogen. You can correct this deficiency by adding nitrogen in the form of bloodmeal, chicken manure, or massive amounts of grass clippings.

Compost must heat up to between 140 and 160° F for good bacterial action to occur. Smaller compost piles lose heat readily, and bacterial action is apt to be slow unless the compost is in a dark, heat-retentive container. A good minimum size for a "quick-cooking" open-air pile is 3 cubic feet.

Every pile needs moisture for decomposition to take place. You can keep the pile's moisture content right by making sure that it remains about as wet as a squeezed-out wet sponge. Just put your hand in the pile and feel. (But watch out, it can be really hot!) If necessary, add water until the pile has the right consistency. Don't overdo it, though—too much water can cut down on the oxygen available to the bacteria.

A compost pile must be turned every two to three days to keep the bacterial action going. Since Vegetable Factory gardens use composters, you can turn the material with a small hand cultivator so the top and sides are moved to the center. This allows air penetration and also brings uncomposted materials to the center, where most of the action is taking place.

For composting in a closed container, I suggest that you use a Compost Tool. This allows you to get air into your compost pile without having to lift the whole thing with a fork. The Compost Tool is a long tube with 4-inch blades on the end. The blades close as you insert them and open as you withdraw. As you pull the blades out they turn, aerating the pile. This tool is available through W. Atlee Burpee Co. See Sources of Seeds and Supplies for address.

When finished or "ripe," the composted materials will be converted into a crumbly brown substance with the fragrance of good earth. The compost is now ready to use. As decomposition proceeds, most piles will shrink to about half their original size; a 5-foot-high pile, for instance, will end up hardly more than 2½ feet tall. One cubic foot of ripe compost is usually enough to cover 4 square feet of a Vegetable Factory garden.

COMPOST IN A CAN

The easiest way to make compost for a Vegetable Factory garden is in a garbage can or a commercial composter, available from a number of suppliers. See Sources

Grass clippings
or leaves

Kitchen scraps

Grass clippings
or leaves

Kitchen scraps

Soil or peat moss

For gardeners with little space, compost can be produced easily in a garbage can tucked out of the way in a corner of the yard or in the garage.

of Seeds and Supplies for sources. These containers can be placed in an out-of-the-way corner of the yard, in the garage or, in a pinch, even in the corner of the laundry room.

Here's what you'll need to do to turn out good garbage-can compost.

1. Buy a galvanized garbage can (20- or 30-gallon size), and punch several small holes in the bottom with a hammer and a large nail. Put the can on a few bricks, and place a pan underneath to catch any liquid that might drain out from the decaying organic matter that you will be adding.

2. Next, put a 3-inch layer of soil or peat moss in the bottom of the can.

3. Add 2 to 3 inches of kitchen scraps, then a 2-inch layer of grass clippings, shredded newspaper, and/or shredded leaves, another of layer kitchen scraps, a layer of grass clippings, newspaper and leaves, and so on until the can is full. Add these materials each day, or every few days as you collect them.

4. Put the lid on the can. The ripe compost will be ready in about 3 or 4 months. If you start the can in the fall, the compost will be ready to add to your garden by spring. You don't need to worry about the moisture content of this kind of pile, nor does it have to be turned.

COMPOST BINS

If you have room, you can expand your operations by composting in a bin. You can make a compost bin with a dozen 1-by-12-inch boards, each 30 inches

You can easily make a compost bin of almost any size boards. Several bins can be stacked together to create a "compost factory."

long. Nail four boards together to make a frame, or bottomless box, and place this on the site. Use the remaining boards to make two more frames, and stack these to complete the bin.

Build your compost in layers. Put down a 6-inch layer of plant refuse, grass clippings, kitchen scraps, and leaves. Add a 2-inch layer of good garden soil on top of this. Repeat this procedure until the pile reaches the top of the bin, then add a 1-inch soil cover.

I also recommend several different types of commercial composters. The Soilsaver Compost Bin is made of polyethylene, with thermal insulated walls and a translucent plastic top that is engineered to trap soil heat. To use, just lift the top and add kitchen scraps, grass clippings, leaves, and weeds. The finished compost comes out the bottom. The Rotocrop Accelerator compost bin has sliding galvanized rust-resistant panels. You can buy composters that will make 21 cubic feet of compost. These can produce finished compost in a few weeks and are ideal for Vegetable Factory gardeners.

SOIL NUTRIENTS

Plants need 16 nutrients to be healthy and vigorous. There are three major nutrients—nitrogen (N), phosphorus (P), and potassium (K)—and 13 minor and trace elements, including calcium, zinc, iron, manganese, copper, sulfur, and magnesium.

New gardeners always want to know whether they should use organic or chemical fertilizers to supply these nutrients. There is general agreement among most soil scientists that there isn't a great deal of difference between chemical and organic nutrients as far as a plant is concerned. But they also agree that chemical fertilizers do nothing for the soil. In fact, overuse of chemical fertilizers can damage soil, killing beneficial microorganisms in the soil and burning plant roots as well. So, for your soil's sake, and therefore your garden's sake, it's better to add organic nutrients. Here's a rundown of nutrients and their sources:

Nitrogen in the soil promotes rapid growth of stems and leaves, and produces a dark green leaf color. It is especially important for leaf crops such as cabbage, kale, lettuce, and spinach. Nitrogen is readily leached out of soil by water, so it is usually necessary to add nitrogen several times during the season.

Nitrogen deficiency causes yellowed leaves and stunted growth. When there is not enough nitrogen to sustain new plant growth, nitrogen moves from the older plant cells to newer, growing ones. This causes the yellowing and dropping of leaves farthest from the growing shoots. Excess nitrogen produces excessive vegetative growth, reduces the quality of fruits, and delays flowering.

Bloodmeal contains 7 to 15 percent nitrogen. It can be mixed as a liquid fertilizer, using one tablespoon to a gallon of water. Hoof and horn meal contains 7 to 15 percent nitrogen. Cottonseed meal contains 6 to 9 percent. Fish meal and

Natural Plant Foods

Type	Source	N	P	K	Ca	Mg
			Composition (%)			
Animal manures (fresh)	Cattle	0.53	0.29	0.48	0.29	0.11
	Chicken	0.89	0.48	0.83	0.38	0.13
	Horse	0.55	0.27	0.57	0.27	0.11
	Sheep	0.89	0.48	0.83	0.21	0.13
Animal manures (dried)	Cattle	2.00	1.80	3.00	—	—
	Horse	0.80	0.20	0.60	—	—
	Sheep	1.40	1.00	3.00	—	—
Animal tankage	Dried bloodmeal	9–14	—	—	—	—
	Bonemeal	1.6–2.5	23–25	—	—	—
	Dried fish scrap	6.5–10	4–8	—	—	—
	Fish emulsion	5–10	2.0	2.0	—	—
Pulverized rock powders	Rock phosphate	—	38–41	—	—	—
	Limestone				40	
	Greensand	—	1.35	4.1–9.5	—	1.63
Vegetable residues	Coffee grounds	2.0	0.4	2.5	—	—
	Cottonseed meal	6.7–7.4	2–3	1.5–2.0	—	—
	Seaweed	1.7	0.8	5.0	—	—
	Soybean meal	6.0	1.0	2.0	—	—
	Wood ashes		1.5	7.0	23	
	Oak leaves	0.8	0.4	0.2	—	—
	Maple leaves	0.5	0.1	0.5	—	—

fish emulsion contain up to 10 percent nitrogen and nearly as much phosphorus. Bonemeal may contain up to 3 percent nitrogen. It is used primarily to supply phosphorus.

Most animal manures are fairly low in nitrogen. The main value of animal manures is as organic material to improve soil structure. Let animal manures decompose before putting them in your garden. Exceptions are chicken manure and guano, which are high in nitrogen.

Phosphorus stimulates early root formation and is necessary for the development of fruit, flowers, and seeds. Plants with a phosphorus deficiency are often dwarfed and spindly; the leaves are dull green with purple tints, while the leaf veins and margins often turn bronze, reddish, or purple. Fruit development is usually delayed.

Phosphorus fertilizers include bonemeal, averaging 20 to 25 percent phosphoric acid, and phosphate rock, a finely ground rock powder. It contains about 30 to 33 percent phosphoric acid, plus minor and trace elements.

Potassium (potash) is essential to the life processes of plants, including the manufacture and movement of sugars and starches within the plant. Potassium hastens maturity and seed production, and is essential to the development of fruit, flowers, and seeds.

Nutrition Problems at a Glance

Nutrient Deficiency	What to Look For
Nitrogen (N)	Yellow leaves starting with older leaves; stunted growth
Phosphorus (P)	Bluish-green leaves followed by bronzing or purpling, drying to a greenish-brown or black
Potassium (potash, K)	Dry or scorched leaves; dead areas along margins, plants stunted, rusty appearance
Magnesium (Mg)	Mottling of lower leaves at margins, tips, between veins; leaves wilt from bottom up
Copper (Cu)	Dark green, olive-gray leaf edges; edges curl upward
Zinc (Zn)	Mottling, yellowing, or scorching of tissues between veins
Iron (Fe)	Yellow leaves; green veins
Sulfur (S)	Young leaves turn pale green to yellow, older leaves remain green
Molybdenum (Mo)	Leaves pale green or yellow, leaves crinkled, stunted
Boron (B)	Scorching of tips and margins of younger leaves

Without potassium, plants tend to grow more slowly. The leaves of plants that lack potassium have mottled yellow tips and edges. Older leaves look scorched at the edges.

Potassium is supplied by granite dust (up to 8 percent potash), hardwood ashes (up to 10 percent), and softwood ashes (about 5 percent). Gather ashes as soon after burning as you can handle them, because potash is easily leached out.

It is sound practice to add humus and fertilizer before you replant each Vegetable Factory garden section with a new crop. You can add dry fertilizers to the soil in the form of a packaged preblended organic mix, or you can mix your own from organic ingredients.

About every two to four weeks, I suggest you give your entire garden a supplemental feeding of fish emulsion. It contains 5 to 10 percent nitrogen, 2 percent phosphorus, and 2 percent potassium. Crops that are heavy feeders will especially benefit from these supplemental feedings. Light feeders can easily get along without them.

ORGANIC FERTILIZERS

I have listed the major organic nutrients that can be used in Vegetable Factory gardens. Now I want to give you three formulas for mixing these ingredients that I find work well. Use any of the three in your own garden.

Formula One

2 pints bloodmeal
4 pints bonemeal
3 pints greensand

Formula Two

4 pints cottonseed meal
4 pints bonemeal
3 pints greensand

Formula Three

2 pints bloodmeal
4 pints bonemeal
2 pints wood ashes

You can substitute any of the nutrients listed here in the formula as long as you keep the same nitrogen: phosphorus: potassium ratio. For instance, cottonseed meal contains 7 percent nitrogen instead of the 15 percent in bloodmeal. This means you will need roughly twice as much cottonseed meal as bloodmeal. Store in small plastic bags to use when you make up your beds. Pints are used as units here because they are easy to handle. You can make up these mixes in any quantities, such as gallons, as long as you keep the same ratios between the ingredients. This holds true for all the formulas suggested in this book.

ACID OR ALKALINE?

Soils are frequently acid (sour) or alkaline (sweet). This is usually expressed in terms of pH (the degree of acidity or alkalinity) on scale of 1 to 14. Seven is neutral, below 7 is acid, and above 7 is alkaline. You must consider your soil's pH, since most vegetables do best in neutral or slightly acid soil.

The Availability of Plant Nutrients in Acid or Alkaline Soil

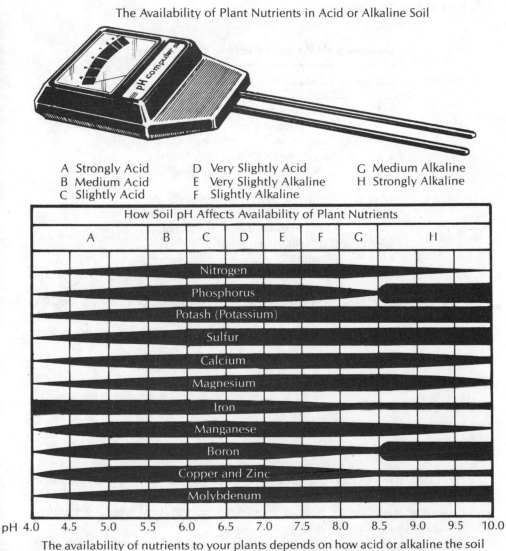

A Strongly Acid   D Very Slightly Acid   G Medium Alkaline
B Medium Acid   E Very Slightly Alkaline   H Strongly Alkaline
C Slightly Acid   F Slightly Alkaline

The availability of nutrients to your plants depends on how acid or alkaline the soil is. A hand-held pH meter will give a reading of the soil's pH after the prongs are inserted in the ground.

Alkaline soil causes plants to have yellow leaves, stunted growth, and burned leaf margins. In extreme cases, heavy brown or white salt deposits are left on the soil surface. The symptoms of acid soil are more difficult to detect.

The easiest way to determine whether your soil is too acid, too alkaline, or in a good growing range is with a pH test, which you should conduct after you have created your "super soil." You can purchase a simple pH test kit from your nursery or most mail-order catalogs for about $3. A pH meter is also available from many garden centers. They cost about $20. Insert its prongs in your soil, and the needle will give you the pH reading.

Optimum pH Range for Vegetables

Soil pH	Vegetable
6–8	Asparagus, beets, cabbage, muskmelons
6–7.5	Peas, spinach, summer squash
6–7	Cauliflower, celery, chives, endive, horseradish, lettuce, onions, radishes, rhubarb
5.5–7.5	Corn, pumpkins, tomatoes
5.5–6.8	Beans, carrots, cucumbers, parsnips, peppers, rutabagas, winter squash
5.5–6.5	Eggplant, watermelons
4.8–6.3	Potatoes

To counteract acid soil, add ground limestone at the rate of 4 pounds per 100 square feet for each unit of pH below 6.5. To correct alkaline soil, add elemental sulfur at the rate of 4 pounds per 100 square feet for each unit of pH above 7.

TOOLS FOR THE VEGETABLE FACTORY

You can build a Vegetable Factory garden with either hand or power tools or a combination.

Hand Tools

The three large hand tools you'll need are a round-pointed shovel, a spade, and a spading fork. A rake is useful for levelling the beds, and a hoe is good for weeding and occasional spot-digging. Besides these, a trowel and hand-weeder are essential for replanting during the season.

When selecting any of these tools, look for straight-grained ash handles. Ash has clearly visible grain lines. Sometimes you will find the type of wood used stamped on a label. Hickory is also acceptable in a tool handle, but it is not as

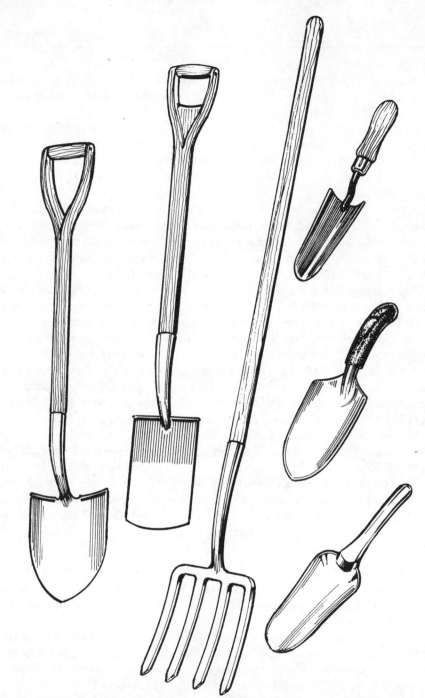

Left to right: The shovel is the gardener's most versatile tool. Closed-back shovels are sturdier than the open-back version. A spade makes a good tool for digging and squaring up any size of bed. A garden spade with an 11-inch blade is recommended for digging most vegetable beds. A short-handled digging fork is essential for digging in rocky soil. The best are made with a one-piece head. Every gardener needs at least one trowel for planting, transplanting and other garden chores.

strong as ash. Ideally the handle of a garden shovel, hoe, or rake should be shoulder high. Some gardeners prefer a short D-handle for spades and forks. Try out both types at a garden store and see which feels best to you.

Forged tools are heavy and durable. A forged tool is heated white-hot and shaped with a press. Rolled-steel shovels and spades are cut from large rolls of steel and stamped out. If this rolled steel is thick and of high quality, it can make a good garden tool; rolled metal tools may be stamped "heavy weight" or "medium weight" metal.

A tool will hold up better if the metal attaching the head to the handle is closed all the way around, rather than open on the back. The best tools have a head and shank made from a single piece of metal. The weakest connection is the tang-and-ferrule. A metal tongue (tang) is inserted into the wood handle and secured by a metal cover (ferrule) attached to the wood.

The round-pointed shovel ($10 to $40) is the tool most often used in the garden. This is the tool you'll be shown if you ask your nursery for a digging shovel. Use it for moving quantities of soil from one spot to another. It is not a good tool for digging the bed, however, since it does not make square cuts; a spade is best for this. The best shovels are forged with a forward-facing lip.

A garden spade ($15 to $40) is an indispensable tool for a dozen garden tasks. Because of its shape, it cuts the sides and bottoms of garden beds square. In addition, the blade is just the right length for digging vegetable beds. The digging fork ($15 to $42) is unsurpassed for loosening and preparing the soil.

Garden rakes ($10 to $20) come in different widths, with teeth that are long or short and straight or curved. Teeth can be widely or closely spaced. Rakes can weigh as little as 3 pounds or as much as 5 pounds. For Vegetable Factory beds in which you need to move soil, break up clods, and smooth beds, I suggest a high quality, light bow rake with straight teeth spaced fairly close together.

Hoes ($7 to $20) are not used often in Vegetable Factory gardens, but you should have one around for miscellaneous digging chores.

Trowels

A steel-bladed trowel ($5 to $18) has a sharp blade that cuts easily into the soil. Unfortunately, many of them use a thin connecting rod in the handle that bends easily with heavy use.

Aluminum trowels ($5 to $10) are usually made in one piece, with plastic-covered handles for sturdiness. Aluminum trowels are not nearly as sharp or as strong as steel trowels. An aluminum trigger trowel ($6 to $8), with a hook under the handle, is especially useful for anyone with arthritis or a weak grip.

A long-handled trowel ($7 to $15) has a handle about 2 feet long and is the choice of gardeners who have trouble stooping. It helps to get into hard-to-reach spots in a Vegetable Factory bed.

The narrow, cupped blade of a transplant trowel ($3 to $8) makes it excellent for transplanting cabbage, cauliflower, tomato, and other seedlings into the garden. It is not useful for general digging. The offset trowel ($7 to $10) has a pointed blade that is good for digging out seedlings from flats.

Power Tools

If you want to dig your garden the easy way, use one of the electric tillers. They turn on a dime and can be used in a 5-by-5-foot bed. You can purchase them at many hardware stores. You can also work up Vegetable Factory gardens fairly easily with the smaller, portable rotary tillers. Most companies that manufacture full-size tillers also manufacture the smaller portable type. See Sources of Seeds and Supplies for addresses.

I suggest that you purchase the highest-quality tool you can afford. I've discovered over the years that cheap tools don't hold up well under garden conditions. I've also found that it pays off to find a garden center that offers a wide selection so that you can try out the various choices. If you don't have such a center nearby, try a specialized mail-order firm that sells high-quality, heavy-duty tools.

Sharpening Your Digging Tools

When you've finished using any digging tool, a good way to clean it is to plunge it into a bucket of sand. If the blade has anything stuck on it, scrape it off first. As a nice extra, wipe the blade with an oily rag. Periodically, wipe down wooden handles with linseed oil and resharpen the blades with a small flat file.

STARTING YOUR GARDEN FROM SCRATCH

The first thing to do is to lay your garden out on the ground. Stake it out, using string. If your garden soil is extremely rocky, you've got some work ahead of you. The easiest way to remove the rocks is to dig out the soil of your Vegetable Factory garden to a depth of 12 inches with a shovel. Or you can work up a larger bed with a small tiller and *then* dig it out. Place the soil in a pile, then set up a screen over your garden and screen out the rocks as you replace your soil. If your bed is bigger than 5 by 5 feet, divide it into quarters. Dig out a quarter at a time. Sift the soil back onto each quarter in stages.

You have already mixed our nutrients. Now you need to mix the organic soil conditioners, add the two together, and use them to create "super soil."

Place these materials in a pile on a tarp near the Vegetable Factory bed. Here are the formulas I like. Pick the one that suits you best.

Formula One

1 bucket animal manure
1 bucket compost
1 bucket peat moss
3 buckets sand
1 bucket vermiculite

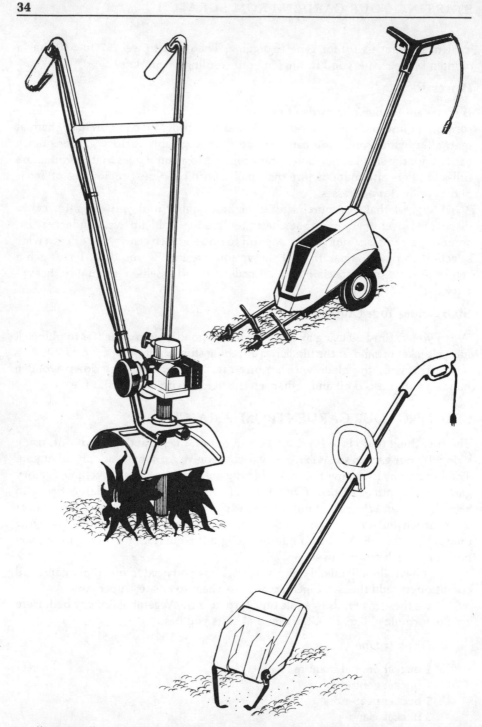

Small rotary tillers, soil blenders, and electric tillers are ideal for making up a Vegetable Factory bed. These small tillers can be easily maneuvered in small spaces.

Formula Two

1 bucket animal manure
1 bucket compost
1 bucket peat moss
1 bucket vermiculite

Formula Three

1 bucket animal manure
1 bucket leaf mold
1 bucket compost
3 buckets sand

Formula Four

3 buckets compost
1 bucket vermiculite
3 buckets sand

You will need to add nutrients to the soil before mixing and turning it into the garden. Use 1 cubic foot of organic material (approximately 3 standard buckets) and ½ cup of mixed nutrients for every cubic foot of soil. You will need to determine how much organic material and nutrients you need for each garden.

For instance, if you are building a 5-by-5-foot Vegetable Factory garden (25 square feet) to a depth of 6 inches, you have 12½ cubic feet of soil. This means you will need 37½ buckets of organic material and 6¼ cups of Vegetable Factory nutrient mix.

A 6-by-8-foot garden (48 square feet) made up to a depth of 6 inches involves 24 cubic feet of soil. You would need 72 buckets of organic material and 12 cups of Vegetable Factory nutrient mix.

Mix the nutrients and all the organic material together on the tarp, using a shovel. Again, you can change the units as you like, as long as you keep the same ratios of ingredients.

WORKING UP VEGETABLE FACTORY BEDS

The final step is to turn both the organic materials and the nutrients into the bed. There are several ways to do this.

You can spread the mixture on the bed to a depth of 2 inches, then turn it in using a small rotary tiller or an electric tiller. When you have this mixed thoroughly, add another 2 inches and turn that in. Repeat until you have thoroughly mixed the organic material and nutrients into the bed. If you put it all on at once, you will have trouble turning it in evenly. When finished, rake the bed until it is smooth.

Alternately, place 3 inches of mixture on the bed and turn it in to a depth of 8 inches, using a shovel. Repeat this until you have mixed all of the organic material into the bed. When finished, rake the bed until you have a fine surface.

THE ULTIMATE BED

This method uses principles developed by Alan Chadwick for creating biodynamic beds. The soil quality is excellent, but you must double dig by hand, so it is several times the work of other methods. Here's how to do it.

1. Cover the entire bed with 6 to 8 inches of your organic and nutrient mixture.

2. Dig a trench along one entire side, about one spade wide and deep, that is, about 9 to 10 inches. Put the excavated topsoil (along with the organic-nutrient mix) just outside the bed; you'll need it in step 6.

3. Loosen the subsoil in the trench that you've just created, digging down another 9 to 10 inches. Don't turn this soil over, just loosen with the shovel. This will give you a fairly coarse mixture at the bottom and a fine mixture at the top.

4. Remove one spade depth of topsoil (including the organic-nutrient mix) from a strip of bed paralleling the trench that you've just opened, filling in that first trench as you go.

5. In the new trench, loosen the subsoil as before, then fill it with the topsoil and organic nutrient mixture from the third strip, and so on.

6. After you've reached the very last row of the bed, fill in this trench with the organic mixture that you laid aside from the first trench.

7. Allow the soil surface to stay rough for a few days so that air can get into the soil. Then, using a spade and rake, work the topsoil to a fine texture. Make sure that you break up all clods.

WOODEN RAISED BEDS

If you are gardening in a landscaped yard, wood-sided raised beds are more attractive than conventional Vegetable Factory beds. Compared to ground-level beds, raised beds eliminate the necessity to plant on your hands and knees, give your garden a neat and permanent appearance, and warm up faster in the spring.

The simplest way to construct them is to nail together a frame of redwood, cedar, or pressure-treated 2-by-12s directly in place. Reinforce the corners with 2-by-2-inch or 4-by-4-inch posts. Extend the posts about 12 inches into the ground to anchor the box in place. To have a place to sit, some gardeners top the box off with a 2-by-6-inch cap.

Before building the box, peel away old sod from your chosen spot and dig down about 10 inches. Place this soil in a pile. Make up your Vegetable Factory organic and nutrient mix. Then build the bed in place, and fill with the original soil and the Vegetable Factory mix—one shovelful of soil to one shovelful of mix.

A 5-by-5-foot raised bed of this type holds 50 cubic feet of soil. To fill it completely, you will need to bring in some outside soil. If you have a source in your yard, use this. If not, buy some good loam from a garden center and fill the bed with one shovelful of soil to one shovelful of organic mix.

Digging the Ultimate Intensive Bed
1. Cover the bed with Vegetable Factory nutrient mix 6 to 8 inches deep. Dig a trench along one side, one spade's depth. Put this topsoil just outside the bed. Loosen the soil in the bottom of the trench another 9 to 10 inches deep.
2. Dig a second trench beside the one just opened. Use the soil from the second trench to fill the first. Loosen the bottom 9 to 10 inches of soil in the new trench. Repeat across the bed.
3. Finish the bed by filling the first trench from the soil placed outside the bed. Rake fine before planting.

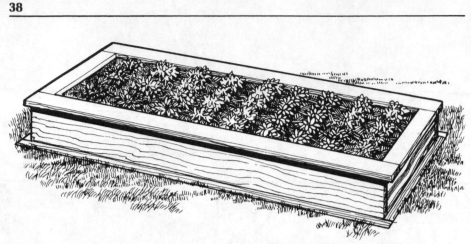

Wooden beds help organize the yard and make the Vegetable Factory bed fit into the landscape. They can be made any size.

Other options to wood-sided beds include framing your raised bed with railroad ties, bricks, or tile. You can even have soil-sided raised beds, but a framed bed keeps the soil in place and creates a focal point for your landscape.

CHAPTER 3

PLANTING THE VEGETABLE FACTORY

THERE ARE THREE MAJOR DIFFERENCES between a Vegetable Factory garden and a conventional one. First, Vegetable Factory gardens are extremely small, the biggest rarely larger than 10 feet by 10 feet. Second, they produce vegetables across the entire bed instead of just a portion of it; unlike a conventional garden, the space between the rows is not wasted. And finally, the space above the Vegetable Factory plot is employed far more efficiently.

Because of these differences, you have to pay close attention to the spacing of each vegetable, the placement of individual plants, and the grouping of the vegetables in a Vegetable Factory garden.

When you combine these elements properly in a small garden, that garden takes on a life of its own. Over the years, I have experimented with Vegetable Factory gardens and conventional gardens, growing them side by side; and invariably the Vegetable Factory gardens grow faster and are considerably more vigorous than those grown any other way, including in many cases intensive-type gardens.

Often, the differences are so striking that you can't believe the two gardens contain exactly the same vegetables, grown in what started out as the same soil.

IT ALL BEGINS WITH SEEDS AND SEEDLINGS

There are two ways to begin the planting process: by purchasing your vegetables as seedlings at the nursery, or by purchasing seeds. Seeds are either planted directly into the soil or started indoors, then transplanted as seedlings into the garden when the weather warms up.

I like to start my vegetables from seed. This gives me the feeling that I'm a part of the gardening process from the very beginning. City gardeners who are short on space and time often prefer to purchase at least some of their vegetables as seedlings from nurseries, rather than starting them indoors six to eight weeks before outdoor planting time.

Some nurseries carry several varieties of a vegetable, but most restrict their selection to just one or two. As you make your choices, be sure to select healthy-looking, compact, dark green, leafy transplants with well-branched stems. Yellow or pale plants indicate a nutrient deficiency, neglect, or overhardening. Wilted plants and those with dead leaf tips may have been allowed to dry out. Torn, damaged plants indicate poor handling. Insect-infested plants (look under the leaves) can infest other plants in your garden. Tall, spindly plants generally have poor root systems that can't support their top growth.

Plants in flats or plant packs cost less than seedlings grown singly in pots, and they usually grow just as well. Cucumbers, melons, and squash, however, must be started individually in peat pots for transplanting into the ground without disturbing their roots.

Shop the seed racks if you need a wider choice of varieties than your nursery can provide. Today you can often find unusual varieties, new hybrid seeds, and even a wide selection of oriental vegetables. Seed racks frequently contain varieties that are suited to your area, but they may also have nationally known varieties that may not adapt well to your climate.

Seed packages list the variety name, disease resistance (if any), number of days to maturity, bare-bones planting instructions, and an expiration date. Make sure you check this date before purchasing your seed. Companies usually change the seed packages seasonally, but you may come upon old seed. Some seeds, such as onions, are short-lived and should be planted as soon as possible (see the table, Seed Germination, on page 43).

Most seed is treated with a chemical fungicide to prevent damping-off (rotting of the seed or emerging seedlings) and other problems. However, you can buy untreated seed from Johnny's Selected Seeds, Nichols Garden Nursery, and several other firms (see Sources of Seeds and Supplies).

Seed tapes are gaining in popularity. In these, seeds are inserted into water-soluble tape at equal intervals. Seed tapes allow vigorous seedlings to emerge without crowding, and eliminate the need for thinning. You can purchase special tape collections such as a full-season lettuce garden (a set of lettuce varieties that reach maturity over an extended period of time) or a children's minigarden (an assortment of easy-to-grow vegetables for kids).

Tapes for sowing seeds in flats (shallow boxes in which plants are grown together) are available in 3-foot lengths, with seeds spaced at ½- or 1-inch intervals. This prespacing makes it easy to sow seeds evenly, and gives each plant adequate growing space.

If you want a wide selection, try shopping at a bulk seed store. Although you won't find as many bulk seed stores around today as you might have a few years ago, they offer a far greater variety than seed racks. Seeds are usually sold in bulk from rows and rows of drawers and seed bins. Many also offer seed through catalogs. Two of the better known firms are Gurney and Seedway.

You'll find local stores listed under "Seeds" in the Yellow Pages. Unfortunately, many metropolitan areas no longer have a seed store.

Order from seed catalogs when you are looking for a large seed selection. Firms often specialize in areas such as heirloom or oriental vegetables. Here are some of the possibilities.

New introductions: Plant breeders at the state Experiment Stations, the U.S. Department of Agriculture, and seed companies are constantly developing new varieties. Many of these have been bred for traits most useful to commercial agriculture (such as the ability to ship well) and are not offered to home gardeners, but those varieties deemed suitable for home gardens and offered for sale by seed companies (such as 'Munchkin' pumpkin) are often spectacular. Practically every seed company offers new varieties each year.

All-America Selections: Each season, several All-America Selections are chosen based on results in test gardens across the United States. To be selected for All-America honors, a vegetable must have superior qualities and be adapted to a wide range of soils and climates. All-America Selections are noted in seed catalogs by AAS.

Choice varieties: Many catalogs single out vegetable varieties with special qualities—the sweetest, the largest, the most flavorful, the easiest to grow in home gardens, and so forth. Burgess notes these special varieties as "Best of Burgess"; Burpee marks its with a bull's-eye.

Catalog exclusives: Most seed firms also feature varieties sold exclusively by them. Examples are the large 1- to 2-pound 'Abraham Lincoln' tomato sold exclusively by R.H. Shumway and the 'Cold-Set' tomato, a heavy-yielding early variety offered by Gurney.

Baby vegetables: So many people have gone crazy over baby vegetables that several firms now offer complete collections, including baby beets, carrots, corn, and squash.

Oriental vegetables: Oriental vegetables are becoming more and more popular with American cooks and gardeners. In the beginning there were only two firms offering a complete selection of these vegetables, Tsang and Ma International and Kitazawa Seed Co. (see Sources of Seeds and Supplies for addresses). Since that time, seed companies have begun to add more varieties every year.

Special collections: Many catalogs also list special seed collections that you may want to investigate. For example, Burgess offers a small-space collection, a slicing cucumber collection, an edible-podded pea collection, and a carrot collection.

Each catalog has its own personality. Gleckler's offers Japanese varieties of broccoli, cabbage, carrots, and melons. Nichols Garden Nursery features gourmet vegetable seeds from around the world, plus herbs and rare seeds. Burpee has one of the most complete catalogs. And Thompson and Morgan, whose agents comb the world for seeds, lists some 3,000 varieties. Seed catalogs are listed and briefly described in Sources of Seeds and Supplies, page 241.

SAVING YOUR OWN SEEDS

Collecting seeds is not difficult. Most require no special treatment other than drying. Seeds of hybrids, however, are not likely to produce plants and fruit that resemble the parent and should not be saved.

Most seed catalogs tell if a variety is a hybrid (denoted by "hybrid" or "F_1 hybrid"). A hybrid is a cross between two parents of different types, each parent having its own particular qualities. Its seeds are "genetically variable," that is, they produce plants of different heights and other characteristics; if you try to save these seeds, plant vigor and crop yield will decrease, and the disease tolerance of hybrid vegetable parents will decrease with each generation. Seeds of non-hybrid or open-pollinated varieties retain the parents' vigor and inbred characteristics.

Seeds must be allowed to mature before you collect them. Those of many warm-weather vegetables are mature when the produce is ready for harvest, including cantaloupes, pumpkins, squash, sunflowers, tomatoes, and watermelons. After removing the seeds, wash them to remove the pulp, and dry them on paper towels in the sun. It may take two weeks or more for seeds to completely dry.

Seeds in pods, such as beans, okra, and Southern peas, should be allowed to mature on the plant. Leave these pods until they shrivel and turn yellow. Then collect the pods and remove the seeds. These also need to be dried in pie plates placed in the sun. Complete drying is essential, since even a small amount of moisture can cause seeds to rot during storage.

The table, Seed Germination, indicates how long seed will remain viable if properly stored. Onion seed will stay good a year or two, cabbage and beet seed about four years. Place dried seeds in jars, and puncture the lids to allow ventilation. Store in a cool, dry area such as a basement or garage.

Use the "rule of 100" to determine where to store your seeds. That is, if you let the combined temperature and relative humidity rise above 100, you run the risk of destroying seed viability. Keep seeds at a constant 45°F and 40 percent humidity, and they will remain good for the time indicated in the table. A few pieces of mothball dropped in the jar will protect the seeds from insect attack. Dried seeds can also be protected from insects by storing them in frozen food containers in the freezer.

Testing Stored Seed

The first sign of seed germination is the absorption of water, lots of water. This activates an enzyme that increases respiration and causes the protoplasm to begin to duplicate itself. Soon the embryo becomes too large for the seed coat, the coat bursts open, and the growing plant emerges.

Before the seed germinates, it is either in a state of dormancy or quiescence (inactivity). Dormancy is caused by internal conditions. Quiescence is caused by

Seed Germination

Crop	Minimum Federal Standard Germination (%)	Seeds Per Ounce (average)	Relative Longevity (years)
Asparagus	60	1,400	3
Bean, lima	70	20–70	3
Bean, snap	75	100	3
Beet	65	2,000	4
Broccoli	75	8,100	3
Brussels sprouts	70	8,500	4
Cabbage	75	7,700	4
Carrot	55	22,000	3
Cauliflower	75	8,600	4
Celeriac	55	50,000	3
Celery	55	76,000	3
Chicory	65	20,000	4
Chinese cabbage	75	7,000	3
Corn	75	140	2
Cucumber	80	1,100	5
Eggplant	60	7,200	4
Endive	70	17,000	5
Kale	75	10,000	4
Kohlrabi	75	9,200	3
Leek	60	9,900	2
Lettuce	80	26,000	6
Muskmelon	75	1,100	5
New Zealand spinach	40	430	3
Okra	50	500	2
Onion	70	8,500	1
Parsley	60	18,000	1
Parsnip	60	6,800	1
Pea	80	50–230	3
Pepper	55	4,500	2
Pumpkin	75	200	4
Radish	75	3,100	4
Rutabaga	75	11,000	4
Salsify	75	2,000	1
Spinach	60	2,900	3
Squash	75	180–380	4
Swiss chard	65	1,500	4
Tomato	75	10,000	4
Turnip	80	14,000	4
Watermelon	70	320	4

SOURCE: J. F. Harrington, University of California, Davis.

external conditions, such as the lack of moisture or oxygen, or the wrong temperatures or light levels.

Before you plant stored seed, you should test it to see whether it is still good (viable). Place a small sponge in a shallow saucer. Add water to the saucer until the sponge is completely saturated. Place ten seeds from your seed jar on the sponge, and set the whole thing in direct light on a windowsill.

Experiments by U.S. Department of Agriculture (USDA) researchers show that a large percentage of small-seeded species require both moisture and a small amount of light from the red part of the spectrum to start the germination process. For instance, when 'Grand Rapids' lettuce seed is moistened, but kept in complete darkness, only 5 to 30 percent of the seeds germinate. When the seed is given a small dose of red light, then placed in darkness, almost all will germinate. See the table, From Seed to Plant, for the number of days required for germination. Add five days to this, then count the number of seeds germinated on the sponge. If eight out of ten seeds have started to germinate on the blotter, for example, your

From Seed to Plant

Crop	Days for Seed to Emerge at Different Temperatures								
	32°F	41°F	50°F	59°F	68°F	77°F	86°F	95°F	104°F
Asparagus	—	—	52.8	24.0	14.6	10.3	11.5	19.3	28.4
Bean, lima	—	—	—	30.5	17.6	6.5	6.7	—	—
Bean, snap	—	—	—	16.1	11.4	8.1	6.4	6.2	—
Beet	—	42.0	16.7	9.7	6.2	5.0	4.5	4.6	—
Cabbage	—	—	14.6	8.7	5.8	4.5	3.5	—	—
Carrot	—	50.6	17.3	10.1	6.9	6.2	6.0	8.6	—
Cauliflower	—	—	19.5	9.9	6.2	5.2	4.7	—	—
Celery	—	41.0	16.0	12.0	7.0	—	—	—	—
Corn	—	—	21.6	12.4	6.9	4.0	3.7	3.4	—
Cucumber	—	—	—	12.0	6.2	4.0	3.1	3.0	—
Eggplant	—	—	—	—	13.1	8.1	5.3	—	—
Lettuce	49.0	14.9	7.0	3.9	2.6	2.2	2.6	—	—
Muskmelon	—	—	—	—	8.4	4.0	3.1	—	—
Okra	—	—	—	27.2	17.4	12.5	6.8	6.4	6.7
Onion	135.8	30.6	13.4	7.1	4.6	3.6	3.9	12.5	—
Parsley	—	—	29.0	17.0	14.0	13.0	12.3	—	—
Parsnip	171.7	56.7	26.6	19.3	13.6	14.9	31.6	—	—
Pea	—	36.0	13.5	9.4	7.5	6.2	5.9	—	—
Pepper	—	—	—	25.0	12.5	8.4	7.6	8.8	—
Radish	—	29.0	11.2	6.3	4.2	3.5	3.0	—	—
Spinach	62.6	22.5	11.7	6.9	5.7	5.1	6.4	—	—
Tomato	—	—	42.9	13.6	8.2	5.9	5.9	9.2	—
Turnip	—	—	5.2	3.0	1.9	1.4	1.1	1.2	—
Watermelon	—	—	—	—	11.8	4.7	3.5	3.0	—

SOURCE: Department of Vegetable Crops, University of California, Davis.

germination rate is 80 percent. Eighty to 85 percent is good for seed stored several years; 50 to 80 percent is acceptable. Just plant more seed to compensate. If the germination rate is below 50 percent, throw the remaining seed away; plants that survive from these batches may have low vigor and are susceptible to disease. See the table, Seed Germination, on page 000 for the Federal Germination Standards.

STARTING SEEDLINGS INDOORS

Many vegetables, such as broccoli, cabbage, eggplant, peppers, and tomatoes, can be started in either flats or individual containers and transplanted into the garden when the plants are six to ten weeks old. Other vegetables, like beets, carrots, and onions, are regularly started from seed directly in the garden. See the table, Starting Vegetables from Seed.

Beginning gardeners often choose to buy vegetable transplants from a local

Starting Vegetables from Seed

Method	Type of Vegetable	
Start directly from seed in garden	Beets Carrots Corn salad Cress, garden Okra	Parsnips Radishes Rutabagas Salsify Turnips
Start indoors, transplant to garden	Broccoli Brussels sprouts Cabbage Cardoon Cauliflower Celeriac	Celery Eggplant Florence fennel Peppers Tomatoes
Start indoors or outdoors	Chinese cabbage Collards Corn Endive, escarole Kale	Kohlrabi Leeks Luttuce Mustard Swiss chard
Start from seed in garden or start indoors in individual biodegradable containers to protect sensitive root systems	Beans Cucumbers Muskmelons Peas	Pumpkins Squash Watermelons
Start in other ways	Artichokes: start from root divisions Onions: start from sets, seeds, or small plants Potatoes: start from potato pieces	

nursery. This is fine, since it saves you a step. But after you have gained experience in Vegetable Factory gardening, I suggest that you start all your plants from seed. There are many reasons for this. The best one I have is that it helps keep you in tune with the natural rhythm of your garden.

Here are two methods for starting seedlings. First, you can sow seeds directly in a small pot or cube made of biodegradable materials. In this "One-Step Method," when seedlings reach transplant size, they are placed in the garden, pots and all. The roots then grow through the pot walls and spread into the surrounding soil.

With the "Two-Step Method," a number of seeds are sown in a container, and the seedlings are moved, when large enough, to individual pots. These plants are then transplanted into the garden at a later date.

THE ONE-STEP METHOD

Use this method to grow the bigger vegetables, such as eggplant, melons, peppers, squash, and tomatoes. The individual pots will allow your seedlings to become larger and more vigorous than they would if grown together in a flat.

The several kinds of containers for transplanting are shown here. Jiffy-7–type pellets are compressed sterile sphagnum peat enclosed in a plastic net.

A wide variety of peat, fiber, and plastic containers are useful for starting seedlings. You can also grow seedlings in "containerless" containers—homemade soil blocks.

When placed in water, the pellets expand to form small containers. Prepackaged pellets in plastic trays are convenient, because you simply add water directly in the tray without danger of spillage. Jiffy-9–type pellets are held together with a binder instead of a net. When planted in the garden, they will disintegrate faster than Jiffy-7 pellets.

Peat pots are hollow containers made of compressed fiber. Pots are round or square and can be purchased individually or in multiple break-apart strips. Fill these with Vegetable Factory planting mix (see page 89) and plant the seed directly into that soil.

Cell pots or Cell-Paks are light plastic pots you fill with planting mix for growing individual pop-out transplants. These pots are often used with a plastic tray and come as single cells and in units of two, three, four, six, or 12 cells.

Here's how to go about the One-Step Method of planting:

1. Choose any of the above containers that appeal to you. Fill the biodegradable pots or plastic cell pots with Vegetable Factory planting mix, which you can mix yourself (see page 89), or with a seedling mix you can purchase at any garden center or nursery.

2. Dampen the cubes or planting mix (Jiffy-7–type pellets need to be thoroughly watered or placed in water so they will expand).

3. Sow the seeds directly into cubes, peat pots, or cell pots.

4. Place the containers on a tray, and put the tray and containers inside a plastic bag. Blow up the bag like a balloon and secure the end with a wire tie.

Use the one-step method to start the bigger vegetables such as eggplant, melons, peppers, tomatoes, and squash.

5. Keep the bag at room temperature, in a bright area but out of direct sunlight. Keep the containers damp but not soaked.

6. When the plants are 4 to 7 inches tall, they are ready to be hardened-off and planted in your garden. Hardening-off means gradually adapting an indoor-grown seedling to outdoor weather.

You may also want to consider the commercial seed-starters used with Jiffy cubes and similar materials. In one design, windowsill greenhouses with sliding vents to control humidity can be either placed on a windowsill individually or stacked three or four high.

THE TWO-STEP METHOD

Use this method when you intend to grow large quantities of small vegetables, such as onions or lettuce. It is also suited to starting broccoli, Brussels sprouts, cabbage, and cauliflower. Beans, cucumbers, melons, peas, pumpkins, and squash should not be planted together in large containers, because their roots cannot take the shock of transplanting into the garden.

For the initial sowing, you can use wooden or plastic flats, aluminum cake or meatloaf pans, milk cartons, large frozen-food containers, or cut-off gallon bleach jugs. You can also buy commercial containers that are divided into rows for easy planting.

For planting in flats, you might want to make a row-maker—just a scrap of board with nailed strips to make the rows. Some gardeners construct a different row-maker for each type of flat. With these row-makers you can regulate the depth of rows by controlling the pressure on the board as illustrated here.

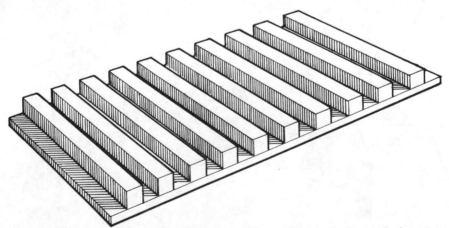

For flats, you can make up to 10 rows at a time by pressing this homemade form into the soil mix. It is especially useful when planting a number of flats at one time.

Make sure the container holds at least 2½ to 3 inches of soil. Anything more shallow will allow the soil to dry out too fast. My favorite container for starting seeds is a throwaway aluminum loaf pan. It is lightweight and will fit easily on a windowsill, yet holds all of any one vegetable that you are going to need. Punch drainage holes with a fork, placing the pan on a dish towel so that the pan doesn't bend.

Germination Media

Does it make any difference which medium you start your seeds in? Absolutely. Theoretically, since the seeds contain their own food supply, they don't need nutrient-rich soil. But one experiment questioned that theory. Tomato seedlings were grown in individual pots filled with commercial potting mix, pure sand, vermiculite, perlite, or a mix of equal parts of sand, vermiculite, and balanced nutrients. Seeds grown in the potting mix grew only an inch in six weeks, while vermiculite and perlite produced 2-inch seedlings, the seedlings grown in sand reached 3 inches, and the tomato seedlings in the nutrient mix grew to 6 inches.

Let's take a quick look at the various germinating materials.

Vermiculite, as we've already seen, can hold a lot of water, yet provides good drainage. See page 22.

Peat moss is organic matter (often sphagnum moss) that decomposed centuries ago. It has a tremendous ability to absorb and hold water. To premoisten it, knead water into it by hand. Peat is slightly acidic and has little or no nutritive value.

Perlite or sponge rock is sterile, expanded volcanic rock that serves the same purpose as sand, though it holds water a bit better.

Blow sand or number 2 builder's sand gives good support to seedlings, but doesn't hold water as well as either vermiculite or perlite. This is a drawback, since seedlings should never be allowed to dry out completely. However, sand improves drainage, adds air space, and gives body to planting mixes.

The Vegetable Factory planting mix is a germination mix I feel works well. Mix equal parts of sand, vermiculite or perlite, and peat moss in a container. Add 3 tablespoons of Vegetable Factory fertilizer (see Chapter 2, Vegetable Factory Soil) to each gallon of germination mix. I suggest that you start all vegetables in this mix. You can keep seedlings in this medium for some time without stunting growth.

You can also start your plants in any of the media listed above, but the seed itself and photosynthesis will supply nutrients to keep the seedlings healthy only until the first true leaves appear. At that time, you must either transfer the plant into a more fertile medium or feed it with fish emulsion.

Here is the Two-Step Method.

Step One

1. Place a layer of coarse material on the bottom of the container. I often use a layer of crumbled dried leaves, then fill the container with Vegetable Factory planting mix. Level off the mix with a knife or stick, then lightly press down and wet the mix thoroughly before planting seeds.

2. For small seeds like lettuce, first mix a quarter of the package of seeds with 2 tablespoons of sand to make it easier to scatter them over the planting mix. Cover the seed with ¼ inch of mix or vermiculite. Pat down and water lightly.

3. For large and medium-sized seeds, sow in furrows made with a pencil or a row-maker. Space large seeds 1 inch apart and medium-sized seeds ½ inch apart. When you finish planting, water lightly.

4. Keep the temperature around 75° F during the day, 60 to 65° at night. For optimum growth, vegetable and herb seedlings need about 12 hours of light a day and a relative humidity of about 80 percent.

To achieve the proper humidity, you can seal the trays or aluminum loaf pans in a clear plastic bag and set them on a bright windowsill, but out of direct sunlight, which can cause the temperature within the bag to become too high. After the seedlings are 3 or 4 inches tall, remove them from the bag and allow them to grow in a south-facing window.

5. Don't water again until after germination—that is, until the little sprouts poke through. After that, add only enough water to keep the soil mix damp. Check by feeling the mix with your fingers; when the mix starts to dry out, add just enough water to dampen it again.

6. When seedlings are 1 or 2 inches high, thin so that they stand about 2 inches apart. Keep the healthy, vigorous seedlings, and remove the smaller, leggy, or weak ones and those that look like they might be diseased. To avoid damaging the entangled roots of nearby plants, don't yank the seedlings, but clip them with a small scissors.

Step Two

1. When the first true leaves have formed, dig out the seedlings and plant them in individual containers. The first two leaflike growths are not true leaves, but cotyledons or "seed leaves"; wait until you see the third and succeeding ones.

Peat pots make good individual containers for seedlings. Simply fill them with the Vegetable Factory planting mix. Many gardeners use quart milk cartons for this purpose. Cut the tops off, make a 2- or 3-inch hole in the bottom, and fill with planting mix. When you transplant into the garden, remove the bottom of the carton, but leave the sides on to protect the plant against insects without restricting the roots. The remainder of the carton will break down in a short time.

Similarly, you can use small cottage cheese and yogurt containers and the larger juice cans. Punch holes in the bottom of the container before you fill with planting mix. When you're ready to plant, cut the container away from the root

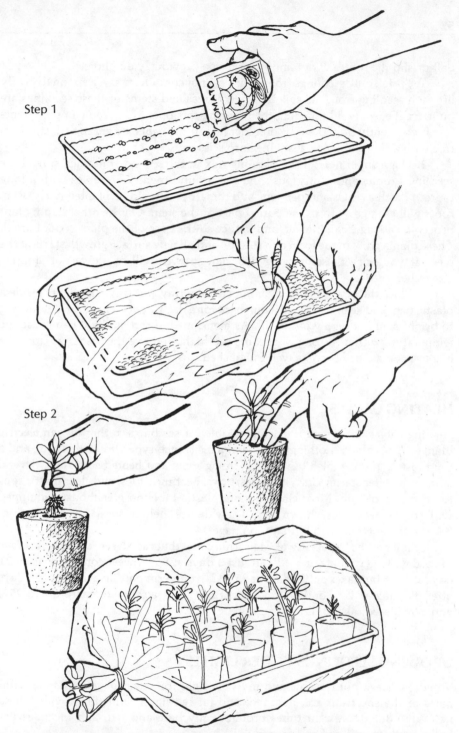

Step 1

Step 2

Use the two-step method to start quantities of small vegetables such as onions, lettuce, and cabbage.

ball or slip the root ball out and plant it in a previously dug hole.

To "prick out" seedlings from their original containers, use a spoon to gently lift each seedling from the soil. The new leaves and stems of these seedlings are quite fragile, so avoid touching them during this operation. You can pull plants free if you gently hold them by an older leaf. If the roots are entangled, cut them free with a sharp knife or a small, sharp scissors.

2. Dig a small hole in the planting mix in the second container, spread the seedling's roots, and gently push the soil around them. Vegetables with a long taproot (such as eggplant, peppers, and tomatoes) should be planted fairly deep; roots will then grow from the buried part of the stem. On the other hand, plant broccoli, cabbage, cauliflower, and lettuce so the base of the plant is not buried. These plants grow in the form of a rosette, and all new surface growth starts at the base. If you bury these growing tips, new growth will be slowed or stopped altogether.

3. Place the newly planted containers on a tray, put tray and plants inside a plastic bag, and keep the bag in a dim light for a day or two. Then transfer the bag to bright sunlight on a windowsill. As mentioned, direct sunlight can cause the temperature within the bag to become too high. Remove the seedlings from the bag as soon as they become well established.

HEATING CABLES

Heating cables make seed flats comfortable for seedlings, rather like an electric blanket. The cable is nothing more than a resistance-type wire with a plug and a thermostat. You can also buy soil-warming mats and heated seed flats. Several companies offer starter kits with cubes, trays, heating cables, and clear plastic tops to keep in moisture. Most elaborate are plastic tabletop greenhouses equipped with soil-heater cables, shown here. These devices help to speed up germination. See the table, From Seed to Plant, on page 44.

Studies at the University of California show that radish seeds take an average of 29 days to germinate at 41° F, but just 3 days at 86°. Sweet corn emerges in 21 days at 50° F, but takes only 3 days at 95°. Carrots germinate an average of 50 days after planting at 41° F and only 6 days at 86°. But raise the temperature to 95°, and carrot seed takes 8 days to germinate.

GROWING SEEDLINGS UNDER LIGHTS

Vegetables need both visible and invisible light for vigorous growth. The vital parts of the spectrum are blue, red, and far-red light. Sunlight provides these naturally. But fluorescent tubes produce only blue and red, and incandescent bulbs produce only red and far-red.

You can start seedlings with two 40-watt cool-white fluorescent bulbs. Some gardeners supplement this with two 25-watt incandescent bulbs to supply far-red

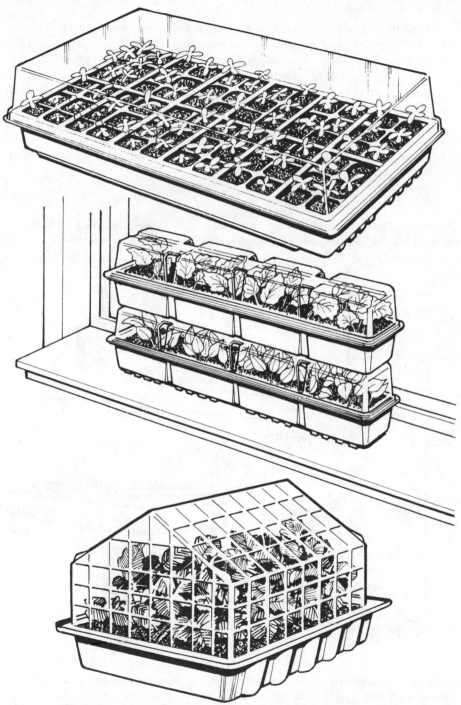

Table-top "greenhouses" speed up seed germination. These can be placed on the windowsill or under artificial light.

light. Both bulbs and fixtures are available at electrical and home centers. Specially designed fluorescent starting units can be purchased through seed catalogs. They can be set up on a table, a desk, a workbench, or wherever handy.

To start vegetables, you need 15 to 20 watts per square foot of surface area. To calculate the watts per square foot reaching your plants, simply divide the total light wattage by the number of square feet you are trying to light.

For example, a fixture holding two 20-watt fluorescent tubes gives off a total of 40 watts. If the fixture and its bulbs cover a 2-square-foot area when mounted one foot from the surface, then that surface is receiving 20 watts per square foot.

$$\frac{40 \text{ watts}}{2 \text{ sq. ft.}} = 20 \text{ watts per sq. ft.}$$

This means that with one 40-watt unit, you can start seedlings over an area of 2 square feet—for example, in nine 4-by-8-inch aluminum trays or four 6-by-12-inch wooden flats.

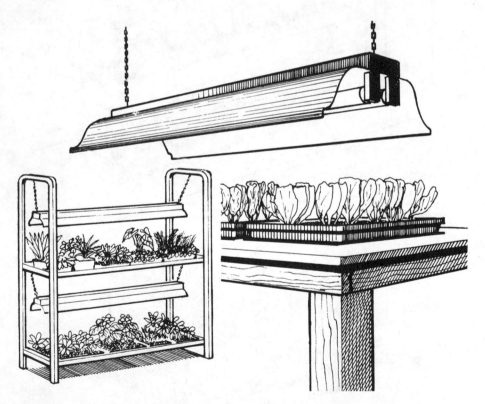

All that's needed to grow seedlings under lights is a place to work and a hanging fluorescent fixture. Fluorescent tubes provide both the heat for germinating the seeds and the light for growing seedlings. More elaborate light carts are useful for houseplants too.

To sprout seeds, position containers 3 to 4 inches below the tubes, then keep the lights on continuously until the seedlings emerge. Once they have sprouted, give seedlings about 12 hours of light a day. An inexpensive timer will take the guesswork out of turning the tubes on and off, and will automatically give your seedlings the correct amount of light every day.

HARDENING-OFF AND TRANSPLANTING

Whether you purchase plants from a nursery or start them indoors, seedlings must be hardened-off (acclimated to the conditions they'll find in the garden).

When they are about ready to be transplanted into the garden, slow their growth by giving them half their normal water supply. For five to seven days before planting, place them outside in the garden during the daytime and bring them back inside at night. You can keep seedlings outside if you place a plastic cover or a cardboard box over them at night. If you are using a heating coil, you can harden-off seedlings inside by gradually cutting back on the heat until you approximate garden temperatures.

PLANTING BY ZONE

I want you to stop a minute and consider exactly what a Vegetable Factory garden is—an extremely small garden that uses all of its growing space all the time. This is accomplished by gardening both horizontally and vertically. A Vegetable Factory garden presents a diagonal wall of plants to the sun, so that when mature it looks something like a wedge. The vegetables in front seldom grow above 2 to 10 inches tall; those in the middle reach 2 to 3 feet tall; and those in back may grow 6 feet or more above the garden bed.

In addition, in these small gardens you must learn to think of the larger plants such as zucchini and tomatoes in terms of one, two, or three plants, not dozens or even five or six.

It is true that you can grow 100 or 200 carrots, beets, or radishes in 2 square feet, but in most Vegetable Factory gardens you have room for only one eggplant, one crookneck squash, or similar vegetable. Now let's look at some of the principles that help us turn even a tiny plot of ground into a real Vegetable Factory.

There are three planting zones in the Vegetable Factory garden, which I'll identify as zones A, B, and C. Vegetables are planted within the zones by height (see the table, Zones for Plants).

Zone A is a 6- to 15-inch strip at the north end of the garden reserved for vine crops. Plant zone A with peas, winter squash, melons such as cantaloupes, cucumbers, and similar vegetables. Grown horizontally in the garden, these crops would take up a tremendous area. Just two watermelon plants, for instance, can easily cover an entire bed if you let them sprawl. But if you grow them vertically up a support and space them about 1 foot apart in zone A, you can easily squeeze

Vegetable Factory Zones for Plants

Zone A	Zone B
Beans, snap	Broccoli
Cucumber	Brussels sprouts
Muskmelons	Cabbage
Peas	Cauliflower
Pumpkins	Celeriac
Winter squash	Celery
	Eggplant
	Okra
	Peppers
	Tomatoes
	Bush varieties of squash, cucumber, muskmelon, and other vegetables

Zone C	Herbs and Flowers For Zones B and C
Beets	Anise
Carrots	Basil
Lettuce	Borage
Kale	Caraway
Mustard	Chervil
Onions	Chives
Parsnips	Marigolds
Radishes	Nasturtiums
Rutabaga	Parsley
Turnips	Peppermint
	Sage
	Sweet marjoram
	Thyme

Plant corn varieties that grow over 5 feet in a solid block in zone A. Plant varieties that grow under 5 feet in a small block in zone B.

in five to ten plants. Don't plant bush varieties in this zone, since they will be shaded out by the taller plants in zone B.

Zone B occupies the next 2 to 4 feet of the bed. This is the intermediate zone in the Vegetable Factory garden, intended for plants that grow 2 to 6 feet tall. These might include one tomato plant in a 6-foot wire cage, pole beans grown around a single pole, such vegetables as broccoli, cabbage, cauliflower, eggplant, peppers, and summer squash, and bush varieties of vine crops such as 'Table King' acorn squash and 'Bush Champion' cucumbers.

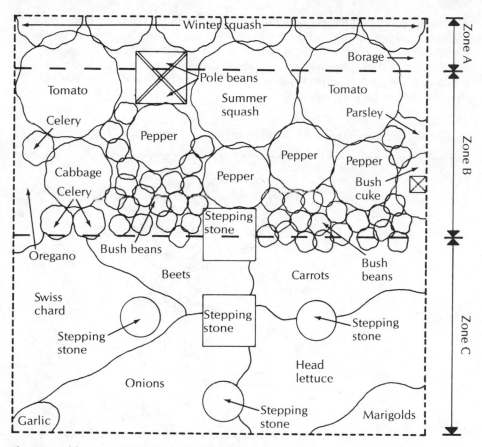

Winter squash

Zone A

Borage

Tomato

Celery

Pole beans

Summer squash

Tomato

Parsley

Zone B

Pepper

Cabbage
Celery

Pepper

Pepper

Pepper

Bush cuke

Pepper

Stepping stone

Oregano

Bush beans

Beets

Carrots

Bush beans

Swiss chard

Stepping stone

Stepping stone

Stepping stone

Onions

Head lettuce

Stepping stone

Garlic

Marigolds

Zone C

The Vegetable Factory garden is divided into three zones: Zone A is a 6- to 15-inch strip at the north end of the garden; zone B occupies the next 2 to 4 feet; zone C occupies the remainder of the garden. The vegetables are planted in each zone by height.

Zone C takes up the remainder of the garden. Here you can grow root and leafy vegetables such as beets, carrots, spinach, and turnips. This arrangement allows you to garden vertically in the northern portion of the garden, while giving shorter vegetables their quota of direct sunlight.

In portions of zone B not shaded by other vegetables and in zone C, I always squeeze in at least two or three herbs such as basil and parsley, and a few flowers such as marigolds and nasturtiums.

DYNAMIC PLANT GROUPINGS

A dynamic plant grouping is simply a small community of vegetables that grow well together. Each grouping is planted roughly in the form of a semicircle, and

A dynamic plant grouping is a community of vegetables that grow well together, planted roughly in the form of a semicircle. A grouping consists of one key producer plant surrounded by secondary vegetables such as peppers and bush beans, and tertiary plantings of leafy and root vegetables. Groupings can be squeezed close together in the garden, or two key producer plants can be treated as one plant to make up a dynamic plant grouping.

1. One key producer plant surrounded by secondary and tertiary plantings.

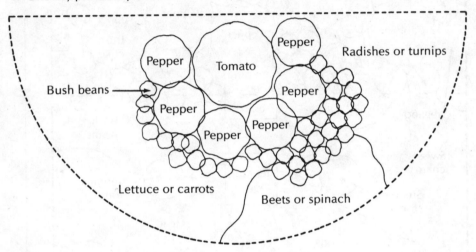

2. Two key producer plants treated as one plant to create a dynamic plant grouping.

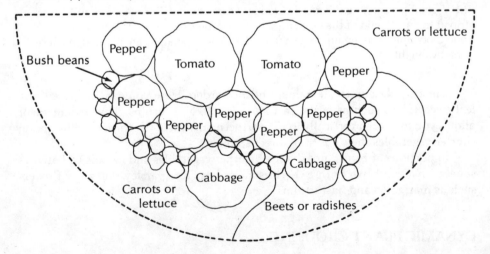

3. Two side-by-side groupings planted close together in the garden.

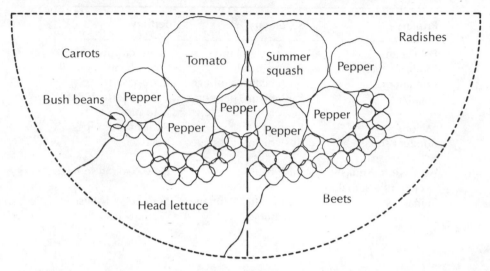

4. Three dynamic plant groupings with overlapping secondary and tertiary plantings.

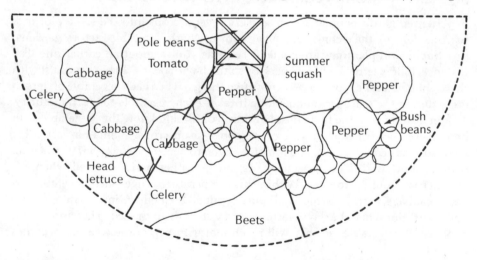

consists of one key producer plant surrounded by secondary and tertiary plants. A key producer plant might be a single cabbage, eggplant, tomato, or bush winter squash. This is the largest and most dominant plant in the group. Each is surrounded by secondary plantings of bush beans, small cabbage, celery, or peppers. Beyond this, plant a semicircle of tertiary plantings of leafy or root vegetables such as lettuce, onions, and radishes. All plantings within the Vegetable Factory garden are irregular in shape (rather than square). The reason for this will be explained later in this chapter.

Dynamic Plant Groupings

Primary	Secondary	Tertiary
Pole beans	Celery, eggplant	Beets, carrots, onions
Cabbage, cauliflower	Broccoli, celery	Spinach, Swiss chard
Cucumbers	Bush beans, cabbage	Radishes
Eggplant	Bush beans, peppers	Carrots, lettuce, turnips
Melons	Peppers	Radishes, turnips
Summer squash	Bush beans, cabbage, peppers	Beets
Bush winter squash, cucumbers, melons	Bush beans	New Zealand spinach
Tomatoes	Bush beans, cabbage, peppers	Lettuce, radishes, spinach

SQUEEZING MORE VEGETABLES INTO YOUR GARDEN

Experienced gardeners manage to squeeze several crops into the same plot in a season. Here are the techniques I suggest for use with Vegetable Factory gardens.

Succession plantings are made as soon as you take out an earlier one. For instance, follow lettuce with peppers, or spinach with beans. To be successful with this tight scheduling, you need to know two things: when each vegetable prefers to grow during the season, and how long it takes each vegetable to reach maturity.

In dealing with the first consideration, you should know that vegetables can be classified as either warm-season or cool-season crops. Plants harvested for fruit, such as beans, squash, and tomatoes, tend to need heat (65 to 85° F) and long days to grow well. Cool-season plants, on the other hand, do well when the weather is about 55 to 75° F. Within this temperature range, such vegetables as beets, cabbage, carrots, lettuce and spinach put all their efforts into forming leaves and roots. But when the days warm up, they start to go to seed. Therefore, plant cool-season vegetables so they will reach maturity before the weather becomes too hot.

Some vegetables will tolerate freezing temperatures, and may be planted in the spring as soon as the soil can be worked. These include broccoli, cabbage, onions, peas, radishes, rutabagas, spinach, and turnips. Other vegetables such as beets, carrots, cauliflower, lettuce, and Swiss chard can be planted two to four weeks before the last frost (see Appendix A). Beans, cantaloupes, cucumbers, eggplant, peppers, squash, tomatoes, and watermelons are damaged by frost and should be planted or transplanted on or after the average last frost date.

The second factor to consider in succession planting is how long it takes a vegetable to grow to maturity. Since radishes mature in about 25 days, you can pop them into the ground early, harvest them, follow with vegetables that need longer to mature such as tomatoes, then finish the season with more radishes.

For a succession of three crops, you generally can (1) plant a cool-season crop that takes less than 50 days to mature; (2) follow that by a hot-weather crop; and (3) follow at the end of the season with a fast-maturing cool-weather crop.

Cool- and Warm-Season Crops

Cool-Season Crops		Warm-Season Crops	
Very hardy (plant 4–6 weeks after last frost-free date)	Hardy (plant 2–4 weeks before frost-free date)	Not cold-hardy (plant on frost-free date)	Needs hot weather (plant 1 week or more after frost-free date)
Asparagus	Beets	Beans, snap	Beans, lima
Broccoli	Carrots	Corn	Cucumbers
Cabbage	Mustard	New Zealand	Eggplant
Lettuce	Parsnips	spinach	Melons
Onions	Potatoes	Okra	Peppers
Peas	Swiss chard	Pumpkins	Sweet potatoes
Radishes		Soybeans	
Rhubarb		Squash	
Spinach		Tomatoes	
Turnips			

The term **intercropping,** as used in Vegetable Factory gardening, means planting quick-maturing crops in spaces between slower-maturing ones. This allows us to make the greatest use of small beds for maximum production.

Intercropping involves long-term and short-term plants, tall plants and short plants, and light- and shade-tolerant plants. For instance, plant lettuce in the same space where you plant one summer squash. The lettuce reaches maturity long before the summer squash does, allowing you to harvest its leaves for a long period of time before it is finally shaded out by the squash. Other possible intercropping plantings are radishes and cabbage, leaf lettuce and tomatoes, green onions and bush cucumbers, and fast-maturing turnips and zucchini.

As you intercrop, you should be aware of the light requirements of your crops. Some plants require full sun, while others tolerate some shade. Lettuce, for instance, is a shade-loving plant that benefits from growing under taller plants like cabbage, eggplant, peppers and tomatoes.

Here's how to intercrop vegetables in zones A and B of the Vegetable Factory. Several weeks before the last frost, plant quick-maturing crops such as green onions, lettuce, radishes, spinach, and turnips across all of zones A and B. Then, at

Vegetable Light Needs

Partial Sun	Full Sun
Beets	Beans
Carrots	Broccoli
Cauliflower	Brussels sprouts
Lettuce	Cabbage
Onions	Corn
Parsley	Eggplant
Peas	Muskmelons
Radishes	Peppers
Spinach	Pumpkins
Swiss chard	Squash, summer
	Squash, winter
	Tomatoes

the proper time, plant the larger, slower-maturing crops such as broccoli, bush vine crops, cabbage, eggplant, peppers, tomatoes, and winter squash. Thin out enough of the quick-maturing crops to make room for them. By the time these larger vegetables cover the soil between plants, you will already have harvested your first crop of fast-maturing vegetables.

In zone C, you can mix radish and carrot seeds together, and plant them in the same space. The radishes will be harvested long before the carrots begin to take hold. This technique is especially useful for increasing the production of a small garden.

The basic rule in Vegetable Factory gardening is: Don't leave bare ground unplanted at any time during the entire growing season. This wastes valuable space and allows weeds to gain a foothold.

WHAT GOES NEXT TO WHAT?

In a small garden, vegetables are squeezed in next to each other, and it is important that only compatible plants are neighbors. Those that don't get along should be planted as far apart as possible.

What does well with what? Over the years, a vast amount of gardening lore has dealt with this question. Unfortunately, very few Agricultural Experiment Stations have conducted formal tests to help us understand the phenomenon of companion planting. It is known that plant roots exude seven major compounds into the soil—amino acids, vitamins, sugars, tannins, alkaloids, phosphatides, and glucosides. These substances may affect other plants grown in the vicinity.

I have tried a number of combinations in Vegetable Factory gardens, and here are some of my observations. Cucumbers do well when paired with bush beans, lettuce, and radishes; they don't do well paired with potatoes. Beans grow well in proximity to beets, cabbage, carrots, cauliflower, corn, cucumbers, savory, and strawberries but don't grow especially well when grown with onions. Peppers do well when planted near carrots, eggplant, onions, parsley, and tomatoes but don't particularly like kohlrabi.

Plant Companions

Crop	Plant Near	Keep Away From
Basil	Most garden crops	Rue
Beans, bush	Beets, cabbage, carrots, cauliflower, corn, cucumbers, marigolds, savory, strawberries	Onions, garlic, leeks, shallots
Beans, pole	Corn, marigolds, potatoes, radishes	Beets, garlic, kohlrabi, leeks, onions
Beets	Broccoli, bush beans, Brussels sprouts, cabbage, cauliflower, lettuce, onions, Swiss chard	Pole beans
Borage	Squash, tomatoes	—
Broccoli, Brussels sprouts	Beets, cabbage, other cole crops, carrots, marigolds, nasturtiums, thyme, tomatoes	Strawberries
Cabbage, cauliflower	Beans, carrots, celery, cucumbers, potatoes, spinach, Swiss chard	Strawberries, tomatoes
Cantaloupe	Corn	Potatoes
Carrots	Cabbage, chives, leeks, lettuce, onions, peas, potatoes, radishes, rosemary, sage, tomatoes	Dill
Celery	Cauliflower, leeks, tomatoes	—
Chives	Carrots, tomatoes	Beans, peas
Corn	Beans, cucumbers, melons, potatoes, pumpkins, squash	Peas
Cucumbers	Beans, cabbage, corn, potatoes, radishes, squash	Potatoes
Eggplant	Beans, peppers, potatoes, tomatoes	—
Garlic	Cabbage, tomatoes	Peas, beans
Kale	Cabbage family	Pole beans, strawberries
Kohlrabi	Beets, carrots, celery, marigolds, mints, spinach, Swiss chard	Tomatoes, pole beans
Lettuce	Beets, carrots, parsnips, radishes, strawberries	Cabbage family
Marigolds	All garden crops except beans	Beans
Marjoram	All vegetables	—
Nasturtiums	Beans, broccoli, cabbage, cauliflower, potatoes, pumpkins, radishes, squash, tomatoes	—

(continued)

Plant Companions—*Continued*

Crop	Plant Near	Keep Away From
Onions	Beets, broccoli, cabbage, carrots, cauliflower, parsnips	Asparagus, beans, peas
Oregano	All vegetables	—
Parsley	Asparagus, corn, tomatoes	—
Parsnips	Onions, radishes	—
Peas	Beans, carrots, corn, cucumbers, potatoes, radishes, turnips	Garlic, leeks, onions, shallots
Peppers	Basil, carrots, eggplant, onions, parsley, tomatoes	Kohlrabi
Potatoes	Beans, broccoli, cabbage, cauliflower, corn, eggplant, marigolds, peas	Cucumbers, pumpkins, tomatoes
Radishes	Cucumbers, lettuce, melons, nasturtiums, peas, root crops	Grapes
Rosemary	Beans, broccoli, cabbage, carrots, cauliflower, sage, squash, tomatoes	—
Sage	Cabbage family	Cucumbers
Spinach	Cauliflower, celery, eggplant, strawberries	—
Squash	Radishes, nasturtiums	Potatoes
Strawberries	Bush beans, borage, lettuce, spinach	Cabbage family
Swiss chard	Bush beans, kohlrabi, onions	Pole beans
Thyme	All vegetables	—
Tomatoes	Asparagus, basil, broccoli, carrots, cauliflower, mustard, onions, parsley, rosemary, sage	Cabbage, corn, kohlrabi, potato
Turnips, rutabagas	Peas	Mustard, potatoes

Plants are placed together in Vegetable Factory groupings because, through experimentation, they have been found to grow well when close to each other. In some cases, they agree with the conventional advice on companion planting. In other cases, these groupings are not yet recommended in companion planting literature.

PUT YOUR GARDEN ON PAPER

We've already discussed this in Chapter 1, Planning the Vegetable Factory. Since you will be dealing with a number of vegetables in a very small space, I suggest that you lay out your garden on paper before you try to plant anything.

Sketch in the zones. Mark in each key producer plant—tomatoes, zucchini, and so forth—including the vining plants in zone A. Lay out secondary plantings such as peppers and bush beans, and the tertiary plantings, including carrots and beets. Sketch in the blocks of vegetables you intend to plant throughout the rest of the bed, including any herbs and flowers. Finally, indicate on your plan the succession planting, intercropping, and catch-cropping sequences you intend to follow.

Before you actually plant, mark out the entire garden on the ground. Stake out the key producer plants and the secondary vegetables with either a commercial plant stake or a Popsicle stick (there are usually only four or five key producer plants at the most, and not too many more secondary plants). Then take a little flour or lime, and mark off the remaining plantings.

In the past, I have tried to simply remember where everything goes. I have also tried laying out the various areas with stakes and string. Neither method works well, because I get in the middle of planting and can't remember the boundaries for each vegetable. By marking the entire garden out on the ground, however, I can see in advance exactly what the finished plot is going to look like.

PLANTING YOUR VEGETABLE FACTORY GARDEN

A Vegetable Factory garden starts to become a functioning unit the minute you begin to put your seeds or plants in the ground. At this point, both the shape of the plantings and the spacing of individual plants becomes extremely important. Let's examine this in detail.

Spacing determines both the quantity of vegetables you can take out of the bed and the vitality of the garden itself. The object is to space the plants within each grouping in such a way that their outer leaves just touch one another when three-quarters mature. When the plants are fully mature, the leaves should virtually carpet the bed. The plants shade their own root zones at maturity, allowing the bed to retain moisture and preventing weed growth. The microclimate and plant groupings also seem to create a vigor that other types of plantings don't have.

All plants should be spaced *slightly under* the distances suggested on the seed packages (see the table, Vegetable Factory Spacings.) Plant peppers, for instance, about 12 inches apart instead of the recommended 18 inches, leaf lettuce 3 to 4 inches apart instead of 4 to 6 inches, and so on. When planting two different vegetables side by side, add the two spacings together and divide by two. For instance, radishes require 2-inch spacing and Swiss chard requires 6; add 2 and 6 and divide by 2, for a spacing of 4 inches.

Most home gardens today use one of three types of spacing: row spacing, square spacing, or equidistant spacing.

As an example of **row spacing,** you might plant a particular vegetable 6 inches apart in rows 2 feet apart—wasting much of the space between rows. In a 5-by-5-foot garden, for instance, you would be able to squeeze in only 33 plants.

Vegetable Factory Spacings

Vegetable	Spacing (in.)	Vegetable	Spacing (in.)
Anise	8	Lettuce, head	10
Asparagus	12	Lettuce, leaf	6
Basil	6–8	Marjoram, sweet	15
Bean, fava	4	Mint	8
Bean, lima-bush	8	Muskmelon	12
Bean, lima-pole	10	Okra	16
Bean, snap-bush	4	Onion, bunching	2
Bean, snap-pole	6	Onion	3–4
Beet	3	Parsley	8
Borage	12	Parsnip	4
Broccoli	15	Pea	2–3
Brussels sprouts	15	Pepper	12–24
Cabbage	14	Potato	4–10
Cabbage, Chinese	10	Pumpkin	12–18
Cardoon	15	Radish	2
Carrot	2	Rutabaga	6
Cauliflower	15	Sage	30
Celeriac	8	Salsify	3
Celery	6	Savory, summer	8
Chervil	6	Shallot	2
Chives	6	Spinach	4
Collards	12	Spinach, Malabar	8
Coriander	6	Spinach, New Zealand	10
Corn, sweet	8	Squash, summer	12
Cucumber	6	Squash, winter	12–24
Eggplant	24	Sweet potato	12
Garlic	3	Swiss chard	6
Horseradish	6	Thyme	10
Kale	8	Tomato	18
Kohlrabi	6	Turnip	3
Leek	3	Watermelon	12–18

With **square center spacing,** plants are treated as squares, with the plant centers placed an equal distance apart. If you plant 6 inches apart in rows 6 inches apart, you'll be able to grow approximately 81 plants in that 5-by-5-foot garden instead of the 27 you'd get using conventional garden row spacing.

With **equidistant spacing,** plants are placed an equal distance apart in all directions. But the plants are treated as circles, and the plantings staggered so the rows can be moved even closer together. You will now be able to grow approximately 99 plants in the 5-by-5-foot garden. This allows maximum production from the space available. Always use equidistant spacing when planting your Vegetable Factory garden.

The most efficient way to plant blocks of vegetables together using equidistant spacing is to plant each block in an irregular shape. Three pepper plants, spaced 12 inches from each other, will create an irregular semicircle. If you plant a block of carrots at 2- or 3-inch spacings up against the peppers, the most efficient way to do this is to squeeze the carrots within 7½ inches of each pepper plant. A square planting here would waste space.

Laying out a Vegetable Factory garden is a bit more challenging than making straight rows. For guides, I cut circles from fairly heavy cardboard—three or four each, in diameters of 10, 12, 15, and 18 inches, with a ½-inch punched in the center. I lay one of the circles on the bed where I intend to put each key producer plant. This gives me the exact spacing of each major vegetable without having to measure. I then put a marker into the ground through the center of each circle, and remove the circle.

I also use 6-, 8-, and 10-inch-square cardboard triangles. I find them extremely handy for laying out vegetables like celery and rutabaga.

Finally, I make up several 1-foot squares of 1-inch mesh chickenwire for planting root and leafy crops that need spacings of 2, 3, or 4 inches. I also find a 12-inch ruler handy at all stages of planting.

Sowing Seeds Outdoors

There are two ways to sow seeds—one at a time, and by broadcast seeding. Planting seeds one at a time may sound tedious, but in most cases you plant fairly limited areas, so the actual work is kept to a minimum. Try to space seed right the first time, so you have to do less thinning.

Medium-sized to large-seeded root and leaf crops are planted using the chickenwire grid. Fine-seeded root and vegetable crops such as carrots and lettuce should be planted by broadcasting the seed across the entire planting area. The biggest advantage of broadcast seeding is that you can plant each section quickly. The disadvantage is that the method is imprecise, and you wind up with some seed bunched up rather than spread evenly over the entire surface.

The way to avoid uneven broadcasting is practice. I suggest that you try "sowing" dry coffee grounds over a piece of clear plastic. Some gardeners I know practice with sand, but sand is too heavy and doesn't broadcast like seed. With a little practice, you will find that you can obtain a reasonably good distribution. One word of warning: Broadcast seed only on windless days, or you will have seed everywhere. After broadcast seeding, spread about ¼ inch of garden soil over the area and water with a fine spray.

Plant large to medium-sized seeds at a depth roughly equal to four times the diameter of the seed. Medium-sized seeds, such as radish and rutabaga seeds, should be ½ inch deep. Large seeds (beans, corn, melons, squash) do best planted 1 to 2 inches deep. Climate and soil conditions should also be considered in determining seed depth. In wet weather or in heavy soils, plant shallowly; in light, sandy soils or in dry weather, plant more deeply.

All vegetable seeds must be kept moist until they have completely germinated or begun to sprout. To make sure that the soil stays moist at all times, water once a day. To keep seed from drying out when it's planted only ¼ inch deep or less, you may have to cover the seedbed after sowing your seeds with ⅛ to ¼ inch of compost, rotted horse manure, or organic mulch. You can also cover the seedbed with a piece of black plastic to keep in moisture. When the seedlings poke their heads out of the ground, remove the plastic.

Transplanting Seedlings

Dig the holes for seedlings with a small garden trowel or a bulb planter. Fill the holes with water, letting it soak in. Water the seedlings thoroughly before removing them from their flats. If seedlings are planted in peat pots or cubes, soak them until they are moist and soft.

If you are transplanting from a flat or a container planted with two or more seedlings, carefully separate the root ball of each plant. If plants are in individual pots and are rootbound, trim off the long roots and rough up the outer roots of the root ball with your hand. If you have uncovered the roots of a plant that you don't intend to transplant immediately, cover the soil ball with a damp cloth or damp soil to keep from damaging the feeder roots.

Trim off about half the leaves of large transplants, being careful not to trim the central growing tip. Set plants like cabbage and lettuce at the same height in your beds that they were growing in the soil. Planting too deeply, as already discussed, can slow down or stop growth. Plant one-third of the stem of eggplant, pepper, and tomato plants below ground level. Additional roots will grow out along this below-ground portion.

Planting the Zones

Plant the vine crops in zone A either from seed or as seedlings, about 6 inches from the back of the bed. You can, if you like, plant two rows in this zone, spacing each plant 12 inches apart using equidistant spacing. Measure the distance between plants with a ruler or a 12-inch triangle.

Lay out the zone B positions for the key producer plants—cabbage, eggplant, tomatoes—using the appropriate cardboard circles. Plant the secondary plantings with the dynamic plant groupings, using either the circles or triangles. Plant the root and leaf crops in zones B and C with the triangles or the chickenwire grids, or by broadcast seeding.

WHEN TO PLANT

Figuring out when to plant your vegetables can be as simple or as complicated as you want to make it. I have a number of engineering friends who figure it all out using their computers. I'm afraid I can't garden that way. I try to keep it as simple as possible. Let me mention a few rules that work well for me.

Look up the approximate date of the last spring frost for your area in Appendix A. This table lists these dates by state and by areas within the state, but these geographical areas are so broad that you will have to estimate the date for your particular location. For instance, I live in the foothills of the Sierra Nevada Mountains of California. The table gives the last date of frost for California's Central Valley as March 1, and the last date of killing frost for California's mountainous areas as April 20. In fact, the last killing frost date for my area lies somewhere between the two, probably closer to April 20 than to March 1.

Of course, the actual date of last frost will vary from year to year. Some years, I can easily plant my warm-weather vegetables on March 15; other years, I need to wait until May 1 if I expect the vegetables to grow vigorously after I put them in the ground. My suggestion is to start with the date given in the appendix table and modify it as you acquire experience.

Using your frost date from Appendix A, now look up the vegetables you wish to plant in Appendix B. This will give you the correct in-ground planting dates for that vegetable. For instance, if the average date of the last freeze in your area is April 10, the table says that you can plant carrots from March 10 to April 20, eggplant from May 1 to June 1, and radishes from March 1 to May 1. Mark these dates on your garden plan, so you'll know when to plant what.

If you intend to start your plants from seed, you will find the number of weeks from seed to transplant size listed in Appendix D. Simply subtract this from the planting dates. If, for instance, you can plant eggplant from May 1 to June 1, and the appendix table says that eggplant takes six to nine weeks to grow to transplant size, then you should start seed at least two months before May 1, or about March 1. Again, if you look up these dates in advance and write them on your plan, you will know when to plant seeds indoors for all your plantings.

When making up a particular Vegetable Factory garden, I usually do more than just mark the dates on my plan. I make a list of the vegetables I intend to grow, then use the tables already mentioned to make up seed-starter and planting timetables for that particular garden. See the illustration on page 70 for a sample timetable for one of my gardens.

If you would like to eliminate most of the planting-date guesswork, try taking your soil's temperature. You can purchase a soil thermometer from a number of mail-order seed firms. As already mentioned, some seeds can't tolerate cool soil, while others thrive in it. Researchers have pinpointed the minimum and maximum planting temperatures, as well as the ideal germinating temperature, for most major vegetables. Refer to the table, Vegetable Seed Germination Temperatures, on page 71.

Seed-Starters' Timetable

(Arrows run from seed-planting date to setting-out date)

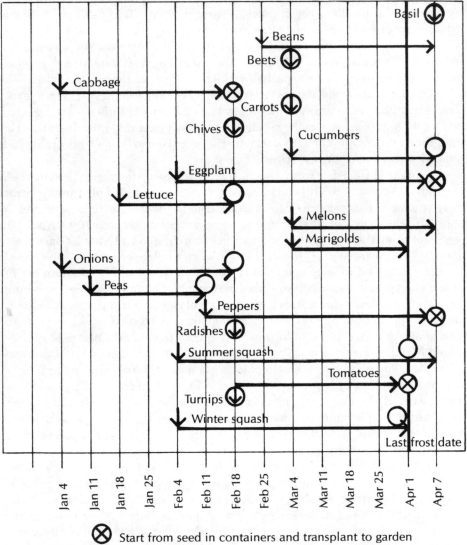

Vegetable Seed Germination Temperatures

Crop	Minimum Temperature (°F)	Optimum Temperature Range (°F)
Asparagus	50	60–85
Bean, lima	60	65–85
Bean, snap	60	60–85
Beet	40	50–85
Cabbage	40	45–95
Carrot	40	45–85
Cauliflower	40	45–85
Celery	40	60–70
Corn	50	60–95
Cucumber	60	65–90
Eggplant	60	75–90
Lettuce	35	40–80
Muskmelon	60	75–95
Okra	60	70–95
Onion	35	50–95
Parsley	40	50–85
Parsnip	35	50–70
Pea	40	40–75
Pepper	60	65–95
Pumpkin	60	70–90
Radish	40	45–90
Spinach	35	45–75
Squash	60	70–95
Swiss chard	40	50–85
Tomato	50	60–85
Turnip	40	60–105
Watermelon	60	70–95

SOURCE: Department of Vegetable Crops, University of California, Davis.

CHAPTER 4

PROTECTION FROM THE ELEMENTS

CLIMATE IS ONE MAJOR VARIABLE that you can't control. The garden doesn't get enough sun. Frost wipes out your peppers earlier than you expected. The weather turns cold in the spring, and your tomatoes don't grow well for several weeks. The wind destroys some of your plants.

With a Vegetable Factory garden, you can modify planting beds to improve growing conditions. This may mean putting up a simple windscreen, adding a reflector to supply more light, heating the soil to speed up germination, or using a variety of devices to protect plants from frost and extend either end of the growing season.

PROTECTIVE DEVICES

You can easily protect vegetables from the weather by placing a cover over individual plants, a section of the garden, or an entire Vegetable Factory bed. These devices make it possible to raise the garden temperature at least 5 to 15° F or more. This allows you to start crops earlier and to extend the season for such warm-season crops as tomatoes and eggplant by two to four weeks.

A **cloche** is any covering that admits the sunlight to warm a bed. In a Vegetable Factory garden, this might mean anything from a plastic cup turned upside-down over a single plant to a bed-wide greenhouse.

When the sun's rays pass through the glazed surface of the cloche, they are stored in the soil as energy. Because this heat energy has a longer wavelength than light energy, it will not pass back out through the glazing. The trapped heat then raises the temperature of the soil and air under the cover. As a result, even simple cloches made from household materials will extend the growing season by at least a few weeks.

Hotcaps and hot tents are the simplest devices to use in a Vegetable Factory bed. They are slightly translucent and let in enough light to support plant growth.

Hotcaps are heavy wax paper cones that protect your plants from the cold. Besides the commercial devices, you can make your own using paper cups or plastic jugs.

You can buy hotcaps and hot tents at garden centers and nurseries or from seed catalogs. Or you can make your own by cutting the bottoms off plastic jugs and by turning plastic containers (such as cake covers) over individual vegetables.

Soft plastics (most commonly polyethylene) are lightweight and inexpensive, and are useful for covering a variety of cloches if you intend to move them around the garden. A drawback is that they don't last as long as rigid plastics. Here are some ideas for making soft plastic cloches.

● Stretch polyethylene over coat hanger wickets to make a plastic tent. Hold down the plastic with rocks.

● Stretch polyethylene over chickenwire tunnels.

● Cover a hinged A-frame with polyethylene. It can be moved around the garden easily and folded for storage when not in use.

● Cover the entire bed or a portion of the bed with a "wicket tunnel." This tunnel is made of construction wire covered with clear plastic. Construction wire is heavy wire mesh used in pouring concrete foundations. Buy it at any lumberyard or building supply store. Cut the wire to fit your bed.

● For plants normally grown in vertical cages, simply wrap polyethylene sheets around the cage and staple them in place.

Rigid plastics (often fiberglass) can be bent over a frame and aren't damaged by wind and rain. One cloche design can be made by drilling a pair of holes in rectangular sheets of acrylic and fastening them together at the top by passing notebook rings through the holes. These can be moved around easily and folded for storage.

Or create a "cucumber incubator" from a flexed sheet of translucent ribbed fiberglass. This incubator traps growth-enhancing heat and carbon dioxide to

Plastic-covered tents and tunnels are extremely useful in the Vegetable Factory garden. They cover several plants at one time and can be moved where needed.

speed up seed-to-harvest time for cucumbers, melons, pumpkins, and squash.

There are several cloche-type devices on the market that offer effective protection.

Portable roll greenhouses can simply be laid out over the whole bed or a portion of the bed. A three-piece miniature greenhouse, resembling a clear plastic garbage can with a shower-cap cover, allows you to set out eggplant, peppers, and tomatoes at least five weeks early; when the plants reach the top, remove the domed lid.

The Wall o' Water consists of a plastic ring of sectioned, cylindrical tubes filled with water. The liquid will hold heat from the day's sun to warm the plants at night. If the water should freeze, heat is still released as the water cools. This device protects plants to 16°F and allows you to water and fertilize without removing the cloche.

The **Sunhat** is a rigid plastic cone that has alternating clear and green stripes. The transparent stripes let sunshine in, while the colored stripes provide shade.

The **floating row cover** requires no wire support. It consists of soft, lightweight polypropylene fabric such as Reemay that allows light and water to pass through. As your crops grow, they lift the cover along with them. Simply roll it out loosely over the seedbed, and secure the edges with soil or mulch.

One word of warning about plastic: on warm, sunny days, the air temperature under plastic cover can quickly become too great for plants. It is therefore essential to provide good ventilation and to check the temperature regularly. The easiest way to do this is to place a thermometer inside the device. When the temperature rises 10°F or more above the maximum for a specific vegetable, remove or open the protective device. Replace or close it only on cooler days.

COLDFRAMES

Coldframes and hotbeds mark the next step in Vegetable Factory evolution. A coldframe is an unheated boxlike glass- or clear plastic-covered structure for protecting plants. A hotbed is a coldframe with an added heat source. Cloches and row covers are designed for short-term use, but coldframes and hotbeds can be used for year-round gardening.

A Vegetable Factory coldframe consists of a wooden or masonry box with a plastic or glass top. For maximum exposure to the sun, the coldframe should face due south. This is easy if you orient your coldframe directly north and south. It doesn't matter if you are slightly off—the orientation can be varied as much as 20 degrees east or west without significantly inhibiting the coldframe's solar gain.

The top should be slanted so that the sun's rays strike it as close as possible to a 90-degree angle. Because the sun's path through the sky changes daily, there is no way to set the top so that it is perpendicular to the sun at all times.

The rule of thumb is: add 20 degrees to your latitude to arrive at the best angle from the horizon. If you live in northern California as I do, or in northern Colorado, southern Nebraska, central Illinois, Indiana, Ohio, Pennsylvania, or New Jersey, you're near the 40-degree parallel, so you should slant the top 60 degrees from the horizon. In northern Oregon, southern Minnesota, and northern Wisconsin through to central Maine, you will need to slant the top 65 degrees from horizontal.

To construct a Vegetable Factory coldframe or hotbed, enclose a bed or a portion of it with 2-by-8- or 2-by-10-inch boards, forming a box. The box can sit on the bed frame, if it has one, or directly on the ground. Make the cover out of 1-by-3-inch boards glazed with either two layers of window glass, two layers of polyethylene plastic, or a combination of glass and plastic. You can also use double-pane recycled windows, if you can find a size that fits your bed.

Soft plastic used for glazing is lighter and cheaper than glass. Rigid plastic can be more expensive. Most plastics, unfortunately, deteriorate rapidly when exposed to the sun and atmosphere. You can fasten polyethylene films and rigid plastics directly to the frame with nails, screws, or staples.

In my own area, the winters are so light that I frequently use single glazing for coldframes. Many expert gardeners in cold-winter climates build the lid with glass

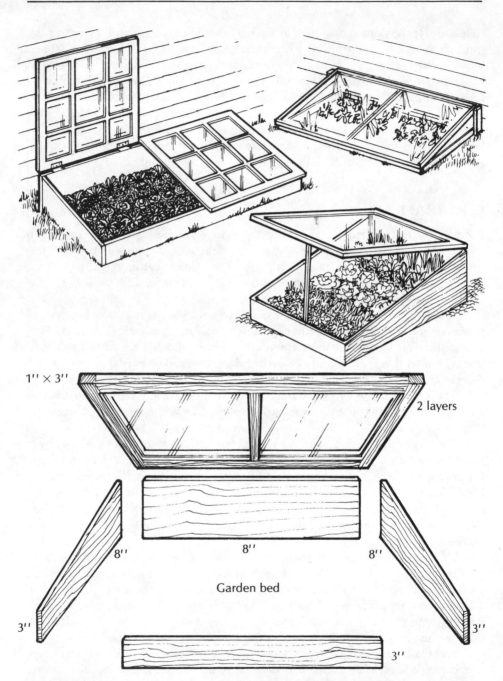

Coldframes take many forms. They range from a simple box to insulated multi-unit frames that grow large quantities of vegetables. You can construct your own coldframe out of 2-by-8 or 2-by-6 boards. Cut two boards to slant to 3 inches at the front. Make the cover of glass- or plastic-covered 1-by-3s or old windows.

Plastic Glazings

A number of plastic films can be used to cover the frame of a coldframe.

Polyethylene film: This film transmits light well and is usually sold in 4- or 5-millimeter thicknesses. It usually lasts only one growing season. Use a double thickness for coldframes, one on the top and one on the bottom of the lid. There are many trade names; simply ask for clear plastic film.

Polyester film: Thin (0.3- and 1.4-millimeter) polyester film transmits light well. Make sure the film you buy is treated with ultraviolet (UV) light absorbers or it will disintegrate rapidly when exposed to sun. Trade names: UV-X, Mylar.

Polyvinyl film: Polyvinyl is expensive, but it lasts about four times as long as polyethylene film. It is sold in gauges ranging from 4 to 12 millimeters. Trade name: Tedlar.

Fluorocarbon film: Fluorocarbon film is extremely resistant to light damage and will last 10 to 15 years. It is available in a variety of gauges. This film is extremely expensive. Trade name: Teflon.

Fiberglass-reinforced polyester: Fiberglass is vulnerable to ultraviolet damage. It can be purchased in rigid flat or corrugated strips. Trade names: Filon, Lascolite, Kalwall.

Acrylic: Acrylic is clear and semirigid. It is resistant to ultraviolet deterioration, and has good light and heat transmission. Trade name: Plexiglass.

Polycarbonate: Twinwall uses two thicknesses of polycarbonate bonded together. This sheet is rigid and structurally strong. It is resistant to ultraviolet deterioration. Trade name: Lexan.

---

on the outside and plastic inside. This insulates better, and the glass screens out ultraviolet rays that are harmful to plastic. What's more, the plastic protects the bed if the glass is broken.

In areas with cold winters, you need to insulate coldframes. I line them with 2-inch-thick foam sheets, because they are easy to cut and handle. Since foam deteriorates with exposure to water and sunlight, paint exposed surfaces with a white latex paint. The frame should be as tight as you can make it. Fill the gaps, corner seams, and other joints with a silicone caulking compound. Make sure you seal air spaces around glass or plastic glazing panels.

In really cold climates, you can add a 2-inch-thick foam panel to the inside of the lid as well as the sides. For large coldframes, glue the foam to a backing of ½-inch plywood, and cut to fit the inside of the lid. Put the panel inside the lid at night to insulate your plants from the cold, and remove it during the day to allow sunlight to enter.

Ventilation is important. Without it, direct sunlight can overheat your coldframe. Waste gases may also increase to harmful levels, and carbon dioxide levels can decrease, slowing plant growth. Finally, humidity can build inside the frame, and condensation inside the box encourages mildew, fungi, and bacteria.

On warm or sunny days, open the top of the frame to allow air to circulate. Unfortunately, if it is extremely cold outside, exposing your vegetables to prolonged cold may harm them. The best way to overcome this problem is to buy automatic vent controllers (about $25) used for greenhouse ventilation panels. They are available from a number of catalog seed firms (see Sources of Seeds and Supplies). These vent controllers open automatically when the temperature in the frame becomes too hot and close when the temperature goes down. If overheating is a consistent problem, place cheesecloth or burlap over the top or paint the glazing white.

You may want to consider buying a ready-made coldframe. A new design from Austria has a peaked roof with four hinged top panels. The top and side panels are made of strong, weatherproof polycarbonate plastic. The lid is double-glazed. You can add units to make the frame bigger as your garden grows.

HOTBEDS

A coldframe with an added heat source becomes a hotbed. By heating the soil in beds, you can speed up the germination time of most vegetable seeds. The seeds of cool-season crops sprout eagerly at soil temperatures as low as 50° F. Seeds of warm-season crops "sulk" and rot when soil temperatures remain below 65°. Within these two categories, each vegetable has its own temperature requirements for seed germination. See the table on page 70 for seed germination temperatures of commonly grown vegetables.

The most efficient heating method is heating cables or mats. Most come with a built-in thermostat that enables you to keep the soil at a constant temperature. To install cables in a bed, lay the cable out on the ground within the frame and spread it evenly over the entire bed in large loops. Place 2 to 3 inches of sand over this, and cover with 3 to 6 inches of garden soil.

To heat the frame naturally, place it on top of a pit containing about 18 inches of green organic material (grass clippings or other lush vegetation) or fresh manure. The bacterial action involved in rotting this material will heat the frame for some time. You can also heat the frame by placing one or more lightbulbs in the box. This is a relatively inefficient way to heat a hotbed, but it works.

BED-SIZED GREENHOUSES

Vegetable Factory gardens are so small that they can easily be converted into bed-sized greenhouses. The frame is covered with polyethylene plastic in early spring, late fall, and winter to create a large cloche or "greenhouse." There are two types of bed-sized greenhouses you might want to consider.

In a Vegetable Factory garden, you can easily build a combination cold frame

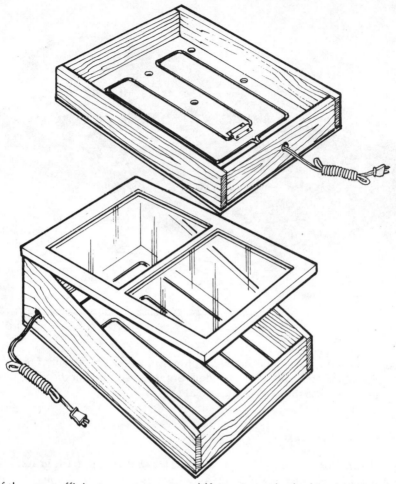

One of the most efficient ways to turn a coldframe into a hotbed is with a heating cable. They can also be used in a flat during hardening-off.

and summer garden. Construct these the exact size of your bed using 2-inch lumber. Build the lid from 1-by-3-inch lumber, and cover top and bottom with two sheets of polyethylene. Attach the lid to the frame with door hinges so you can pull the pin in the summer and remove the lid entirely. This allows plants that require greater height, such as tomatoes, to grow to maturity.

The PVC pipe greenhouse shown on page 80 can be built of 1-inch PVC pipe and polyethylene sheets. Determine the length of pipe you need by arching a length across your bed. The greenhouse should be at least 4 feet high in the middle. Cut all cross-pipes the same length, and space them at 3- or 4-foot intervals along

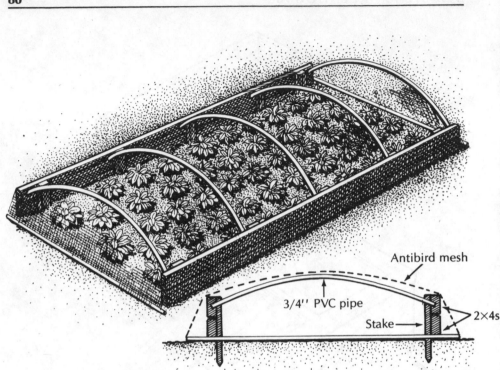

To make this greenhouse, simply arch PVC pipe over a bed. The height of the greenhouse will be determined by the length of pipe used. Anchor the pipes directly into the ground or into the sides of the bed as shown.

the bed. To anchor each one, shove both ends 6 to 8 inches into the ground. Cover the frame with polyethylene plastic. As with other types of cloches, the plastic must be removed or pulled back on warm days.

Some commercial greenhouses can also be extremely useful for Vegetable Factory gardens. Small ones can be tucked into any available space in the yard. A good one is a greenhouse called a poly tunnel that fits into a corner of the yard. It can be installed completely over your garden. Vegetable Factory gardeners often heat their greenhouses with soil cables, soil mats, or small electric greenhouse heaters.

AN EARLY START IN SPRING

You will nearly always produce better and more consistent results if you follow a season-stretching plan each year. Here is my spring/summer timetable.

First, look up the average date of the last spring frost in your area in Appendix A. Then find the first safe spring date for planting in your area from Appendix B. This gives you a date for planting or transplanting each vegetable in the open without protection. Next, subtract the number of weeks of protection afforded by each protective device you plan to use. As a rule of thumb, subtract 2 weeks for hotcaps, 4 weeks for plastic tunnels and other cloches, and 8 to 16 weeks for coldframes and Vegetable Factory plastic greenhouses. Insulated coldframes, of course, will extend the season even longer. In addition, simple coldframes and plastic greenhouses can be used all winter long in mild climates.

Now subtract the time needed to germinate seed and grow seedlings to transplant size. This gives you the date to start that particular vegetable for transplanting.

EXTENDING THE FALL SEASON

If you intend to extend the fall gardening season as long as possible, follow these steps.

Look up the average date of the first fall frost in your area in Appendix A. Then find the range of safe fall planting dates in Appendix C. This gives you the range of safe fall dates for planting for transplanting in the open without protection. Subtract the time needed to germinate the seed of each particular vegetable and to grow the seedlings to transplant size (see Appendix D). This gives you the date on which to start your plants for transplanting.

To extend the season two to ten weeks for warm-weather crops, and to keep cool-weather crops growing at their optimum rate, put protective devices in place when the temperature drops below 50 to 60° F. On sunny days, be careful not to burn plants under the plastic.

TO MULCH OR NOT TO MULCH?

In a Vegetable Factory garden, the plants themselves create a living mulch that conserves moisture and encourages growth. This doesn't work well, however, until the leaves touch each other. To conserve moisture before this stage in the season, I have tried a number of mulches, from straw placed on top of the bed to shredded newspaper. I have found all of these methods to be unsatisfactory. If anything, they keep the soil cool and retard growth.

On the positive side, however, plastic mulches seem to speed up production of tomatoes and other hot-weather plants. Over the years, I have tried a number of plastic and synthetic roll mulches.

Ordinary **polyethylene film,** 1½ mils thick, comes in rolls 3 to 6 feet wide. Clear plastic heats the soil about 10° F, and black plastic just 3 to 6°. Use clear plastic to promote the early germination of cool-season crops. Black plastic is effective for accelerating the growth and increasing the yield of most warm-season crops. I have found that I can double the size of the plants in a given period by using black plastic. It can extend the season two to three weeks for such crops as eggplant, peppers, and tomatoes. The problem with polyethylene is that it restricts the flow of air and holds moisture in, which can help create disease and insect problems. As a result, many gardeners have tried and then abandoned it.

Sky-blue plastic can also be used to heat the soil in beds. It has the additional advantage of repelling some insects.

Ordinary **aluminum foil** increases light intensity, helping vegetables grow in shady parts of your garden. Foil lowers the soil temperature about 10° F and helps keep lettuce from going to seed during hot weather. Experiments show that kitchen foil is an effective control against aphids, because the insects seem to dislike light reflected under leaf surfaces.

Nonwoven polyester and nonwoven polypropylene have good air and water penetration and can be cut with scissors. Both are produced in UV-resistant formulas.

Biodegradable paper is now on the market. This thick, dark material holds down weeds for an entire season. Instead of removing it at the end of each garden year, you work it into the soil.

Perforated plastic sheets have small holes every inch or so, allowing air and water to reach the soil easily. It lasts only one season unless you cover it with soil or gravel.

Woven plastic also allows air and water to penetrate easily. It can be used for several years.

To use a plastic mulch, soak the soil first, then lay down a strip as wide as the bed, securing it with soil on the ends and sides. Cut out planting holes with a tin can, and cut occasional X-shaped slits about 3 inches long for watering with a hose.

WIND

When there is no wind, there is very little difference between the temperature of a plant and the air surrounding it. When air moves, however, heat is carried away from the plant, slowing down its development. That's because wind increases transpiration, and water may be pulled from plants faster than they can replace it, causing leaves to wilt. Wind may cause some plants to divert their growth processes to protection instead of setting or producing fruit.

You can screen vegetables from wind with the same devices used for frost protection, although they can be less elaborate if your wind conditions are not severe. Try propping up shingles or half milk cartons in front of individual plants, staking a 2-foot-high plastic wall on the windward side of your beds, or staking grocery bags with the bottom cut out around each plant.

HEAT AND LIGHT

Most vegetables need a minimum of six to eight hours of sunlight a day to grow properly. Unfortunately, small city gardens may be jammed between a fence and a wall, sandwiched between two buildings, or crammed into an oddly-shaped corner so plants are shaded most of the day. If one of these is your problem, don't give up. You can add to the natural light with a reflector panel or wall. Make reflector panels by stapling or gluing aluminum foil to large sheets of cardboard or plywood. Typical sizes are 4 by 4 feet, 4 by 6 feet, and 5 by 8 feet.

To construct a reflector wall, mount a large reflector panel on a wall facing your garden and cover it with aluminum foil. Make the reflector panel the same length as the garden.

Since the sun comes up in the east, travels through the southern sky, and sets

Light reflectors are especially useful for narrow side areas that receive little morning sun and are in the shade in the late afternoon. Aluminum foil reflectors like this one placed on both the east and west sides of the garden will illuminate an entire bed all day long.

in the west, light reflectors should be set up on the east, west, or north side of your garden—or all three. You'll have to experiment to determine the size and placement that works best for you. In some cases, one panel or wall will do. In others, you will need three to produce adequate light. In difficult-to-light areas, you may have to place a reflector at an angle to direct the light where you want it to go.

Still another way to raise the temperature in a garden is with a heat reflector such as a white wall behind the garden. You can set up white plywood panels behind individual plants, or even arrange sheets of white cardboard on the north side of wire cages. The reflected light and heat help speed the growth of many warm-weather crops, including eggplant, peppers, and tomatoes, by two weeks or more.

In areas where hot summers are the norm, you have the opposite problem. Try stretching the season for cool-weather crops by planting them early and shielding them during the sunniest part of the day. Shade your garden with a piece of plywood or a lath frame mounted on posts. Single heat-sensitive plants can be protected with slotted milk cartons. Cut out carton-length strips 1 inch wide and 2 inches apart all the way around the carton.

CHAPTER 5

THE VEGETABLE FACTORY CONTAINER GARDEN

MOST VEGETABLES ARE AS MUCH AT HOME in a 2-foot container on an apartment house terrace as on a 40-acre farm. In fact, some of the best tomatoes I've ever eaten came from plants growing in a bushel basket on a balcony eight stories above the street. Just give your container vegetables good soil and the other conditions they need, and they will add generously to your bounty. This chapter tells how to grow a significant number of vegetables on a balcony or patio.

CONTAINER VEGETABLES

You can garden in almost any kind of container. In a Vegetable Factory garden, however, containers often become part of the garden itself. They will spotlight a single vegetable such as an eggplant, or become an overall part of your motif on a balcony or patio. Before you decide what to use, I suggest that you go on a treasure hunt through a variety of garden centers, hardware stores, import shops, and supermarkets to find unusual containers. Consider ceramic animals, all sizes and shapes of ceramic and clay pots, baskets, wastebaskets, garbage pails, and even ice buckets.

Select containers that hold a minimum of 3½ gallons of soil. That's the amount you would use in a 12-inch clay pot. A cubical planter measuring 1 foot high and 1 foot wide holds 7½ gallons of soil. The exceptions to this are some leafy and root vegetables, which can be grown on a small scale in 4- and 8-inch pots (see page 90).

Now let's look at the individual types of containers.

Pots

Clay pots can be plain or fancy. Before you place a seedling in a clay pot, soak it in water so it won't rob moisture from the soil and the roots of the plants.

Glazed pottery can be highly decorative. If you select a decorative container that does not have a drainage hole, grow the plant in a slightly smaller clay or plastic pot slipped inside it.

Plastic pots are lighter and hold water longer. Plastic pails and plastic wastebaskets may not look impressive, but they are relatively inexpensive and will grow almost any kind of vegetable. Rubbermaid and other companies manufacture attractive plastic planters in many shapes and sizes. Paper-pulp pots are also popular because they are lightweight and easy to move from one spot to another.

After harvesting a crop, wash the emptied containers before refilling and replanting them. This prevents disease organisms from being transmitted from one crop to the next. Put clay pots in a bucket of hot, soapy water and let them stand a couple of hours before scrubbing with a brush. Plastic and glazed pots need to be soaked first.

Wooden Containers

Wooden fruit boxes and old-fashioned bushel baskets are excellent for growing corn, tomatoes, and zucchini. Line them with black plastic and fill with the Vegetable Factory container soil described below.

Redwood planters look great and are long-lasting. They hold moisture well and need less watering than clay pots. Many vegetable gardeners use half whiskey barrels as a cheaper alternative. Wooden sides provide excellent insulation for the roots of plants.

When buying a tub or half whiskey barrel, look for a nursery that keeps them stacked upside down; this keeps the bands from slipping toward the base. Barrels must be coated inside or they will rot in a few years. Make sure the barrel is completely dry, then cover the inside with asphalt roof patching compound.

You can also build your own wooden planters. To build the simple cubical planter shown on page 88, you'll need five 1-foot-square pieces of 1-inch lumber or ¾-inch plywood, 2 feet of 2-by-2-inch stock, and a few dozen small nails. Nail four sides to the base. Cut the 2-by-2 into four equal sections and nail them inside the four corners as supports. Also shown is a plan for a large planting box for root and leafy vegetables.

Wooden containers made of redwood or cedar resist decay. The interiors may be lined with black plastic or coated with a preservative paint or asphalt compound. Trellises attached to the backs of these containers provide vertical growing space for vines.

All containers need holes to drain the excess water that percolates through the soil. Without this hole, the soil becomes so saturated that oxygen is cut off from the plant roots. Containers less than 10 inches across need a hole ½ inch in diameter; larger containers should have two to four holes. For plastic containers, punch holes about ½ inch up on the sides; holes in the bottom will weaken the base too much for the weight of the wet soil. Place saucers, foil pans, or trays under containers if there is any chance that water will stain floors, furniture, or windowsills.

Wooden barrels now come in a variety of sizes and shapes. Choices range from mass-produced new containers to well-used half whiskey barrels.

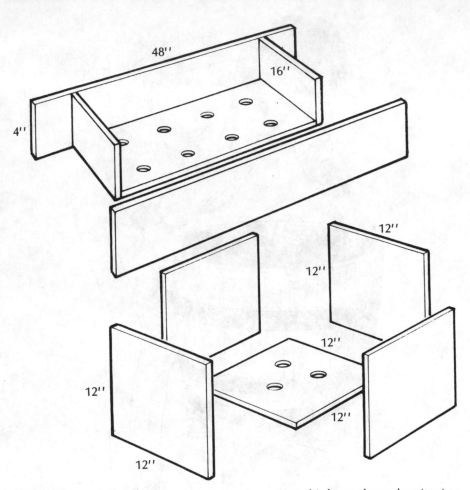

Redwood or cedar resist decay, but you can construct this large planter box (top) or simple cubical planter (bottom) of any type of wood lined with plastic or coated with a preservative paint.

THE PERFECT CONTAINER SOIL

Do not use garden soil to grow container vegetables. It becomes compacted much more easily in a pot than it does in the ground. It also dries out faster and drains poorly. A good container mix combines organic material and minerals. It must provide the right nutrients for vegetable growth and enough air space to allow air and water movement.

Many gardeners grow container plants in "soilless" growing media based on formulas developed by Cornell University and the University of California. These

A trellis fastened to the back of a container will support tomatoes, bush cucumbers, or bush winter squash.

are sold under such trade names as Jiffy Mix, Metro Mix, Pro Mix, and Supersoil. Unfortunately, these mixes all use chemical fertilizers.

I have developed an alternative that I'll call Vegetable Factory container soil. Here is the recipe:

Container Soil Formula

- 2 gallons garden soil
- 2 gallons vermiculite
- 2 gallons shredded peat moss
- 2 tablespoons lime
- 10 tablespoons bloodmeal
- 10 tablespoons bonemeal
- 5 tablespoons greensand

These quantities are arbitrary. I selected the quantities used here because they can be mixed easily on a small tarp or in a 10-gallon garbage can. You can make up the mix in any amounts you like, as long as you keep the ratios the same.

Many gardeners first sterilize the garden soil to kill disease organisms, pests, and weed seed. You can do this by spreading the soil in a shallow pan and baking it in the oven for one hour at 275° F. To reduce the odor of the cooking soil, soak it thoroughly before putting it in the oven. Some gardeners don't sterilize their soil because it destroys beneficial microorganisms. Personally, I dislike the muss and fuss that go with the sterilization process and prefer to take the chance that there might be something harmful in the soil.

To mix your Vegetable Factory container soil, place a large square of black plastic or a plastic tarp on the ground and pour separate piles of garden soil, vermiculite, and peat moss on it. Sprinkle the bonemeal, bloodmeal, greensand, and lime on top of the three piles. Take shovelfuls from each pile in turn, depositing them in a fourth pile. Then shovel this pile into another, to mix the container soil.

PLANTING CONTAINER VEGETABLES

Soak the soil thoroughly before planting. Sow beet, carrot, lettuce, radish, and turnip seed directly into the container. You can also plant cucumber, melon, and squash seed directly in the container, or start the seed in peat pots and transplant into your containers. Start broccoli, Brussels sprouts, cabbage, and tomatoes in peat pots and transplant them into your containers. Or you can purchase seedlings for container planting directly from a local nursery.

Plant at the depth directed on the seed package. But here's a difference: don't dig holes in the container soil. Instead, place the seeds on top of the soil, then cover with soil to the recommended depth. And here is a second difference: The spacing for container vegetables may be closer than for vegetables grown directly in the garden. Broccoli and cabbage, for instance, can be planted 10 inches apart. In addition, you need to think in terms of allotting enough soil for each vegetable. Cabbage, cauliflower, eggplant, and indeterminate tomatoes, for example, need approximately 5 gallons of soil for one plant and 8 gallons for two plants. Container-type tomatoes can be grown in less soil; see chapter 9, Vegetable Wizardry: Beans to Watermelons.

How Many Vegetables Per Pot?

Vegetable	Plants in 4-Inch Pot	Plants in 8-Inch Pot
Beets	2-4	8-10
Carrots	2-4	8-15
Garlic	2-4	4-10
Green onions	4-8	12-25
Looseleaf lettuce	1	2
Mustard greens	1	3
Radishes	4	10-20
Turnips	2-3	4-10

HANGING BASKET WIZARDRY

Hanging wire baskets make fine containers for lettuce, radishes, and even small tomato plants. Round baskets can be hung from the ceiling; half-round ones should be attached to a wall.

To prepare a wire basket, stuff sphagnum moss between the two top wires until you have a neatly packed collar around the rim. Place burlap or an aluminum pie tin in the bottom to keep the soil from washing out. Line the basket with pieces of moss, overlapping them to hold the soil better. The basket should have an even layer of moss about 2 inches thick. Trim off straggly moss with scissors.

Start all your vegetables in peat pots, then transfer them directly into the container when they are several inches tall. To start the leaf and root vegetables, poke your fingers through the moss and push the plants through from the outside. Place about 15 plants where you want them in the moss around the basket, so that the crown of each is about at the same level as the outside of the basket. Fill the container with soil, and plant across the top at the required spacing for each vegetable. This intensive planting virtually covers the container with vegetables!

To prepare a 10- or 12-inch plastic hanging pot for planting, make four or five 1½-inch holes in the side of the pot (about halfway down) by drilling. Also punch small drain holes near the bottom of the pot. Enlarge the upper holes by melting them with a soldering iron. Cut a 3-inch square of black plastic and slip it around the stems of the plants. Tuck the plastic and the plants through the holes. Now fill the basket with soil mix, and add the remaining plants at the top.

Container tomatoes and bush cucumbers also do well in hanging baskets; see chapter 9 for suitable varieties. Simply fill either type of basket with soil and plant one tomato or cucumber at the top. Wire baskets must be packed with sphagnum moss before they are filled with container soil.

CARE AND FEEDING OF CONTAINER VEGETABLES

All containers need to be watered daily. You can immerse them in water, or use a drip watering system (see chapter 7, Watering the Vegetable Factory). Watering vegetables in containers is especially important, because the limited volume of soil dries out faster than the soil around plants in a garden. If the soil is allowed to dry, the plants seldom recover the lost momentum.

When the days are short, cloudy, and moist, your container vegetables will use less water than during long, sunny days of warm weather. Glazed and plastic pots restrict evaporation through the soil surface, but plants in clay pots lose water through the walls as well. So they need more frequent watering. Wooden containers fall somewhere between these two.

Water all containers until the soil is completely saturated. Don't water again until the soil is dry to a depth of 1 or 2 inches. To check, poke your finger into the

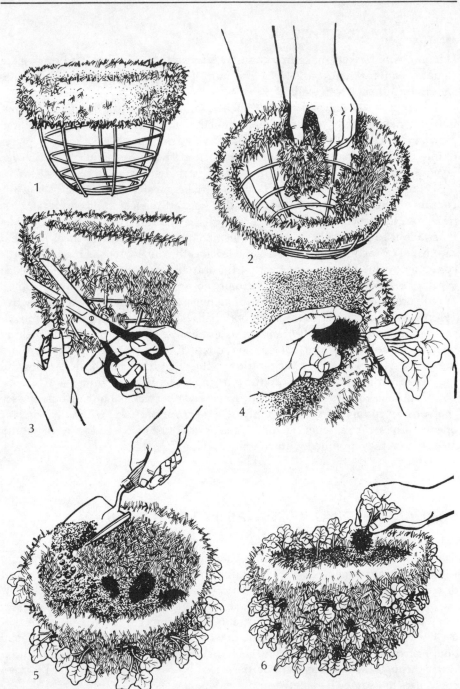

A basket like this can be planted with leafy vegetables or root crops. Plant all the way around the sides, then across the top.

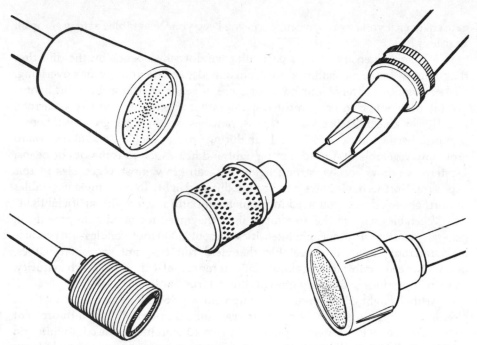

Water-breaking nozzles like these deliver a large volume of water without disturbing the roots of seedlings.

soil and rub a bit of it between your fingers. If it feels dry, then water. You can use a moisture meter to obtain a more accurate measurement.

Water large containers from above with a watering can or a hose. Mist-spray nozzles are good for leafy plants like lettuce and spinach. Water-breaking nozzles will deliver a high volume of water without disturbing the soil. The shepherd's watering extension (a long wandlike extension) is excellent for watering hanging containers.

Drip irrigation systems also make it easy to water a number of containers. Spaghetti tubes with drip emitters can deliver water directly to each container. These more sophisticated systems are described in chapter 7.

Give all containers a supplemental feeding of fish emulsion every week or two. Because container cultivation requires more water than an in-ground garden, nutrients are leached out faster. Fish emulsion applied once a week keeps vegetables growing vigorously. Follow the instructions on the bottle.

GROWING VEGETABLES INDOORS

You can also grow vegetables indoors both in a window and under lights. Indoor gardening is a must if you're an apartment-dweller or don't have room for a garden. Even if you have a garden, it lets you keep your Vegetable Factory going all year long!

The light intensity on any particular windowsill depends on the direction that window faces, on shadows cast from outside, and on your home's overhang. Eastern windows receive four hours or more of gentle morning sun. This light is not intense enough to grow most warm-weather vegetables, but beets, carrots, cauliflower, chard, lettuce, onions, peas, radishes, and spinach grow well here.

Southern windows receive full sun during most of the day, and allow you to grow any vegetable that needs strong light and heat, such as tomatoes or beans. Western windows receive strong light. You can grow most vegetables in this exposure. Northern windows receive only diffused light. To grow most vegetables in northern windows, you need to supplement natural light with artificial light.

Vegetables vary in the amount of light they need for maximum growth. In general, plants require low light intensities—about 1,000 foot-candles—to produce leafy and root growth. But vegetables that yield fruit (eggplant, squash, tomatoes, and such) need a minimum of about 2,500 or more foot-candles to reach maturity. They will produce good leafy growth (but no fruit) at lower levels.

Artificial light will do more to pep up your windowsill garden than anything else. If your light is minimal or if your vegetables do poorly, place a fluorescent fixture about 6 inches above the plants. Use two 40-watt units, one cool-white and one warm-white tube. These tubes together give the plants about the right balance of red and blue light needed for good growth. Simply hang fixtures from the top of the window on small chains. Start by burning them two hours a day, and increase the time if you are not obtaining good vigorous growth or if your vegetables become spindly.

You can also use lights to grow vegetables elsewhere in your home or apartment. A 4-foot fluorescent fixture with two, three, or four 40-watt tubes will light a growing area 2 to 4 feet wide. Two 4-foot, two-tube fixtures mounted parallel will illuminate a 3-by-4-foot area. Two 8-foot, two-tube industrial fixtures (side by side) will light a 2-by-8-foot area. Place the longer tubes 12 to 15 inches above the plants.

Special plant grow-lights reduce the output of the yellow-green spectrum, which are not useful for plant growth, and increase the production of beneficial red and blue light. They are sold commercially as Gro-Lux, Plant-Light, Plant Gro, and other brand names. Do not buy lamps with the designation "white" or "daylight" printed in small letters on the end of the tube. These are not adapted to plant growth.

You can even grow a few vegetables in 4- and 8-inch pots on a windowsill or under lights on a table. An average 4-inch pot contains just 2½ cups of soil. To make sure this will support good vegetable growth, you must adhere strictly to spacing requirements. This means two to four carrots, for example, or four to eight radishes (see the table, How Many Vegetables Per Pot?).

Large numbers of small containers can be moved in a child's wagon. Larger containers can be rolled on a dolly or wooden dowels.

MOVING YOUR CONTAINERS

If you're not a weightlifter, you will have to make some provision for moving larger containers from place to place. A filled 14-inch clay pot feels as if it weighs a ton. A 1-foot wooden cube may be nearly impossible to move.

I suggest using a child's wagon or a throw rug to pull containers that aren't too heavy. It's also possible to install casters on the heavier wooden containers. As an alternative, consider buying a small dolly (a wheeled platform) from a hardware or building supply store. You can also roll heavy planting boxes on pipes or wooden dowels 2 or 3 inches in diameter. Of course, the simplest solution is to put the empty container where you want it, fill it with soil, and leave it there until you harvest the crop. Then empty the soil, and store the container or move it to another location.

CHAPTER 6

VERTICAL GARDENING

CUCUMBERS, MELONS, PUMPKINS, SQUASH, and other vine crops require tremendous amounts of ground space. When they're grown above the garden, however, they produce huge quantities of fruit in a surprisingly small area.

Just one untrained cantaloupe will sprawl over an area of 16 square feet. But the same plant trained up a vertical support requires only 1 square foot of ground space. And several studies suggest that the yield per square foot for all vine crops can be doubled by growing them vertically.

In a Vegetable Factory garden, any vegetable that produces a vine or rambling stem can be grown vertically. This includes cucumbers, all melons, New Zealand spinach, peas, pole beans, most summer squash, tomatoes, and all winter squash. Many of these plants will climb by themselves, grasping the support with their twisting tendrils. Others need to be attached with strings or twist ties.

TRAINING PLANTS TO GROW VERTICALLY

Before looking at garden structures, let's examine the peculiarities of some individual vine crops.

Beans: Pole beans are better adapted to a small garden than the bush varieties. They grow well vertically and produce throughout the season. Bush beans, on the other hand, mature all at once, then stop. Because of their size, plant bush beans in zone B in front of the major producer plants such as zucchini.

Cucumbers: All cucumber varieties are ideally suited to vertical growing. They can be pruned to a single stem or allowed to develop all of their side branches. Just one or two plants of two or three different varieties should be enough for most families.

Melons: All melons (except watermelons) can be grown vertically without any special support for the fruit. One danger, however, is that a melon slips easily off the stem when ripe. If a ripe melon isn't picked soon enough, it will fall to the ground. You can prevent this by attaching each melon to the support with a "sling" of netting or old stockings.

Make it a habit to think vertically. Every time you plant a garden, try to include as many vine crops as possible. Besides the support frame at the north end of the garden, you can scatter a variety of vertical supports throughout zone B.

Summer squash: When grown on the ground, the fruits of summer squash form only at the end of the vine. When grown vertically, the vine produces blossoms and fruits along its entire length. Summer squash varieties that vine, such as 'Yellow Straightneck', will climb right up the vertical supports. Tie them at 1-foot intervals. All summer squash do well when grown in small wire cages.

Tomatoes: Tomatoes are classified as either determinate or indeterminate. The terminal bud of determinate or bush tomatoes sets fruit and stops stem growth. All blossoms and fruit develop on a plant at about the same time. Smaller determinate tomatoes grow well in containers, but aren't good producers in a Vegetable Factory garden. Consider only the larger indeterminate varieties for planting in outdoor beds.

The terminal bud of an indeterminate tomato plant does not set fruit. It keeps producing leaves and more stems from the growing tip. The vine can grow indefinitely if it isn't killed by frost. As a result, indeterminate tomato vines produce the greatest number of fruit in a Vegetable Factory garden. They can be grown up any kind of structure, including strings. But I recommend that you use only wire cages for your tomatoes in a Vegetable Factory garden. The details of growing tomatoes in a cage will be covered later in this chapter.

Winter squash: You can grow almost any kind of squash vertically on either chickenwire or a large wire mesh fence. Nearly all of them, except the larger 'Hubbard' and 'Banana' squash, will grow without extra support for the fruit.

SUPPORT FRAMES

A vertical frame is the most important vertical support used in the Vegetable Factory garden. It spans the entire north end of the garden and extends upward at least 6 to 8 feet. It can be made out of 2-by-4s, iron pipe, or electrical conduit. I suggest that you stretch 1-inch-mesh chickenwire across the support to give the vines something to cling to. You can also use field wire (standard fencing wire used by ranchers) or rectangular wooden trellises (sold by most nurseries to support vines) nailed to the frame. Grow melons, peas, pumpkins, and winter squash on this frame.

The most important vertical frame in the Vegetable Factory garden is the back support located at the north end of the garden. Grow full vining varieties of peas, melons, pumpkins, and winter squash up this frame.

Using the same materials, make one or two smaller vertical frames to use in zone B for bush varieties of cucumber and melon, including watermelon. These frames should be 2 to 4 feet wide and 3 to 4 feet tall.

WIRE CAGES

Since its introduction only a few years ago, the wire cage has become an invaluable garden organizer, especially in small gardens. This device seems to bring out the productive best in such vegetables as tomatoes and cucumbers. It keeps greedy space-gobblers like zucchini from crowding out everything in sight, and helps you to squeeze the maximum number of plants into a small patch of ground. Cages keep fruit and foliage off the ground, so they stay clean and rot-free, as well as providing support.

A tomato plant allowed to go its own way in a wire cage will put out more foliage, protecting its fruit and vines from sunscald, and the plant will produce

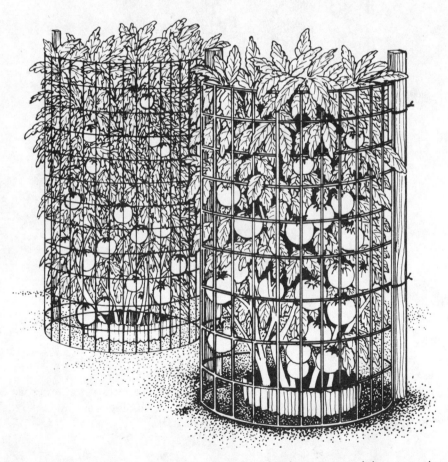

Production Towers: Wire cages produce more fruit for the space used than any other vertical support. The taller ones (4 to 6 feet) are especially good for tomatoes. Shorter cages (3 to 4 feet) are useful for growing cucumbers and bush varieties of melon, pumpkin, and winter squash.

more tomatoes per square foot than if grown any other way. Cages turn a single vine into a production tower. In my own garden, I have gotten 150 to 300 tomatoes from one vine growing in a cage measuring 18 inches in diameter and 6 feet high.

Six cucumber plants grown in a 3- to 4-foot-high, 18- to 24-inch-diameter wire cage go wild trying to outproduce themselves. In several tests at a southern university, one wire cage with only six cucumber plants outproduced shoulder-to-shoulder cucumber plants sprawled over 15 square feet of ground.

The size of a cage will depend on the vegetable you grow in it. Large bush or container types of tomato do best in cages 18 inches in diameter and 2 to 4 feet tall. An ideal cage size for large indeterminate tomato varieties is 18 to 24 inches in diameter by 5 to 6 feet tall. Simply put the cage over individual plants when small and let them go.

Cucumbers do well in 20-inch-diameter, 3- to 4-foot-tall cages. Plant six plants per cage, but don't close the circle—make it a horseshoe shape, leaving a 10- to 12-inch opening on one side for easy access to the cucumbers.

Summer squash, including zucchini, do well in 24-inch-diameter, 2- to 3-foot-tall wire cages. If a plant grows out of the mesh, put it back. If it becomes impossible to keep in check, pick off the fuzzy growing tip.

Some gardeners make their cages of 6-inch-mesh concrete-reinforcing wire because it gives solid support and allows them to reach the fruit easily. I find this wire too stiff and hard to work with and prefer a lighter galvanized fence wire, which is available at most building supply stores. This lighter wire is available either welded or woven and in several mesh sizes. You'll need at least a 4-inch mesh to be able to put your hand in comfortably and remove the fruit. For easy access, you can simply cut a hole on one side of the cage.

To secure a cage, bend 20-inch lengths of standard coat-hanger wire in half, place them over the bottom rim of the cage at 12- to 18-inch intervals, and poke them into the ground. You can also drive wooden stakes about 6 inches into the ground and wire them to the cage.

Recently a number of commercial wire cages and plant supports have appeared on the market. All that I have seen are inferior to those you can make yourself.

FOLDING WOODEN CAGES

Folding cages work well in Vegetable Factory gardens for cucumbers, melons, and tomatoes. They can be moved anywhere in the garden and are easily folded for winter storage.

The cage is made with four 5-foot uprights and 12 2½-foot crossbars, as illustrated on page 102. Vertical bolts placed at the ends of the crossbars serve as pivots so the cage can fold flat. The feet of the vertical members are pointed so they can be pushed in the ground.

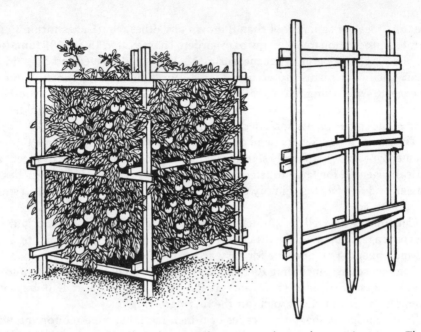

Folding wooden cages perform the same function in the garden as wire cages. They are, however, much easier to store.

Plant four cucumber, melon, or bush squash plants, one at each corner, or plant two indeterminate tomato vines per cage and let them grow as they will. A diagonal lacing of twine helps to contain cucumber, melon, and squash vines. Tomatoes do well without them; just keep pushing the vines back in as they try to get out.

A-FRAMES

The A-frame, like the wire cage, is creating a gardening revolution. It can easily turn a small garden into a cornucopia of vine crops: cantaloupe, cucumbers, pumpkins, watermelons, winter squash, and other plants that usually waste ground space.

The A-frame shown here is made from 2-by-2s and 1-by-2s, and can be designed to fit into any space you have available. Even a relatively small A-frame tucked away in an odd corner will produce large quantities of vine crops. A 6- to 9-foot structure will yield 50 to 60 'Acorn' squash or 100 to 300 cucumbers. An

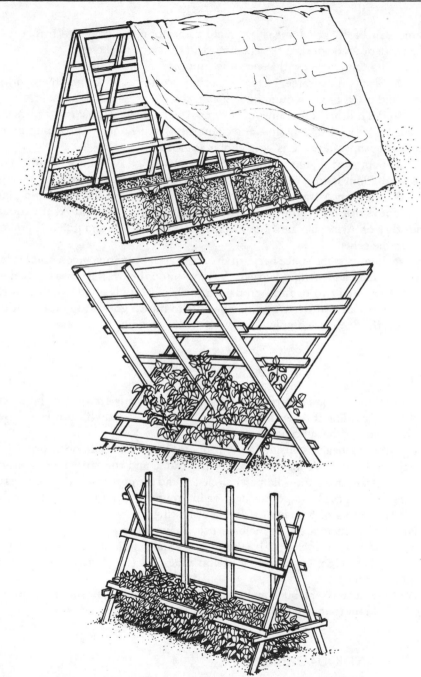

Every small garden needs at least one A-frame. They are useful for both vertical and horizontal gardening.

A-frame can be hinged for easy moving and storage. Cover the frame with chickenwire or wooden slats to accommodate different vine crops.

Here are some uses for this versatile support:

● Place the A-frame, instead of a support frame, at the north end of the garden, and use it to grow pumpkins, watermelons, or winter squash.

● Put five or six A-frames of various sizes to work in the same garden. Use small frames for bush cantaloupes and cucumbers, larger ones for bush pumpkins, summer squash, watermelons, and winter squash.

● Supplement your regular garden by placing an A-frame in another part of the yard. Plant it with cantaloupes, cucumbers, or winter squash.

● Make an A-frame your only garden. Face it east and west, and plant peas on both sides; follow the peas with pole beans on one side and 'Acorn' squash on the other, or 'Armenian Yard-Long' cucumbers on one side and Italian 'Romano' beans on the other.

● Intercrop the space beneath the A-frame by planting green onions, leaf lettuce, radishes, and turnips. Harvest the lower crops before the vines shade them out. I've harvested two or three crops of radishes before losing the space. If the A-frame faces east and west, you may be able to raise a good crop of leaf lettuce even when the frame is completely covered with vine crops.

POSTS

The post is another great garden organizer. It takes little space, can be placed anywhere (providing it doesn't shade out other crops), and will produce prodigious harvests for the space used.

For growing beans, consider an X-frame post, an umbrella post, or a bean-pole garden. Drive nails into the post or the frame and run strings between the nails. Plant beans in a 1-foot-diameter circle around the post and train the vines up the strings. Use these bean posts singly or in groups of two or three. Plant other vegetables within 4 or 5 inches of all bean plantings.

For raising cucumbers or melons, use a cucumber post. You can make a cucumber post with dowels, 2-by-2s, or large nails stair-stepped around it as illustrated. Plant eight cucumber or melon vines, spaced about 8 inches apart, around the post.

For bush cucumbers, bush melons, and summer squash, posts should be 3 to 4 feet high. Plant four vines 12 inches apart and tie them to the post.

TRIPODS AND QUADRIPODS

Tripods (three-legged frames) and quadripods (four-legged frames) make good vertical garden organizers for beans. The bean vines grow up the supports, then cascade down. You can easily reach all parts of a frame to pick the bean pods.

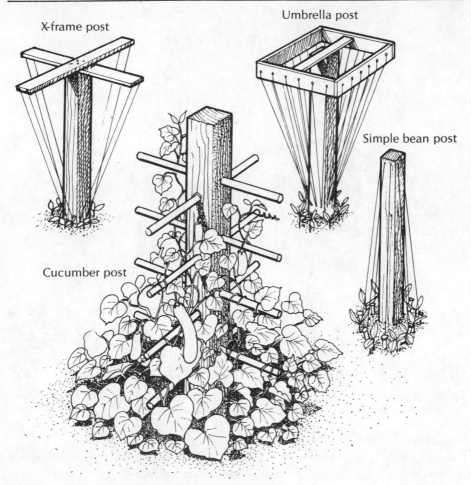

X-frame post

Umbrella post

Simple bean post

Cucumber post

Bean and Cucumber Posts: Pole beans outproduce bush beans in a Vegetable Factory garden. One post with six to eight plants is sufficient for a small garden. Cucumbers grow well up almost any type of 4- to 8-inch post. Use cross-supports to hold the vines. Posts like these can also be used for melons.

Because it's easy to see the beans, you can pick them at the perfect stage—when they're tender and flavorful, before they grow tough and stringy. It's also easier to keep an eye out for Mexican bean beetles, and handpick these pests or apply a botanical spray. Tripods and quadripods get bean foliage up off the ground, where air can circulate freely among the leaves, so you'll have fewer disease problems. Even rampant growers like limas flourish on these tepee frames, and such gourmet varieties as scarlet runner beans are real showstoppers with their fountains of red

Quadripods: These vertical supports are a cross between a bean post and an A-frame. Their advantage is that they can be moved easily around the garden.

sweetpealike flowers. Another advantage is that the structures can be moved anywhere in the garden and are easily taken down for winter storage.

Make the legs from 8-foot lengths of 1-by-2 lumber. Hinge the tripods at the top. Plant three bean seeds at the base of each pole.

Vertical space is really the new frontier of vegetable gardening. A lot has been done, but there is still more experimenting to do. Try these devices, then see if you can dream up some of your own. Who knows, maybe what you create will someday help double and triple production in all small vegetable gardens.

CHAPTER 7

WATERING THE VEGETABLE FACTORY

VEGETABLES NEED TO MATURE RAPIDLY, with no check in growth. Too little water will stress them and can set them back beyond recovery. Without enough water, bean pods produce only a few seeds, and the rest of the pods shrivel. Beets become stringy, radishes become pithy, and cucumbers just stop growing. Plants that are consistently overwatered, on the other hand, often appear weak and spindly.

Critical Watering Periods

Vegetable	Critical Period
Beans	Pollination and pod development
Broccoli	Head development
Cabbage	Head development
Carrot	Root enlargement
Cauliflower	Head development
Corn	Ear development, silking, and tasseling
Cucumber	Flowering and fruit development
Eggplant	Flowering and fruit development
Lettuce	Head development
Melon	Flowering and fruit development
Onion	Bulb enlargement

SOURCE: Rutgers University.

Vegetable Root Depths

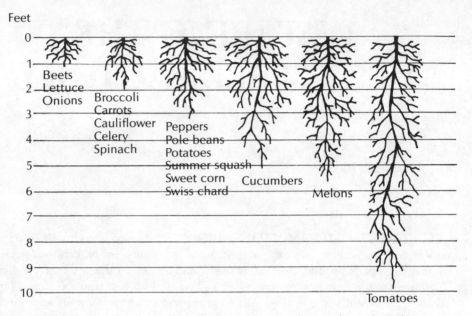

Vegetable roots can reach deeper than most gardeners realize. To keep them from concentrating in the upper level of the soil, you must water as deeply as possible.

THE SOIL-WATER RELATIONSHIP

The soil in your beds will be roughly half air and half solid material. If you continuously soak the soil and displace the air spaces with water, you prevent the exchange of oxygen and carbon dioxide from taking place. Your plants will literally drown.

You also need to consider how deep to water. Each plant has a maximum depth to which its roots will grow. In order for your vegetables' roots to reach this depth, water should ideally penetrate at least as far as the roots go down.

Carrots, broccoli, eggplant, and potatoes put down roots from 2 to 3 feet deep. Cucumbers, cantaloupes, and pumpkins sink their roots 5 to 6 feet, and tomatoes often reach 8 to 10 feet deep or more.

To get an idea of how deeply you're wetting your soil, you can push a ¼-inch metal rod into the ground. It should be relatively harder to push when it hits dry soil. Water at least an hour or two each time, then allow the bed to dry to a depth of 4 to 8 inches; check this with a trowel or a moisture sensor (a small meter that measures the moisture content of the soil).

Now let's look at the three major ways to water a Vegetable Factory garden.

HAND-WATERING

Hand-watering uses less water than overhead techniques (watering from the top with a sprinkler or nozzle), although it is not as efficient as drip-watering. If you want to hand-water, there are many special-purpose nozzles on the market. The most popular are fan sprays and water bubbles.

A hand-held wand is effective for reaching underneath the leaves. They come with special seedling nozzles that produce a fine mist for newly planted seedbeds and with soft rain irrigation nozzles for general purposes.

Here are some imaginative water-stretching techniques that work well in Vegetable Factory gardens.

You can deliver water directly to the roots through a plastic or metal pipe 2 inches in diameter and 18 inches long. Drive it into the ground near the base of such vegetables as eggplant, peppers, and tomatoes. When you're irrigating your vegetables, pour water directly into the pipe. This method encourages vigorous

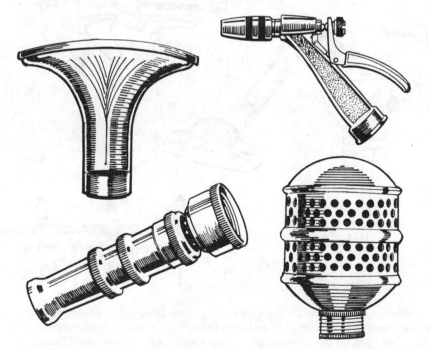

Many gardeners prefer to water all vegetables by hand, and nozzles can be as efficient as the drip-watering devices.

growth, yet uses little more than half the water of overhead methods. You can also accomplish this by sinking large clay or plastic flowerpots into the soil within 2 to 5 inches of the base of large plants. If possible, fill the pots several times a day during hot weather.

A variation of this is to perforate a half-gallon milk carton or plastic gallon jug and cut off its top. Set it in the ground. The water will soak into the soil over a period of time.

OVERHEAD WATERING

Vegetable Factory gardens can be watered with overhead sprinklers in less time than with any hand-watering methods. However, as the plants grow, it becomes more difficult to put the volume of water you need into the ground. I have found that even after an hour or two of watering, there will be dry areas under the

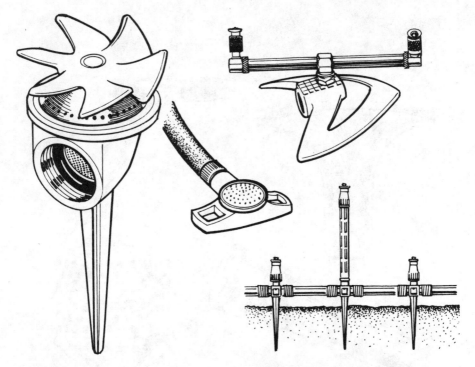

You can easily water an entire bed in a small garden using either a rotating or stationary sprinkler. After the leaves begin to overlap, however, it becomes increasingly difficult to water the ground thoroughly under the leaves. Small sprinklers (at right) plug directly into a hose. They are adjustable from a 2- to 10-foot radius.

leaves of a mature garden. And some gardeners feel that overhead watering increases the danger of disease spreading throughout the garden. You can help prevent problems by watering in the morning to allow the leaves to dry out fairly quickly.

Use either a small sprinkler with rotating arms or a nonrotating sprinkler with holes in the top that throws water in a 10- or 15-foot-diameter circle. Most efficient are the new "minisprinklers" that plug into a hose or dripline (described below) and deliver a spray 4 to 20 feet.

DRIP SYSTEMS

A drip-watering system supplies water in small amounts to your plants at ground level. There are two major types. An ooze system releases small droplets along the length of a porous hose. Perforated plastic tubing has small holes punched in its walls. And a trickle system delivers a low volume of water from small nozzles, called emitters. Any of these can cut water use by up to 50 percent over the hand- and overhead watering techniques.

To lay out an **ooze system,** connect ½-inch nonperforated plastic tubing to a garden hose or spigot. Lay the tubing across the south end of the garden, and run perforated or porous ooze watering lines from it every 12 to 18 inches. Run these lines the length of the garden. Rearrange the lines until they water the garden evenly.

After a trial run of a few hours, check by punching holes a foot or two deep in the ground with a stick. Make sure the soil is moist to this point. Once the system is set up properly, water thoroughly to a depth of about 3 feet, then don't water again until the soil has dried out to a depth of 4 to 8 inches.

An **emitter system** consists of small nozzles, or emitters, that are attached to nonperforated plastic tubing by spaghetti microtubing. The emitters drip or trickle water onto the garden bed. The easiest way to set up a system is to run one nonperforated tube around the perimeter of the garden, and another through the middle of the bed. Attach spaghetti tubing to the nonperforated tubing and run them wherever needed. Attach emitters at the end of each tube.

Each widely spaced broccoli, cabbage, cauliflower, eggplant, pepper, summer squash, and winter squash plant should have its own emitter. But where vegetables like carrots or lettuce are placed close together, one emitter will easily water a 1- or 2-foot-square block. Some gardeners don't bother with emitters and simply allow the water to drip from the end of the microtubing directly onto the bed. You will need to experiment to see what method works best for you.

You can also easily water container gardens with an emitter system. Several types of emitters are useful for containers: spray heads, which spray water like a

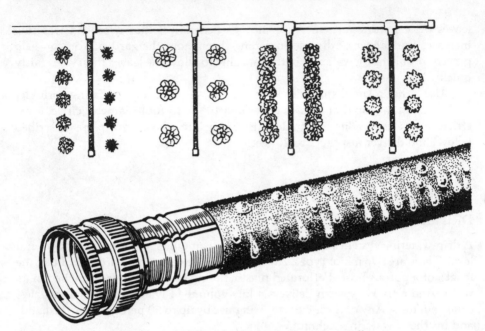

Water is released along the entire length of an ooze hose in small amounts. An ooze hose is extremely effective for watering root and leafy vegetables. Ooze lines should be run through the middle of all plantings. In a Vegetable Factory garden, space them 12 to 18 inches apart from one end of the garden.

nozzle; bubblers, which bubble water slowly over the entire surface of the container; and water loops, which are placed around the perimeter of round containers.

By attaching a filter-strainer to a system, you can prevent foreign matter from clogging the hose and emitters. A ball valve or pressure regulator and gauge will allow you to control the water flow rate and pressure.

AUTOMATIC WATERING

I highly recommend that you hook your watering system up to an automatic timer, and let the watering take care of itself. A clock operates a valve turning on the water for a given time each day, even if you're away for days or weeks. Simple ones cost about $30. More complicated timing devices operate several valves, allowing you to water a Vegetable Factory garden, a lawn, and containers on independent schedules.

Sensors

Water sensors can take almost all the guesswork out of watering. They are buried 6 to 10 inches deep in the garden soil. Some systems turn on the water as soon as the sensor dries out. With others, you dial the moisture level you think your plants need, and the sensor turns on the water when the moisture in the soil drops to that preset level.

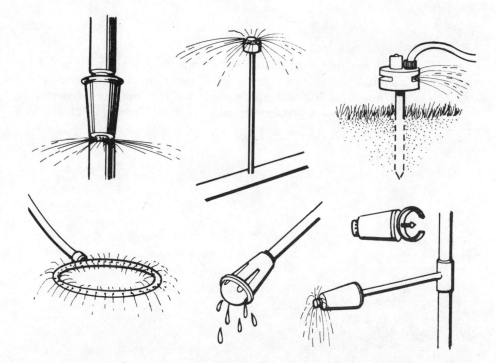

Emitters come in several shapes and sizes. Sprinkler spikes, sprayers, and misters (top row) are useful for watering root and leafy vegetables. Spot emitters and spaghetti tubes (bottom right) are extremely effective for delivering water to the roots of larger plants like tomatoes, peppers, and eggplant. A water loop (bottom left) is useful for watering a container.

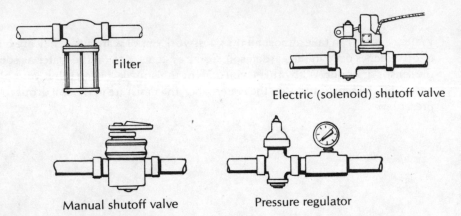

Filter

Electric (solenoid) shutoff valve

Manual shutoff valve

Pressure regulator

You will need a filter, pressure regulator, and either a manual or electric shutoff valve for your drip system. They are placed between the delivery garden hose or pipe and the drip lines.

All of the watering systems discussed in this chapter are a far cry from standing around for a couple of hours with a hose. Ground-level systems save water and cut down on diseases. And automation cuts out the guesswork of watering. Whichever system you install, your Vegetable Factory will thank you for it!

CHAPTER 8

VEGETABLE FACTORY PEST CONTROL

MY OWN VEGETABLE FACTORY GARDENS grow vigorously and present few problems. Occasionally, however, I find a few bugs on the leaves. The summer squash may pick up a little mildew, or the birds will eat a few more of the early lettuce plants than I like. When you garden organically, however, you must learn to use preventive techniques that other gardeners don't know or may ignore.

PREVENTION

Here are some simple prevention rules to catch problems before they need to be controlled.

Keep your garden clean. Get rid of all weeds, clean up piles of trash, and remove crop residue. This debris provides a place for diseases and insects to multiply and hibernate during the winter. If you have severely diseased plants or rotted fruit, don't put them in the compost pile, as the problem may eventually find its way back into your garden.

Start with healthy plants and seed. Buy disease-free seed and healthy-looking transplants. Disease-free seed can be purchased through seed catalogs and at garden centers, and it will be marked "certified disease-free." Many stores and catalogs sell seed treated with Captan, a powdered fungicide, but you can buy untreated seed from Nichols Garden Nursery, Johnny's Selected Seeds, and others. See Sources of Seeds and Supplies for listings.

Most nurseries sell healthy plants. To make sure you're getting the best, select only vigorous-looking, stocky plants without spots on the leaves.

Beware of overhead watering. Mildew and other diseases frequently occur on leaves that stay wet. Water in the morning so the sun dries the foliage quickly; hand-water under the leaves; or use a ground-level drip-irrigation system.

Plant resistant varieties and pest-repellent plants. You can avoid many diseases and insects by growing resistant varieties. Certain types of bean, for example, are

Pest-Repellent Plants

Insects	Repellent Plants
Ants	Pennyroyal, spearmint, tansy
Aphids	Garlic, nasturtiums, spearmint, stinging nettles
Asparagus beetles	Tomatoes
Cabbage maggots	Mint, rosemary, sage, tomatoes
Cabbage moths	Celery, hyssop, mint, rosemary, sage, thyme, tomatoes, wormwood
Carrot flies	Leeks, onions, rosemary, sage
Colorado potato beetles	Eggplant, flax
Cucumber beetles	Radishes, summer savory, tansy
Cutworms	Oakleaf mulch
Flea beetles	Head lettuce, mint, wormwood
Mexican bean beetles	Potatoes, rosemary, summer savory
Nematodes	African and French marigolds
Potato bugs	Horseradish planted at corners of the potato patch
Squash bugs	Nasturtiums, tansy
Whiteflies	Nasturtiums

rust-resistant, and several tomato varieties are resistant to nematodes and to fusarium and verticillium wilts.

Some plants are not attractive to insects; others, such as marigolds and garlic, contain oils that repel insects. Still others are unaffected by insect attack.

Rotate your crops. If you grow vegetables in the same spot year after year, certain diseases may spread rapidly. Broccoli, cabbage, and cauliflower will be more prone to clubroot, for example. In a Vegetable Factory garden, rotate the vegetables within the bed. Plant zucchini where the cabbage was, and cabbage in place of eggplant.

Watch your timing. Time your plantings to avoid peak insect buildups. Insects generally appear at about the same time every year. In some areas, flea beetles will destroy radishes and turnips planted in early summer, but if you hold off a few weeks until the adult (beetle) stage has passed, you will suffer little damage. Many other insects can be avoided in the same manner.

BUGS IN YOUR GARDEN

Before you start to fight back, it helps to know just a little about the insects themselves and what kinds of damage they can do.

Chewing insects: Both beetles and caterpillars eat parts of the leaves and fruit. This damage may range from tiny pinpoint holes in the leaves to the destruction of entire leaves and fruits. Here are the culprits.

Beetles have chewing mouthparts and hard forewings that cover membranous hindwings; the larvae of many beetles can be extremely destructive. Caterpillars are the larvae of moths or butterflies; of their four stages (egg, larva, pupa, and adult moth or butterfly), the larva is the most destructive in the garden.

Among the other chewing insects you may find in the garden are earwigs (an insect with a pair of forceps at the rear of the abdomen), grasshoppers, slugs, and snails.

Sucking insects: Aphids, leafhoppers, spider mites, true bugs, and whiteflies suck plant juices out of vegetables. This causes a spotty or yellow discoloration of the leaves or shoots. All except leafhoppers may attack plants in large groups or colonies.

Insect Problems

Insect	Damage	Description	Prevention	Control
Leaf-Chewers				
Beetles	Irregular holes in leaves	½- to 1-inch insects with biting mouthparts, hard front wings	Keep the garden free of refuse; plant marigolds throughout to discourage beetles	Pick beetles off by hand; spray with pyrethrum, rotenone, or ryania
Caterpillars	Chunks chewed out of leaves	1- to 3-inch brown to green worms	Dispose of garden refuse; remove weeds	Pick by hand; use *Bacillus thuringiensis*
Earwigs	Holes in leaves	Night-feeding insects with "pincers"	Dispose of garden refuse	Trap in rolled newspapers
Grasshoppers	Large holes chewed in leaves; plants stripped	1- to 2½-inch insects with long rear legs	Turn soil under in fall to bury eggs deeply	Trap in quart jars filled with 1 part molasses, 7 parts water; spray with rotenone or hot peppers; use traps

(continued)

Insect	Damage	Description	Prevention	Control
Leaf-Chewers — Continued				
Slugs, snails	Leaves eaten; trails of silvery slime	Slimy, legless creatures with or without shells	Remove hiding places by keeping garden free of debris; use protective borders of sand or ashes	Drown in a shallow saucer of beer; trap by scattering cabbage or lettuce leaves at night, and picking up in morning
Weevils	Chunks out of leaves or roots eaten by grubs or adults	Beetles with long beaks	Dispose of garden refuse; spade deeply in the spring to kill larvae	Pick adult beetles by hand; spray with rotenone
Juice Suckers				
Aphids	Colonies of sucking insects on leaves	Tiny (⅛- to ¼-inch) black, yellow, or green insects	Repel with spearmint, garlic, nasturtiums	Remove with blast from a garden hose or spray soap solution; mulch with aluminum foil; control with lacewings, praying mantids, or ladybugs
Leafhoppers	Leaves appear scorched or wilted	Wedge-shaped brown or green insects	Use resistant varieties; clear weeds near garden	—
Spider mites	Leaves turn pale green; dusty webs between leaves (tap over a sheet of paper — the moving specks are mites)	Minute spiderlike insects	Avoid working among infected plants to keep from spreading mites	Remove with blast from garden hose; control with ladybugs, lacewings, or predacious mites

Insect	Damage	Description	Prevention	Control
Thrips	Scars on foliage; leaves may be brown-edged, spotted or streaked; white blotches on onions	Thin, 1/25-inch needlelike black or straw-colored insects	Keep weeds out of garden; keep garden clean	Control with green lace-wings; spray with rotenone
True bugs	White or yellow blotches appear where bugs have fed; if attack severe, leaves wilt, turn brown, and die	Small (1/10- to 5/8-inch) insects with sucking beaks	Fertilize plants to keep growing vigorously	Destroy bugs that collect under leaves at night; use sabadilla; crush egg masses; spray with pyrethrum, rotenone, or ryania
Whiteflies	Cloud of white wings fly when plant disturbed	Small (1/10-inch) white-winged, sucking insects	Repel with marigolds	Remove with blast of garden hose; control with wasp parasite *Encarsia formosa*; use sticky yellow traps; oil sprays suffocate adults, nymphs, and eggs

Borers

Insect	Damage	Description	Prevention	Control
Corn earworm	Kernels at tip of corn ear are brown and eaten away; bores into fruit of other plants	2-inch green to brown caterpillars	Plant corn varieties with long tight husks: 'Dixie 18', 'Golden Security', 'Silver Cross Bantam'	Apply drops of mineral oil inside the ears when the silks first appear

(continued)

Insect Problems — *Continued*

Insect	Damage	Description	Prevention	Control
Borers — *Continued*				
Leafminers, fly maggots	Small tunnels in leaves	Small (¼-inch), thin maggots	Spade deeply before planting to help control maggots; cover plants with Reemay or cheesecloth	Remove affected leaves or plants
Stem borers	Sudden wilting of leaves; holes in stems	Worms that bore inside stems	Clear debris and weeds from garden	Slit stem with knife, take out borer; control with ladybugs or trichogramma wasps; use *Bacillus thuringiensis*
Soil Insects				
Beetle or moth larvae (wireworms, cutworms, white grubs)	Plant growth stunted; worms bore into roots; young plants cut off at soil line	Wormlike insects in soil	Keep garden free of refuse; push cardboard collars into soil around plants to keep cutworms away from plants	Use barriers of damp wood ashes, mulch of oak leaves; scatter cornmeal where worms have been a problem; control with *Bacillus thuringiensis*
Maggots	Tunnels in bulbs; yellowing leaves	Soft legless wormlike larvae of flies	Delay planting until late spring or summer	Scatter onion plants throughout garden; add sand or wood ash to soil around plants

Borers: Borers are either grubs (the larvi stage of beetles), caterpillars (the larvi stage of moths), or maggots (the larvi stage of flies). These insects bore into fruits, buds, roots, leaves, and stems. A few of the more destructive ones are the European corn borer, spinach leaf miner, and squash vine borer.

Soil pests: These insects attack vegetables from below the soil line. The most destructive are root maggots, nematodes, and root-feeding grubs. Some examples are the cabbage maggot (the larva of the cabbage-root fly), onion maggot (the larva of the onion fly), wireworms (the larvae of click beetles), and cutworms.

SIMPLE CONTROLS

The first thing I want to urge you to do is to learn to live with some insect damage. What appears like an all-out invasion one day may well turn out to be nothing the next. I always suggest a wait-and-see attitude. If, after a few days, you feel that enough damage is being done to affect the harvest, then you can take the steps described here.

Handpick beetles and caterpillars. I squash these with my heel or a stick. Spray sucking insects like aphids with a garden hose. This won't stop all of them, but it cuts down on their numbers significantly.

Try traps and barriers. You can trap whiteflies with 12-inch-square pieces of cardboard painted bright orange or yellow and coated with mineral oil or Tanglefoot (a commercial product). By spreading aluminum foil on the ground around your plants, aphids, leafhoppers, Mexican bean beetles, and thrips will be discouraged. Earwigs eat your plants at night but will hide in rolled newspaper by day. You can dump them in a pail of water or burn them, newspaper and all. Trap snails and slugs in saucers of stale beer placed around the garden. Trap maggots by placing sticky squares of paper between the plants; coat the paper with Tanglefoot.

Use soapy water or mineral oil. Mix about 20 tablespoons of soap flakes (like Ivory) or 3 ounces of Ivory Liquid in 6 gallons of water, and spray the mixture directly on the plant leaves. This helps control aphids and other sucking pests. Use real soap, not a detergent.

In recent years, a number of insecticidal soaps have been introduced. In a test by University of California entomologists, these soaps were found to have some value against whiteflies and cabbageworms. None of the commercial insecticidal soaps worked any better than Ivory Liquid.

If the corn earworm is molesting your corn crop, inject half a medicine dropper of mineral oil in the tip of the ear as the silks begin to dry.

Try aromatic sprays. Make your own spray from plants that have a disagreeable odor—chives, garlic, marigolds, and anything else you think might confuse an insect and keep it from finding your plants. Put the garlic cloves, petals, leaves, or whatever into a pot, add water to cover, and bring the mixture to the boiling point. Strain, and allow the concoction to cool, then dilute it and spray it on your plants. Some gardeners swear that if you can stand the smell, this method works wonders.

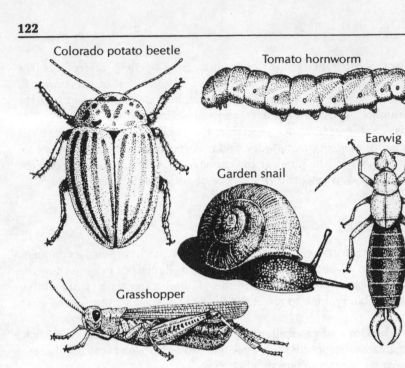

Colorado potato beetle

Tomato hornworm

Earwig

Garden snail

Grasshopper

Aphid

Thrips

Leafhopper

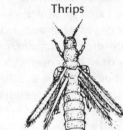

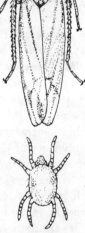

Greenhouse whitefly

Harlequin bug

Spider mite

1. Beetles, caterpillars, earwigs, grasshoppers, slugs, and snails are chewing insects that eat parts of plant leaves and fruit. This damage ranges from tiny pinholes to the destruction of entire leaves.

2. Many insects suck the sap of plants, causing foliage to wither and plants to lose vigor. Aphids, leafhoppers, whiteflies, spider mites, and true bugs are in this category.

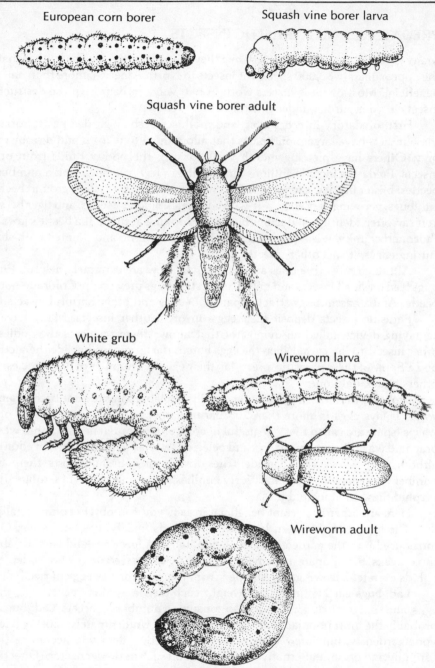

European corn borer

Squash vine borer larva

Squash vine borer adult

White grub

Wireworm larva

Wireworm adult

Cutworm

3. Borers enter a plant as eggs or by eating their way in after hatching. The entry holes are often so small that they are hard to detect. The European corn borer leaves castings outside tiny holes on the stalk.

4. A number of larvae destroy vegetables by boring into bulbs, large roots, and stems.

PREDATORY AND PARASITIC INSECTS

Many gardeners assume that every bug they see is destructive. The truth is that of the approximately 80,000 species of insects in North America, more than half are beneficial. Most of these insects work in two ways to help keep the destructive insects in your garden under control.

First, predatory insects, mites, and molluscs destroy garden pests. Some of these insects have large mouthparts that allow them to tear up and devour their prey. Others have piercing mouth parts to suck the bodily fluids from other insects. Predators include antlions, dragonflies, a few true bugs, and a number of beetles: blister beetles, carrion beetles, checkered beetles, fireflies, ground beetles, ladybugs, net-winged beetles, soft-winged beetles, soldier beetles, and tiger beetles. You can often identify predacious beetles by looking at them. If a beetle's jaws are short and chunky, it is a plant-eater. If the jaws are long and pointed with sharp cutting edges, it eats other insects.

Although most true bugs are destructive, a few are extremely helpful. Pirate bugs feed on small insects and mites. Some stinkbugs prey on the Colorado potato beetle. And assassin bugs attack Japanese beetles and other harmful insects.

Parasitic insects deposit their eggs on or in other insects. Many have an egglaying device called an ovipositor that allows them to pierce the bodies of other insects to lay eggs. When the eggs hatch, the larvae feed inside the victim's body. Some of these parasitic insects lay their eggs in a number of host species, but others attack only one.

Probably the most popular commercially available parasite is the **trichogramma wasp.** It lays eggs in more than 200 harmful species. And thousands of other wasps (some are called flies) are useful in controlling garden pests—aphid wasps, braconid wasps, ichneumon flies, and pelecinid wasps, to name a few. In addition, although almost everyone considers flies obnoxious household pests, there are a number of predacious and parasitic fly families, including aphid flies, robber flies, syrphid flies, and tachinid flies.

Here are other important beneficial insects you can obtain commercially.

The larvae of the **green lacewing** eat aphids, mealybugs, and scale. Once introduced into the garden as eggs, they hatch in a few days and feed for about three weeks, then pupate and emerge as adults. Adults feed on the honeydew that aphids excrete. Lacewings are shipped from the insectory as eggs in rice hulls.

Ladybugs eat 2½ times their weight each day in aphids, mealybugs, moth eggs, and spider mites. The larvae also consume a number of insects. Ladybugs are probably the most popular of all beneficial insects. Unfortunately, most will leave your garden within a few days of being released, unless you acclimate them carefully and provide alternative sources of food such as flower nectar. (Directions will be sent with your order.)

The **mealybug destroyer** is a member of the ladybug family that prefers mealybugs. The larvae consume aphids as well.

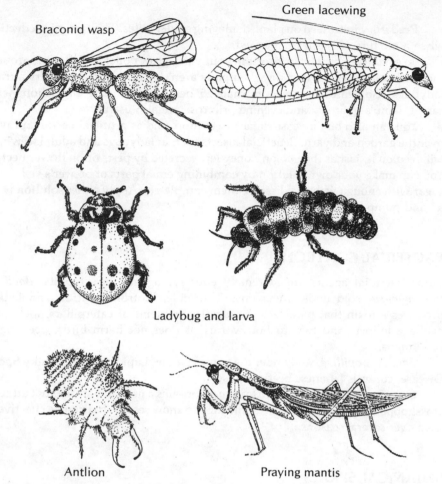

Braconid wasp

Green lacewing

Ladybug and larva

Antlion

Praying mantis

Predators, including lacewings, ladybugs, antlions, and praying mantids, devour insects on the spot or paralyze them to eat later. Parasites like the braconid wasp lay eggs on or in the host insect. Their larvae feed on the host, eventually destroying it. (Not to scale.)

Parasitic nematodes attack borers and soilborne grubs. A few firms offer them for sale.

Of the **parasitic wasps,** *Encarsia formosa* attacks whitefly larvae, *Aphytis melinus* attacks red scale, and *Trichogramma* spp. parasitize the eggs of cabbageworm, corn earworm, and other larval pests.

The **praying mantis,** a large, vicious-looking insect, consumes huge quantities of beetles, caterpillars, and grasshoppers. The young eat aphids, flies, and other small insects.

Predatory mites feed on plant-damaging spider mites. They are most effective when a mixture of species is released.

To encourage beneficial insects in your yard, grow pollen-rich flowers around the garden for them to feed on when pests aren't plentiful. Strawflowers attract ladybugs. Goldenrod hosts more than 75 beneficial species. Dandelion, wild carrot, lamb's-quarters, and evening primrose are also useful.

You can also buy a yeast-sugar insect food sold as artificial nectar. Spray it over the garden and yard. Beneficial insects such as ladybugs and adult lacewings will feed on it, just as they do on honeydew secreted by pests or on flower nectar. You can make your own solution by combining equal parts of brewer's yeast and sugar with enough water to dissolve them completely. Apply either solution with a hand-pump sprayer.

BACTERIAL CONTROLS

Some bacterial agents are extremely effective against insect pests. *Bacillus thuringiensis*, sold under the names Thuricide, Biotrol, Agritrol, and Dipel, produces a toxin that paralyzes the digestive systems of caterpillars, including cabbage loopers and tomato hornworms. It does not harm birds, bees, pets, or humans.

Bacillus popilliae, sold under the names Doom, Lapidemic, and Milky Spore Disease, controls Japanese beetle grubs.

Grasshopper spore *(Nosema lowstae)* contains a natural parasite that attacks grasshoppers. This parasite takes some time to show results, but can be effective if used over several seasons.

BOTANICAL SPRAYS

Plants themselves are the source of some of the strongest insecticides around.

Pyrethrum is made from the dried and powdered flowers of *Chrysanthemum cinerariifolium*, a close relative of the garden chrysanthemum. Pyrethrum is extremely effective against aphids, leafhoppers, leaf miners, and thrips.

Rotenone is an insecticide derived from the roots and stems of tropical shrubs and vines in the genera *Derris* and *Lonchocarpus*. Rotenone acts on contact and is also a stomach poison. It controls many sucking and chewing insects, including aphids, beetles, caterpillars, leafhoppers, and thrips.

Ryania is derived from the ground stems of *Ryania speciosa*, a tropical South American shrub. It is especially effective against the European corn borer, as well as a variety of other insects.

Sabadilla, made from the seeds of a lilylike Mexican plant *(Schoencaulon officinale)*, is sold as a wettable powder. It works as both a contact and a stomach poison against squash bugs.

PLANT DISEASES

Even with your best preventive efforts, you may encounter some diseases in your garden. Here is a quick rundown of the most common.

Bacterial diseases: Bacteria are one-called microorganisms. Most are beneficial in your garden, but a few are harmful to vegetables.

Bacterial spots, soft rots, and wilts cause most of the problems. *Bacterial spot* (or *blight*) may start as dark green spots or streaks on leaves and stems, later turning gray to red-brown. The spots may drop out and leave ragged holes.

Bacterial soft rot may infect leaves, branches, and fruit. The infected area is usually bordered by pale yellow or tan. When the infection is advanced, it oozes a gelatinous fluid.

Bacterial wilt invades the water-conducting tubes of the plant. If you slice the stem of an infected plant, it will ooze a gelatinous fluid. Often, vigorous-looking plants infected with bacterial wilt simply dry up and wilt. Bacterial wilt is often spread by insects.

Fungal diseases: Eight types of fungus are found in the garden: mildews, rusts, rots, cankers, scab, spots, wilts, and smuts.

There are two types of mildews, powdery and downy. *Powdery mildew* appears as white to light gray patches on the upper surface of leaves. *Downy mildew* shows up as pale green or yellow areas on the upper surface, and as light gray or purple patches below.

Disease Problems

Disease	Damage	Prevention or Control
Bacteria		
Bacterial spot	Dark green spots or streaks that later turn gray, brown, or reddish; can ooze gelatinous fluid	Rotate crops; keep plants vigorous with supplemental feedings
Bacterial soft rot	Infected areas on leaves, branches, or fruit bordered by yellow or tan; advanced infection causes large sunken dark areas, frequently oozing gelatinous fluid	Avoid planting in undrained soil; rotate crops on long rotation
Bacterial wilt (spread by insects)	Plants wilt and die; symptoms identical to those of fusarium and verticillium wilts	Destroy infected plants; plant resistant varieties

(continued)

Disease Problems — *Continued*

Disease	Damage	Prevention or Control
Fungi		
Mildew	Grayish patches on upper surface of leaves (powdery mildew); or pale green or yellow areas on upper surface, light gray or purple below (downy mildew)	Rotate crops; avoid overhead sprinkling; plant resistant varieties
Rust	Yellow, orange, red, or brown pustules on underside of leaves and stems	Destroy nearby weeds that show rust; collect and destroy infected plants when first seen
Rots	Stems, leaves, roots, or fruit become mushy and spongy	Plant in well-drained soil; collect and destroy infected plants; keep fruit off soil
Canker	Sunken or swollen discolored dead areas that may girdle stem	Destroy infected plants; use four-year rotation; purchase healthy-looking seedlings
Scab	Roughened, crustlike, raised or sunken area on leaves, stem, fruit, roots, or tubers	Use four-year crop rotation; plant resistant varieties; remove weeds
Fungal leaf spots, blights	Spots on leaves; centers may fall out; spots may enlarge to form blotches	When severe, collect and burn infected material
Wilt	Leaves turn pale green to yellow; plants wilt and die	Plant resistant varieties; use four-year rotation; collect and destroy infected plants
Smut, sooty mold	Dark brown to black sooty-looking masses inside swollen white blisters	Pick off and burn infected parts before blisters open; plant resistant varieties
Viruses	Distortion of leaves, flowers, fruit; stunted plants; yellow streaking or mottling	Destroy diseased plants; keep down weeds; viruses may be transmitted by insects, so control with botanical sprays
Nematodes	Yellowing, stunting, wilting, dieback; knots on roots	Destroy infected plants; plant resistant varieties; rotate plantings; interplant or cover-crop with marigolds

Rust appears as bright yellow, orange, red, reddish-brown, or black blisters (pustules) on the underside of leaves. Only occasionally will it kill vegetables.

Rot is not one disease but several. Root decay may cause the roots to be mushy and spongy. This is caused by either fungi or bacteria. When seedlings rot, collapse, and die before or just after emergence, it is called damping-off. Rots can attack practically all vegetables.

Cankers are simply irregularly oval dead areas on stems. They are often sunken or swollen and are usually discolored. Blackleg of cabbage is the most serious canker found in the garden.

Scab appears as roughened, crustlike raised or sunken areas on leaves, stems, fruit, roots, and tubers. It is caused by a wide range of fungi and a few bacteria.

Fungal *leaf spots* vary in size, shape, and color. The centers of the spots may fall out. Anthracnose, black spot, and tar spot are a few of the named types of this disease.

Fungal wilt plugs up the vessels inside the plants. Fusarium and verticillium wilts are caused by fungi. Both start at the base of the stem and proceed upward.

Smuts and *soot molds* show up as a mass of sooty black spores. Both look bad, but they cause little damage to most plants.

Viral diseases: Viral diseases appear as distortions of leaves, flowers, or fruits; as yellowing or streaking of leaves; and as stunted plants. A few viruses that affect vegetables are *aster yellows* (yellow and stunted plants), *curlytop* (dwarfed plants with curled, bunched leaves), *mosaic* (leaves with mottled yellow or light green areas), *ringspot* (yellow or brown concentric rings), and *yellows* (uniformly yellow plants, may wilt and die). Many viruses are spread by sucking insects such as aphids and leafhoppers.

Damage from all diseases can be minimized by rotating your vegetables, pulling and destroying infected plants, planting resistant varieties, and avoiding overhead watering when possible. Rust damage can be minimized by destroying nearby weeds that show rust.

PROTECTION FROM ANIMALS

Dogs, cats, gophers, birds, and other animals can be a nuisance in the garden. I try to live and let live with dogs and cats. But when an animal rips up a freshly planted bed of carrots, I draw the line.

Physical barriers are especially useful for preventing bird damage. You can protect individual seedlings with paper caps. Groups of plants can be surrounded by window screen cages. Commercial netting will fit over the entire garden. Three-foot fences will keep out dogs and other small animals, but cats can climb right over.

I don't recommend traps that kill animals, but live traps allow you to turn the intruder loose somewhere else. These are effective with rabbits, raccoons, and other small suburban pests.

Plants can be protected from birds with simple devices such as gutter wire or bird netting spread over the garden. Inflatable owls and snakes can also be used to discourage birds from nibbling on vegetables.

Aromatic materials and plants can be used to repel many animals. They range from mothballs to lion dung (available from some zoos). A number of manufacturers offer dog and cat repellents in both stick and aerosol form. The results are mediocre to fair, but if you're desperate, pick up one at the nursery and try it.

Still another tactic is fear. Strips of aluminum foil may scare off birds and small animals; scarecrows, rubber snakes and owl decoys are traditional gardener's allies. See the table Animal Problems for some controls.

AN EIGHT-STEP PEST MANAGEMENT PLAN

This plan is based on the principles of integrated pest management — making use of a variety of strategies, including cultural methods, plant resistance, pest-specific diseases, and beneficial insects. The idea is to garden in balance with nature, and use controls only when absolutely necessary. Here is the sequence of eight steps, from least invasive to the garden environment to most invasive. Try to go no further than necessary in this sequence.

Step 1: Schedule regular fall and spring cleanups. Get rid of weeds and refuse in and near the garden. During the growing season, place garden waste such as radish and carrot tops in the compost pile to keep the garden clean.

Step 2: Ask your county agricultural agent or gardening neighbors if you can avoid any insects and diseases by planting crops early or late. And by learning the names of the worst pests and diseases, you can select varieties, that are resistant to them.

Step 3: Rotate as much as possible. Move key producer plants back and forth in zone B. In zone C, plant root and leafy crops in a different section each season.

Step 4: Encourage beneficial insects to inhabit your garden by planting pollen-rich plants. If your garden is particularly bothered by aphids or whiteflies, consider purchasing beneficial insects to control them.

Step 5: Include plants that repel insect pests in your yearly garden plan. In addition, check the list of preventive methods discussed earlier in this chapter.

Step 6: Check your garden carefully every day for insects and disease. Pick off any beetles or caterpillars that you are certain are destroying your plants. Destroy any diseased leaves or branches you find. If an entire plant is infected, remove it from the garden.

Step 7: Move to more direct controls if insect damage becomes severe. Use cardboard squares for whiteflies, try aluminum foil to repel aphids, use rolled newspaper to trap insects. Try sprays of soapy water or aromatic mixtures.

Step 8: If the damage still persists at unacceptable levels, apply either a bacterial control or a plant-based insecticide.

Animal Problems

Animal and Control	How to Use	Advantages; Disadvantages
Birds		
Dixie cups	Cut off tops, place over individual seedlings	Inexpensive
Hotcaps	Place over individual seedlings	Easy to use; expensive if many are needed
Mosquito, bird netting, floating row covers	Place on stakes over entire seedbed	Good for beds of lettuce and other leafy vegetables; must be remove to weed
Scarecrow	Make of crossed stakes, old clothes	Durable; only partially effective
Screen caps	Cut 8-inch square from window screen, staple to form a cone	Protects small groups of seedlings; not large enough to cover entire crop
Dogs and Cats		
Chickenwire cages	Install 2- to 3-feet chickenwire cages around individual beds of carrots, radishes, other root and leaf vegetables	Completely effective; takes time to build
Chili powder, ground garlic	Mix in equal parts, sprinkle around garden; replenish weekly	Easy to prepare; washes away easily and only partially effective
Commercial repellent stakes	Place in ground around garden	Long-lasting; only partially effective
Commercial sprays or aerosol repellents	Spray around garden, replenish every few days	Easy to use; washes away
Fence	Install 3- to 4-feet chicken wire or mesh fence around garden	Positive control over dogs; not effective for cats
Stale cigars	Scatter tobacco around garden; replenish as needed	Inexpensive; washes away easily, only partially effective
Rabbits		
Animal lard	Rub on plants	Inexpensive, easy to use; partially effective
Chili powder, ground garlic	Mix in equal parts; sprinkle around garden; replenish weekly	Easy to prepare; washes away

Animal and Control	How to Use	Advantages; Disadvantages
Commercial box traps	Place around garden; bait with lettuce leaves, carrots	Safe, and rabbits are released elsewhere; expensive
Commercial repellent	Spray around garden; replenish every few days	Easy to apply; washes away
Fence	Install 2-foot-high chickenwire or mesh fence (mesh must be smaller than 2 inches)	Effective: fairly expensive, and makes it difficult to get into garden
Mineral repellent (ground limestone, talcum, powdered rock phosphate)	Sprinkle around garden	Easy to use; ingredients hard to find in small quantities
Mint leaves	Scatter around garden; replenish weekly	Easy to use; only partially effective
Wood ashes	Scatter around garden; replenish as needed	Fairly effective; washes away

Raccoons, Woodchucks, Skunks

Animal lard	Rub on plants	Easy to use; partially effective
Chili powder, ground garlic	Mix in equal parts; sprinkle around garden; replenish weekly	Easy to prepare; washes away
Garlic	Plant around perimeter	Long lasting; partially effective
Mothballs, naphthalene flakes	Scatter around garden	Easy to use; partially effective

Mice

Mint leaves	Scatter around garden; replenish weekly	Easy to use; partially effective
Mothballs, naphthalene flakes	Scatter around garden	Easy to use; partially effective

Gophers and Moles

Battery-powered gopher stakes (scares gophers, moles with vibration)	Place stake in ground; effective for 100-foot diameter	Good results; expensive, $50 each

(continued)

Animal and Control	How to Use	Advantages; Disadvantages

Gophers and Moles— *Continued*

Animal and Control	How to Use	Advantages; Disadvantages
Castor beans	Plant around edge of garden	Easy to plant; the beans are poisonous to animals and humans
Chili powder, ground garlic	Mix in equal parts; sprinkle in main tunnel; replenish weekly	Inexpensive; partially effective
Commercial box traps	Place in main tunnel	Gophers trapped alive and released elsewhere; lots of work
Elderberry cuttings	Place in holes and runs	Easy to use; must be replaced frequently
Gopher windmill (sold as Klipity klop), manufactured as a gopher deterrent	Place in garden about 12 feet apart; sets up ground vibrations	Many gardeners report excellent results, one will protect a Vegetable Factory garden; costs about $12
Homemade repellent spray	Mix 1 teaspoon castor oil and 1 teaspoon liquid detergent in gallon of water; spray on plants	Ingredients readily available; partially effective
Human hair	Sprinkle liberal amounts in main runways	Inexpensive; may be hard to get
Metal sheets (1-foot square)	Drive 1-foot-square sheets into ground to blockade main tunnel every 10 feet	Can be handled above ground; partially effective
Mole plant	Plant around garden	Easy to grow; limited effect on gophers
Mothballs, naphthalene flakes	Place in main tunnels	Easy to use, old-time control; gophers and moles sometimes toss mothballs out of tunnels, and naphthalene flakes hard to get into tunnels
Scilla bulbs	Plant throughout garden	Easy to grow; partially effective
Wine or pop bottles	Bury in a row up to their necks around perimeter of the garden; wind whistling over them creates a vibration that scares animals	Inexpensive; requires a lot of work

CHAPTER 9

VEGETABLE WIZARDRY: BEANS TO WATERMELONS

THIS CHAPTER IS A REFERENCE FOR PLANTING, caring for, and harvesting the major vegetables grown in Vegetable Factory gardens. Each section has a variety chart that lists popular varieties, baby and gourmet vegetables, and some of the more unusual varieties especially suited for the Vegetable Factory. Oriental vegetables and herbs will be detailed in Chapter 10, Special Gardens. Seed-saving instructions are included with each vegetable. Save open-pollinated varieties only, not hybrids. The seed package will indicate if a variety is a hybrid. Note that page references for particular techniques and materials are included in the bean section below, though they are applicable to all the vegetables.

BEANS

Pole beans produce the greatest yield for a given garden area, since they provide a steady harvest all season long. Grow them on freestanding supports (see Chapter 6, Vertical Gardening) or up the wire frame at the north end of the garden. Bush beans do not produce as high a yield, but they will provide beans earlier than the pole type. Plant them in zone B as a part of one of the dynamic plant groupings (see page 56). For a continuous harvest of bush beans, make several plantings throughout the season.

Planting. All beans, except fava beans, are warm-weather crops. Plant in the spring after the ground has warmed to at least 60° F. You can start them under glass or polyethylene from two to four weeks before the last frost.

Plant bush snap beans 1 to 2 inches deep and 4 inches apart; pole snap beans 1 to 2 inches deep, 6 inches apart; bush lima beans 1½ to 2 inches deep, 8 inches apart; and pole lima beans 1½ to 2 inches deep, 10 inches apart. Feed each plant 1 tablespoon of any Vegetable Factory organic fertilizer (see page 28), or apply fish emulsion every three or four weeks according to the instructions on the bottle.

Container planting. Plant bush beans 3 inches apart in containers. Plant pole beans 9 inches apart. Cover with 1½ inches of planting mix (page 89). Grow pole beans up a garden trellis attached to the back of a large container; or insert a 2-by-2-inch post in a half whiskey barrel and grow beans up strings.

Companion planting. Plant near beets, cabbage, carrots, cauliflower, cucumbers, marigolds, strawberries, and summer savory. Keep away from garlic, leeks, onions, and shallots.

Problems:

● *The beans won't sprout or only a few come up.* They were started outdoors too early. Don't plant until the soil warms up to at least 60° F.

● *The vines look fine but don't produce a good crop.* Overmature pods are left on the vine. This greatly reduces the oncoming crop. Keep the beans picked as they mature.

● *The ends of the pods shrivel.* The soil has dried out. Keep the soil moist during the entire growing season.

● *Vines flower, but flowers drop off without producing beans.* This is caused by the temperature jumping from cool to 90° F and above. It also occurs when the weather is dry and especially windy. Avoid planting varieties susceptible to blossom-pod drop: 'Blue Lake', 'Kentucky Wonder', and pole limas.

● *Reddish or pale brown spots and streaks appear on the pods.* The pods are exposed to the hot sun following cool, overcast weather. To avoid sunscald, plant in well-drained soil.

● *Diseases and pests.* Bacterial blights and molds: avoid tilling when the ground is wet; rotate crops each season. Bean leaf beetles and Mexican bean beetles: pick egg clusters from undersides of leaves; plant in early June to mature between generations of beetles; clean up plant debris after harvest.

Harvesting. Harvest snap beans when the pods snap readily but the tips are still pliable. To keep beans producing, pick the pods frequently. Pick lima beans when the pods are well filled but still bright green and fresh. The end of a pod should feel spongy when squeezed.

Seed-saving. Pull up the plants when the pods turn brown or tan and the beans rattle in the pods. Cut pole bean vines into a convenient size, and hang to dry in an airy place. When dry, remove the bean seeds and store in a cool dry place in a jar with holes in the lid.

Bean Varieties

Variety	Days to Maturity	Description	Catalog Source*
Pole Snap			
Blue Lake	60	Oval, 5½ to 6 inches, dark green pods	1, 2, 6, 8, 11, 13, 14, 26, 28, 31, 32, 33, 35, 36, 40, 43, 48, 50, 57
Kentucky Wonder	65	High-quality, flat pods, 6 to 7 inches, rust-resistant	1, 2, 7, 8, 10, 11, 13, 20, 25, 28, 29, 32, 33, 43, 47, 48, 50, 54, 57
Kentucky Wonder Wax	60–68	Long, brittle, meaty, yellow, almost stringless	2, 5, 8, 13, 17, 26, 30, 33, 36, 48, 50, 54, 57
Romano	65	Flat, wide Italian bean	1, 2, 6, 8, 10, 13, 17, 29, 30, 35, 36, 44, 45, 51, 52, 57
Scarlet Runner	65–70	Flat, scarlet flowers, 6 inches, vines 10 to 12 feet	1, 2, 8, 11, 29, 44, 47, 48, 51, 57
Bush Snap			
Blue Lake Bush	52–60	Long, round, dark green pods, 5 to 6 inches, 18-inch plants	1, 2, 5, 7, 8, 10, 11, 13, 14, 31, 33, 40, 43, 48, 51, 52, 54, 58
Contender	58	Plump pods, 5 to 7 inches, bushy, vigorous	1, 2, 5, 7, 8, 10, 11, 13, 14, 31, 33, 40, 43, 48, 51, 52, 54, 58
Roma II	59	Upright plants, 4½ inches, smooth pods, big yields	6, 8, 18, 26, 29, 33, 34, 36, 40, 45, 46, 47, 54, 55, 58
Royal Burgundy	50–60	Curved, round, purple pods, 12 to 15 inches, bush, turns green when cooked	6, 8, 10, 13, 14, 17, 26, 28, 32, 35, 36, 44, 46, 48, 50, 51, 52, 54, 55
Slenderette	53	Dark green, slender, 5 inches, erect bushes	36, 46, 55
Venture	48	Long green, lumpy pods, 6½ inches, easy to grow	20, 25, 36

(continued)

Bean Varieties — *Continued*

Variety	Days to Maturity	Description	Catalog Source*
Bush Yellow Wax			
Goldcrop	45	Shiny, yellow, 5 to 6 inches, stringless, pods at outer edge of foliage	2, 12, 26, 28, 32, 36, 45, 48, 54
Goldkist	59	Long slender, golden-yellow pods, harvest when young	36
Roc d'Or	57	Yellow, long, straight round pods, buttery flavor, resistant to bean virus, anthracnose	25, 46
Pole Lima			
King of the Garden	90	Large, flat beans, 3 to 5 per pod, climbs 8 feet or more	6, 8, 10, 13, 17, 26, 28, 29, 32, 44, 45, 48, 54, 55, 58
Bush Lima			
Henderson Bush Baby	65–81	3 inches, flat, slightly curved pods, ideal for freezing and canning, small erect plants	2, 5, 6, 7, 11, 13, 25, 28, 30, 32, 34, 40, 43, 44, 55
European Gourmet Beans			
Aiguillon	55	Dark green, bush, pencil-thin, French gourmet bean	31
Aiquille Verts	55	Dark green, bush, pencil-thin pods	24, 31
Aramis	55	Pencil-thin, 7 to 9 inches long, bush, pick when young	56

Variety	Days to Maturity	Description	Catalog Source*
Cristal	65	Climbing French type, pencil-thin pods	31
Daisy Haricot Nain	50	Dark green, long, round, stringless	24
Dandy	54	Round, dark green, pick at 4 inches	10, 35
Dutch Stringless Green Pod	50	Long, pencil-thin, stringless	57
Fin de Bagnols	63	Pencil-thin, 6 to 7 inches, pick very young, 14-inch bush	19, 24, 31
Perfect Improved	55	Thin, green, 4 to 5 inches, stringless	57
Prelude	45	Bush, pencil-thin, stringless	57
Stankette	53	Deep green, string-less, 5 inches, pick young	46
Triomphe de Farcy	53	Thin, straight, 6 to 7 inches	19, 24, 25
Vernadon	55	Long, round, pencil-thin (when 3 to 4 inches long), anthracnose-resistant	46

*Listings correspond to seed companies listed under Sources of Seeds and Supplies.

BEETS

Beets are an excellent crop for a Vegetable Factory garden because you can grow a large quantity in a small space. You have a number of choices of shape, ranging from round to cylindrical, and colors from white through yellow to red. Try some of the new baby beets that grow about 1 inch in diameter.

Planting. Sow the knobby seed clusters about 2 inches apart across the bed, ½ to 1 inch deep. Thin to stand 3 inches apart. You can plant about 20 beets per square foot. Make the first sowing two to four weeks before the last average spring frost date in your area. Then sow additional crops every two weeks or so.

The minimum soil temperature for beets is 40° F. Apply ¼ cup of Vegetable Factory organic fertilizer per square foot about midway in the growing season, or feed once during the season with fish emulsion, according to the instructions on the bottle.

Container planting. Stagger plantings in large containers. Plant in at least two sections, two to three weeks apart. Scatter beet seeds on a 2-inch spacing over the entire container surface. Cover with ¾ inch of soil mix and keep moist. When the beets reach 2 to 3 inches tall, thin to stand 3 inches apart.

Companion planting. Plant with broccoli, Brussels sprouts, cabbage, cauliflower, lettuce, onions, and Swiss chard. Keep away from pole beans.

Problems:

● *Roots are tough and stringy, beets have a bland flavor.* There are several reasons for this. (1) Beets were exposed to temperatures of over 85° F. Grow in early spring or fall, when the temperatures are below 85°. (2) Soil was allowed to dry out. Beets need to grow at full speed without a letup. Water deeply, then don't water again until the soil has dried out to a depth of 4 to 8 inches. Check with a trowel. (3) Beets were left in the ground more than two weeks after reaching edible size. Harvest when beets are about 2 inches in diameter.

● *Spotty germination.* High soil temperatures (over 85° F) keep seed from germinating. Seed will not come up well when soil dries out during the germination period. Place organic mulch over the seedbed. Water twice a day until the seedlings emerge.

● *White ring* (whitish rings inside the beet). Caused by drought or heavy rains following a period of high temperature. No cure for heavy rains. Keep soil from drying out during drought conditions.

● *Diseases and pests.* Leaf spot, curly top virus: control through garden cleanup and crop rotation; destroy affected plants. Aphids and blister beetles: control aphids with rotenone, blister beetles with sabadilla.

Harvesting. Start harvesting beets when they reach ¾ inch in diameter. If allowed to grow larger than about 3 inches, they lose flavor and may become woody.

Seed-saving. Cut stalks when seed clusters are dry and brown, then hang them to dry. Strip seeds from stalk. Beets and Swiss chard may cross.

Beet Varieties

Variety	Days to Maturity	Description	Catalog Source*
Cylindrical			
Cylindra	60	Long, narrow, carrotlike	2, 5, 6, 7, 8, 10, 13, 14, 17, 26, 31, 32, 44, 51, 52, 54, 55, 57
Round			
Detroit Dark Red	55	Round, glossy tops, dark red, All-America Selection	1, 2, 5, 6, 7, 10, 11, 12, 13, 14, 17, 18, 29, 30, 32
Red Ace	51	Deep red, plants 14 inches tall	6, 13, 17, 25, 26, 30, 32, 33, 36, 47, 48, 50, 52, 55
Semiround			
Ruby Queen	52	Dark red, short top, All-America Selection	7, 8, 10, 11, 12, 13, 17, 28, 29, 30, 32, 33, 34, 45, 54
Baby Gourmet Beets			
Badger's Baby	47	Deep red, 1 inch, perfect for pickling	13
Dwergina	58	Intense red, sweet, small taproot, Dutch	20, 25
Fire Chief	52–70	Small, deep red, bronze-tinged top	48
Little Ball	50	Smooth, 1-inch ball	6, 28, 46, 48, 50, 52, 54, 57
Spinel	52	Red, ½ inch	35, 51
Other			
Albion Vereduna	50	White globe-shaped, spinach-type greens	13, 44, 48, 50, 51
Burpee's Golden Beet	55	Golden color, small round beet	1, 6, 11, 13, 17, 20, 26, 28, 29, 31, 32, 35, 44, 46, 48, 51, 56
Green Top Bunching	53–61	Bright red roots, medium tops	30, 34, 45, 57, 58

*Listings correspond to seed companies listed under Sources of Seeds and Supplies.

BROCCOLI

Some broccoli varieties put out lots of side branches in addition to a main head; others have a central head but produce few side branches; still others produce side branches but no central head. The best for small gardens are the varieties that produce good-sized central heads and lots of side branches.

Planting. Grow the plants indoors from seeds or buy seedlings from a nursery. Transplant them into your garden 15 inches apart. You can plant broccoli in the ground four to six weeks before the average frost-free date in your area. The minimum soil temperature is 40° F. You can also plant broccoli in midsummer for a fall crop. Broccoli is a heavy feeder; apply 2 tablespoons of Vegetable Factory organic fertilizer once a month per plant, or feed with fish emulsion every four weeks according to the instructions on the bottle.

Container planting. Grow broccoli in 5- to 10-gallon containers, one plant per container.

Companion Planting. Plant broccoli near beets, cabbage and other cole crops, carrots, marigolds, nasturtiums, thyme, and tomatoes. Keep it away from strawberries.

Problems:

● *Broccoli forms premature small, scattered heads.* This occurs when young plants are subjected to temperatures below 40°F before or shortly after planting. Prevent by protecting small plants with hotcaps or other protective devices.

● *Broccoli stops producing buds.* As soon as some broccoli heads flower, the plant stops putting out young buds. To eliminate the problem, keep the broccoli crop harvested. Pick the developing buds as often as every three days as long as the plant continues to produce.

● *Broccoli flowers prematurely.* Temperatures over about 85°F force broccoli to flower. Solve the problem by planting early varieties ('Green Comet Hybrid', 'Spartan Early', 'Premium Early') to mature ahead of the heat. Or plant broccoli in midsummer for a fall crop.

● *Diseases and pests.* Black rot, bacterial blight, club root: control diseases through crop rotation; avoid tillage when soil is wet. Flea beetles: control by placing wood ash around the plant, or sprinkle a spoonful of ashes on each plant two or three times a week. Cabbage looper: control with *Bacillus thuringiensis*. Cutworm: set a cardboard collar deep in the soil around each plant.

Harvesting. Cut the terminal bud 5 inches below the head on the edible stem. The plant will send up additional shoots. To encourage production, keep the shoots harvested.

Seed saving. Cut stalks when seedpods are dry and brittle, dry pods on trays, then separate seed from chaff.

Broccoli Varieties

Variety	Days to Maturity	Description	Catalog Source*
Calabrese	85	Bluish-green central head with many side branches	1, 8, 10, 12, 35, 44, 45, 47, 48, 51, 55, 57, 58
Green Comet	55	Solid large central head, red side-shoots, All-America Selection	6, 8, 12, 17, 18, 29, 30, 32, 33, 34, 36, 54, 55, 57, 58
Packman	60–80	Central head, good sideshoots	13, 17, 25, 29, 30, 32, 34, 35, 40, 48, 54, 57, 58
Premium Crop	58–82	Central head, no sideshoots, blue-green, disease-resistant, 16 to 18 inches tall	2, 6, 8, 12, 13, 17, 18, 20, 25, 28, 29, 32, 34, 35, 36, 40, 45, 46, 48, 54, 55, 58
Romanesco	85	Pale green, large head on a large-leafed plant	1, 31, 44, 46, 51
Royal Cruiser	85	Sideshoots almost as large as main heads	31
Waltham 29	75	Dark blue-green, medium-large heads	1, 2, 7, 8, 14, 26, 29, 30, 33, 34, 43, 45, 47, 50, 51, 55
White Sprouting	70	Many creamy yellow buds over a large plant	31

*Listings correspond to seed companies listed under Sources of Seeds and Supplies.

BRUSSELS SPROUTS

Brussels sprouts are a cool-season vegetable. They don't grow well in areas with hot dry summers, but they are winter-hardy. Once a plant starts producing, you think it's never going to stop.

Planting. Grow from seed started indoors, planted ½ inch deep in peat pots, or buy plants from a nursery. In cool-summer areas, transplant to the garden eight to ten weeks before the last frost. Where summers are hot, plant in mid-August for

Brussels Sprouts Varieties

Variety	Days to Maturity	Description	Catalog Source*
Jade Cross Hybrid	80	Blue-green, oval sprouts, All-America Selection	5, 8, 13, 17, 28, 29, 30, 36, 40, 48, 55
Long Island Improved	90	Produces good crop of 1½-inch sprouts	1, 2, 7, 8, 10, 13, 14, 17, 18, 28, 29, 31, 32, 33, 34, 36, 44, 45, 48, 52, 57, 58

Gourmet Varieties

Variety	Days to Maturity	Description	Catalog Source*
Aries	102	English, medium-hard oval sprouts	50
Dolmie	102	European, oval, dark green sprouts	48
Fieldstar	100	Dutch, hard, light green sprouts	50
Valient	102	Dutch, buttonlike sprouts, rot-resistant	46

*Listings correspond to seed companies listed under Sources of Seeds and Supplies.

a fall harvest. Space 15 inches apart. The minimum soil temperature for Brussels sprouts is 40° F. Supplement this heavy feeder with 1 tablespoon of Vegetable Factory organic fertilizer per plant about once a month, or apply fish emulsion every three or four weeks according to the instructions on the bottle.

• **Container planting.** Plant one plant per 5- or 10-gallon container, transplanting as seedlings. As the plants mature, remove all excess leaves, except those at the top.

Companion planting. Plant near beets, cabbage and other cole crops, carrots, marigolds, nasturtiums, thyme, and tomatoes. Keep away from strawberries.

Problems:

● *Large, leafy, "loose" sprouts.* Brussels sprouts need temperatures below 75° F to produce compact sprouts. To prevent the problem, plant so that the crop matures in the cool temperatures of fall.

● *Wartlike projections on leaves and stems.* These are injuries caused by soil particles blowing against the leaves. Protect the plants on the windward side. These projections do not affect the quality of the sprouts.

● *Diseases and pests.* Black rot, bacterial blight: control disease through crop rotation; avoid tillage when the soil is wet. Flea beetles: control with ashes scattered around the plant. Cabbage loopers: control with *Bacillus thuringiensis.*

Harvesting. Snap or trim off the sprouts when they are firm and deep green. Sprouts have the best flavor when they are about 1 to 1½ inches in diameter. Mild frost improves the flavor. Pick the lowest sprout each time and break off any leaves below the sprout. Don't remove the top leaves.

Seed-saving. Brussels sprouts is a biennial and needs to be wintered over with a heavy mulch before flowering the next spring. Cut stalks when seedpods are dry and brittle. Dry on trays, then separate the seed. Broccoli, Brussels sprouts, cabbage, cauliflower, collards, and kale are members of the same species, and any of the others may cross with Brussels sprouts if they flower together.

CABBAGE

You can grow a surprising number of cabbage varieties: red cabbage, which ranges from bright red to dark purple in color; savoy, the dark green leaves with a bubbly surface; round, with forms varying from perfectly globular to slightly flat; flat, which vary from wide to flat to almost egglike in shape; and pointed, which are heart-shaped cabbages.

Planting. Start seed indoors, or buy transplants from a nursery. Set seedlings in the beds at 14-inch intervals. You can squeeze cabbage into a spacing of about 10 inches, but the heads will be smaller. You can also space your cabbages 6 inches apart and cut every other plant for greens. The minimum soil temperature for cabbage is slightly above 40° F. Set out transplants eight to ten weeks before the last frost. Cabbage is a heavy feeder, so supplement each plant with 2 tablespoons of Vegetable Factory organic nutrient mix once a month; or supplement every three or four weeks with fish emulsion according to the instructions on the bottle.

Container planting. Plant two cabbage plants per 3- to 5-gallon container. Remove the weakest plant in a few weeks, and allow the strongest to grow to maturity.

Companion planting. Plant with bush beans, beets, carrots, celery, onions, potatoes, and aromatic herbs. Keep cabbage away from pole beans, strawberries, and tomatoes.

Problems:

● *Cabbage suddenly starts to flower.* This is caused by exposure to temperatures of 40 to 50° F for three or four weeks. Cabbage planted to overwinter often flowers and fails to produce heads. To solve this problem, plant slimmer, pencil-sized transplants.

● *Cabbage heads split.* This afflicts plants that are allowed to dry out and then are watered. The center and outer portions develop at different speeds. The heads of early varieties often split in warm weather.

● *Multiple heading early cabbage grown in northern climates.* This results from injury of the main growing tip by frost when the plants are young. To solve the problem, plant locally grown seedlings.

● *Diseases and pests.* Blackleg, bacterial blight: control diseases through crop rotation; collect and burn plant material after harvest. Cabbage looper: control with *Bacillus thuringiensis.*

Harvesting. Cut heads when firm. Cut the stem off squarely and leave it in the ground so small cabbages will form. Harvest Chinese cabbage as early as possible (the long types should be 15 to 18 inches tall), since the large compact heads tend to elongate and bolt into flower when the hot days arrive. You can harvest cabbage in summer by planting in the spring; plant in the summer to harvest in late fall and all winter long in mild climates.

Seed-saving. Cut stalks when seed pods are dry and brittle. Dry them on trays and separate the seeds.

Cabbage Varieties

Variety	Days to Maturity	Description	Catalog Source*
Flat			
Late Dutch Flat	110	Late, bluish-green, good winter keeper	10, 26, 29, 30, 34, 43, 58
Conical			
Early Jersey Wakefield	65	Dark green, 2 to 3 pounds, extra-early	1, 5, 6, 8, 10, 13, 14, 25, 28, 29, 30, 32, 35, 44, 52, 55, 57
Red			
Red Acre	86	Dark red head, 6 to 7 inches across, 4 to 5 pounds, early to midseason	2, 5, 6, 8, 10, 12, 13, 14, 17, 18, 29, 40, 43, 47, 52, 58
Ruby Ball	70	Ball-shaped, 5 pounds, All-America Selection, early	18, 29, 30, 32, 34, 40, 50, 54

Variety	Days to Maturity	Description	Catalog Source*
Round			
Danish Ballhead	105	Large, solid heads, 3 to 5 pounds, late	1, 2, 6, 7, 8, 10, 12, 14, 17, 18, 26, 29, 30, 32, 33, 44, 45, 50, 52, 55, 57
Savoy			
Chieftain Savoy	85	Blue-green, 8 inches across, flattened, 4 to 5 pounds, All-America Selection	1, 8, 10, 13, 18, 29, 30, 33, 34, 45, 48, 50, 55, 58
Baby and Gourmet Cabbage			
Baby Early	50	2 pounds, red, tight head	8
Badger Babyhead	69	2 to 3 pounds, good flavor, baby	13
Green Italian Savoy de Vertus	75	European, dark green richly textured leaves	13
Holland Winter Export	90	Large, white, excellent for coleslaw	31
Libra	85	Grapefuit-size, Dutch variety	31
Red Savoy San Michele Italian	100	Large red cabbage, deeply veined leaves	31

*Listings correspond to seed companies listed under Sources of Seeds and Supplies.

CARROTS

Carrots are a near-perfect plant for Vegetable Factory gardens. They take little space, they aren't too fussy about temperature, and they'll stay in the ground a long time without spoiling. Carrots come in a variety of shapes: long slender, medium, short fat, round, and midget bite-sized.

Planting. You can grow about 60 carrots in one square foot of space. To enjoy them all season long, plant a small section approximately every two weeks.

Broadcast seed directly on the ground, about an inch apart, and cover with ½ inch of soil. If you have trouble distributing the seed correctly, practice with dry coffee grounds, as described in Chapter 3, Planting the Vegetable Factory.

Carrot seeds are sometimes difficult to germinate, especially in hot weather. To reduce loss due to drying out, spread a ¼- to ½-inch layer of compost or rotted manure on top of the bed. Some gardeners also place a black plastic sheet over the mulch to reduce moisture loss even further. When seedlings start to show, remove the plastic. Once the young seedlings have reached about 3 inches tall, thin them to stand 2 inches apart. The minimum soil temperature is 40° F. Carrots are light feeders. They will benefit from ¼ cup of Vegetable Factory organic nutrient mix per square foot of bed, or feed in midseason with fish emulsion according to the instructions on the bottle.

Container planting. Plant by scattering the seeds across the container surface, roughly 1 inch apart. Cover with about ½ inch of soil. After a few weeks, thin to

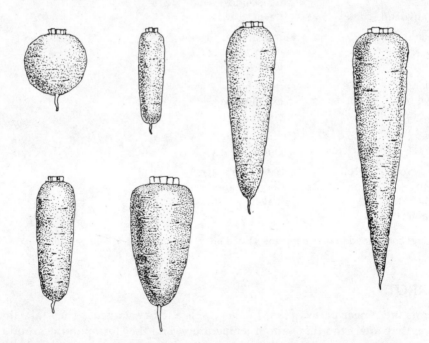

Carrots come in a variety of shapes and sizes. Baby carrots are a favorite of many gardeners today. From left to right: round type, 'Amsterdam', intermediate type, long type; bottom row: 'Early Nantes', and 'Royal Chantenay'.

2 inches apart (use the young carrots in cooking or eat them raw). In large containers, plant twice, ten days apart. Note that if the carrot tip touches the bottom of the pot, the carrot will not develop to full size; make sure your container is deep enough for the variety you intend to grow.

Companion planting. Plant near cabbage, chives, leeks, lettuce, onions, peas, potatoes, radishes, rosemary, sage, and tomatoes. Keep carrots away from dill.

Problems:

● *Carrots crack badly.* This is a watering problem. If you let the soil dry out, watering will cause the roots to crack open as they start to grow again. Water deeply, then don't water again until the soil dries out to a depth of 4 to 8 inches.

● *Carrots don't come up well from seed.* This results from a failure to keep the soil wet during the germination period. Keep the soil moist until the carrots poke through the ground.

● *The top of the carrot (the shoulder) turns green.* Too much exposure to light causes chlorophyll to develop. This makes the carrot inedible. It can be prevented by covering the shoulder with soil.

● *Diseases and pests.* Carrot rust fly: to prevent damage, delay planting until late spring or summer.

Harvesting. Start pulling carrots when they reach finger size, and continue until they reach about 1½ inches in diameter. Small carrots are usually much sweeter than larger ones.

Seed-saving. Carrots are a biennial and must be wintered over to flower in the spring. When seed heads are ripe and brown, cut the stalks and dry them. Rub the seeds from the heads.

Carrot Varieties

Variety	Days to Maturity	Description	Catalog Source*
Long Slender			
Imperator	77	Wide shoulders, 8 to 9 inches, deep orange, tender	6, 12, 28, 55, 57, 58
Orlando Gold	65–80	Smooth, slender, 10 to 11 inches, small core, bolt- and crack-resistant	13, 17, 34, 40, 48, 57

(continued)

Carrot Varieties — *Continued*

Variety	Days to Maturity	Description	Catalog Source*
Medium			
Danvers Half Long	78	Medium slender, 5 to 6 inches, deep orange, mild flavor	2, 6, 10, 12, 13, 17, 32, 33, 36, 43, 44, 47, 55, 57, 58
Red Core Chantenay	70	Medium plump, 5 to 6 inches, sweet	1, 10, 12, 13, 14, 17, 28, 33, 43, 45, 48, 57
Scarlet Nantes Half Long	70	Cylindrical, blunt end, 6 to 8 inches, coreless	1, 2, 5, 6, 8, 12, 13, 14, 17, 18, 20, 25, 26, 29, 30, 32, 34, 36, 48, 52, 57
Spartan Bonus	75	Medium plump, tapering, 5 to 7 inches	12, 14, 36
French Forcing Round			
Golden Ball	58	Round, 2 inches in diameter, golden	10
Parmex	50	Bright orange, 1 inch in diameter, excellent flavor	25
Plant	55	1½ inches in diameter	44, 46, 48
Baby, Space-Savers, Gourmet Types			
Kinko 6	50	Cone-shaped, 6 inches long	44
Little Finger	50–65	Nantes type, 3½ inches long, ⅝ inch wide, extra sweet	5, 8, 28, 32, 36, 52, 54, 57
Minicor	55	Baby Nantes, smooth, rounded tip, harvest at 3 inches, sweet	13, 20, 31, 48
Ox Heart	75	Short and fat, 4 to 6 inches long, 4 inches wide	1, 10, 33, 44, 57

Variety	Days to Maturity	Description	Catalog Source*
Short 'N' Sweet	68	Bright orange, 3 inches, sweet	6, 12, 28
Sucram	70	Nantes type, 3 to 4 inches	35, 44
Suko	55–60	Orange, 2½ inches, does not need thinning for high yields	51
Tiny Sweet	62–65	Golden-orange, 3 inches long, sweet	36
Vita Sweet 500	50	Smooth, bright orange, 4 to 5 inches long, ¾ inch wide, extremely sweet	54

*Listings correspond to seed companies listed under Sources of Seeds and Supplies.

CAULIFLOWER

Cauliflower is more difficult to grow than other members of the cabbage family. It needs to mature in cool weather and is fairly frost-hardy.

Planting. Set plants out in the garden four weeks before the last killing frost. If summers are hot in your area, you may want to grow cauliflower in the autumn. Start seeds indoors, or buy plants from a nursery, and transplant into your garden 15 inches apart. When the cauliflower begins to head (to flower by showing buds), blanch the head to prevent it from turning green: Pull a few outer leaves over the head and tie them in place loosely with a string or rubber band. The minimum soil temperature is 40° F. Give this heavy feeder monthly applications of 2 tablespoons per plant of Vegetable Factory organic nutrient mix, or feed each month with fish emulsion according to the instructions on the bottle.

Container planting. Plant singly in containers for use on the patio, or group containers together to form a cauliflower patch. Each cauliflower plant requires 3 to 5 gallons of soil.

Companion planting. Plant with beans, celery, cucumbers, potatoes, spinach, and Swiss chard.

Problems:
● *Cauliflower heads are small.* The soil was allowed to dry out. Water deeply, then don't water again until the soil dries out to a depth of 4 to 8 inches. Make sure there is moisture in the soil throughout the entire growing season.

● *Cauliflower curds gradually turn brown.* This is caused by a boron deficiency. Apply ½ ounce of borax for every 24 square feet of garden soil.

● *Diseases and pests.* Black rot: control by rotating crop; avoid tilling when soil is wet. Cabbage looper: control with *Bacillus thuringiensis.* Cutworms: place cardboard collar around individual plants and push 1 inch into soil.

Harvesting. Pick heads as soon as they enlarge and are white and firm. Softness of the head or flowering indicates overmaturity.

Seed-saving. Cut stalks when seedpods are dry and brittle. Dry them on trays and separate the seeds.

Cauliflower Varieties

Variety	Days to Maturity	Description	Catalog Source*
Purple Head	85	Large purple head, turns green when cooked	6, 26, 57
Self-Blanche	68	White, self-wrapping 6- to 7-inch head	2, 5, 12, 13, 14, 17, 18, 30, 32, 33, 34, 44, 45, 48, 54, 57
Snow Crown	60	Tight white domes, 5 to 9 inches, up to 2 pounds, All-America Selection	6, 8, 12, 18, 25, 26, 29, 31, 32, 33, 34, 35, 40, 45, 48, 50, 51, 54, 57
Super Snowball	55	Ivory white, 6 inches, dwarf plant, short-season	2, 6, 7, 12, 13, 14, 29, 34, 54, 55
Baby Cauliflower			
Garant	82–86	Quick-growing, 1½ to 3½ inches	51
Predominant	94	Harvest when 1½ to 3½ inches	51
Gourmet, European			
Alpha Blanza	88	Large head, slow grower, Dutch variety	50
Alpha Paloma	93	Dense head, good flavor	50

*Listings correspond to seed companies listed under Sources of Seeds and Supplies.

CELERIAC

Celeriac is a form of celery grown for its swollen root, which may be peeled. It is used in soups and stews. Celeriac is a cool-season, frost-hardy plant.

Planting. Start seed inside four to six weeks before transplanting, or sow them in the bed four to six weeks before the average date of last frost. Space plants 8 inches apart. The minimum soil temperature is 40° F. Celeriac needs extra nitrogen and phosphorus, so give each plant 2 tablespoons of Vegetable Factory organic nutrient mix halfway through the season, or feed with fish emulsion according to the instructions on the bottle.

Container planting. Plant one or two plants per 3 to 5 gallons of soil.

Companion planting. Plant with beans, cauliflower, leeks, and tomatoes.

Problems:

  ● *Diseases and pests.* Mosaic: control aphids (they spread mosaic) with soapy water. Blight: rotate crops each season.

Harvesting. You can simply pull up the plant when the root has swollen 2 to 4 inches wide and cut off the top. Or snip off the side roots and hill the soil over the swollen root as it is beginning to form. This partially blanches it. Harvest when the root is 3 or 4 inches wide.

Seed-saving. Heavily mulch plants for overwintering. Harvest seed heads the following summer when ripe. Shake seeds into bags, crush the heads and screen them.

Celeriac Varieties

Variety	Days to Maturity	Description	Catalog Source*
Giant Smooth Prague	110	Turnip-shaped roots, 3 to 4 inches	8, 10, 26, 29, 30, 33, 48, 57

*Listings correspond to seed companies listed under Sources of Seeds and Supplies.

CELERY

Celery can be either green or golden yellow. The green varieties have green leaves, stalks, and stems. At one time, gardeners blanched all green varieties to make them white. The golden-yellow types are generally self-blanching, with white stems and yellow-green leaves.

Planting: Plant seed outside, leaving 6 inches between plants. Celery grows best in cool weather. In mild-winter areas, celery can be grown as a winter crop. To blanch, place a cardboard collar around each plant two weeks before harvest, then mound up soil or place a heavy mulch around the collar to keep it in place. The minimum soil temperature is 40° F. Celery needs extra nitrogen and phosphorus:

give each plant 2 tablespoons of Vegetable Factory organic nutrient mix at midseason, or supplement with fish emulsion according to the instructions on the bottle.

Container planting. Plant two or three plants per 3 gallons of soil.

Companion planting. Plant with cauliflower, leeks, and tomatoes.

Problems:

● *Ragged, crosswise cracking of celery stems.* Stems are stiff and brittle, and the edges of the young leaves may be streaked. The leaves begin to turn brown. This is a boron deficiency. Apply 1 teaspoon of borax in 4 quarts of water per 30 feet of row. Plant resistant varieties: 'Dwarf Golden Self-Blanching,' 'Giant Pascal,' 'Utah 52-70,' and others.

● *Celery produces lots of leaves but no stalks.* This is caused by sudden fluctuations of temperatures in early stages of growth (up to about 4 inches tall). Protect plants by covering with hotcaps or other protective devices. Remove when the temperature warms up.

● *Diseases and pests.* Mosaic: control aphids that spread mosaic with a water spray. Blight: rotate crops; select a blight-resistant variety. Celeryworm: handpick or control with *Bacillus thuringiensis.*

Harvesting. Harvest younger stalks when the plants are two to four weeks from maturity. Celery stores well in a cool place. You can also leave the surplus celery in the soil during early winter. Pile dirt and straw around the stalks to protect against freezing.

Seed-saving. Mulch plants over winter. Harvest seed heads following the summer when ripe. Shake seeds into bags or crush the heads and screen them. Celery varieties will cross with each other and with celeriac.

Celery Varieties

Variety	Days to Maturity	Description	Catalog Source*
Green			
Giant Pascal	134	Green, tall, solid stalks	2, 5, 8, 10, 30, 43, 44, 55
Golden Self-Blanching	96	Compact, 20 inches, self-blanching	6, 8, 12, 13, 26, 30, 32, 33, 35, 40, 43, 44, 50, 51, 55, 57, 58
Utah 52-70	124	Upright, compact, 24 to 28 inches, tender	1, 8, 18, 26, 30, 36, 45, 52, 57

Variety	Days to Maturity	Description	Catalog Source*
Gourmet, European			
Cutting	110	Stalks hollow and brittle, pungent, cut the leaves as you would parsley, good for soups	31
Kintsai Oriental Wild	110	Widely used in Asian cooking, related to European cutting cabbage	31
Pink Celery	120	English variety, color remains pink after cooking	44

*Listings correspond to seed companies listed under Sources of Seeds and Supplies.

COLLARDS

Collards resemble a lanky, open-growing cabbage with smooth, dark green edible leaves. They are usually regarded as nonheading, but several types form rather loose heads.

Planting. Plant seed outdoors in late spring in cool-summer areas. In other areas, plant in mid- to late summer for a fall and winter harvest. The mature plants are frost-hardy. Sow seeds ½ inch deep and 6 inches apart, and thin to stand 12 inches apart. If you leave collards about 6 inches apart, you will produce bunchy dwarfed plants. Minimum soil temperature is 40° F. Give each collard plant 2 tablespoons of Vegetable Factory nutrient mix about once a month, or feed with fish emulsion according to the instructions on the bottle.

Container planting. Grow two or three plants in containers holding 3 to 5 gallons of soil.

Companion planting. Plant with beets, cabbage and other cole crops, and marigolds.

Problems:

● *Diseases and pests.* Cabbage looper: control with *Bacillus thuringiensis*. Harlequin bug: destroy eggs (small white pegs with black loops in neat rows); pick off the bugs.

Harvesting. Harvest the entire plant, or leave the first six to eight leaves to sustain the plant, then harvest the young leaves over a period of weeks. If you harvest several leaves at a time, never harvest the central growing point or you will delay production until sideshoots form.

Seed-saving. Cut stalks when the seedpods are dry and brittle. Dry them on trays, and thresh to separate seeds from chaff.

Collard Varieties

Variety	Days to Maturity	Description	Catalog Source*
Georgia	75	Crumpled blue-green leaf	6, 10, 24, 29, 30, 32, 33, 34, 35, 40, 43, 44, 54, 55, 56, 58
Vates Non-heading	75	Smooth leaf, broad-spreading plants	1, 6, 7, 8, 10, 13, 18, 28, 29, 30, 33, 34, 50, 52, 54, 55, 56, 58

*Listings correspond to seed companies listed under Sources of Seeds and Supplies.

CORN

Corn takes up a lot of space, but it can be planted in 2-foot-square and larger blocks in the Vegetable Factory garden. Varieties include yellow, white, yellow-and-white, super sweet, popcorn, and ornamental. In areas experiencing cool summers, plant early varieties. If you want corn all summer long, plant early, midseason, and late varieties. Corn will cross-pollinate, so plant only one variety in a Vegetable Factory bed.

Planting. Corn is wind-pollinated. The tassels contain the male flowers, and the silks that come out of the ears are part of the female flowers. Wind-borne pollen from the tassels of one plant falls on the silks of another. Because the wind can't carry pollen very far, you must group the plants as closely together as possible or the ears won't fill out.

Plant corn 1 to 2 inches deep and 8 inches apart after the last spring frost. The minimum soil temperature for corn is 50° F. Corn is a heavy feeder, so apply ½ cup of Vegetable Factory nutrient mix per square foot of corn patch each month, or supplement every three or four weeks with fish emulsion according to the instructions on the bottle.

Container planting. Plant corn in containers with a soil depth of at least 8 inches. Space seeds 4 inches apart, then cover with 1 inch of soil. Grow at least a dozen corn plants close together for proper pollination.

Companion planting. Plant with beans, cucumbers, peas, potatoes, and squash.
Problems:

● *The kernels often wind up white, yellow, and other colors on the same ear.* Cross-pollination is the culprit. Plant only one variety in a Vegetable Factory garden.

● *Ears only partially filled with ripe kernels.* Each individual kernel must be pollinated. Kernels that don't receive pollen don't fill out. Plant at least a 2-square-foot block, never a single row.

● *Leaf edges roll inward.* The plants don't have enough water. Corn needs to make rapid growth just as the ears start to mature. Lack of moisture will affect ear size. Place 2 or 3 inches of organic material on top of the soil to reduce moisture loss. Water corn two or three hours at a time, then don't water again until the soil dries out to a depth of 4 to 8 inches.

● *Stalks produce small ears.* The corn plants were spaced too close together. Space them at least 8 inches apart.

● *Diseases and pests.* Leaf spot: avoid late plantings. Root rot: rotate crops; bury or burn stalks after harvest. Corn earworm: handpick, or place a drop of mineral oil on silks just inside the ear.

Harvesting. Pick corn when the silks turn dark and begin to shrivel. The kernels should be plump and milky. Squeeze a kernel with your thumbnail—it will squirt a milky juice, indicating it is at the peak of sweetness. Corn remains in this stage for two to five days.

Seed-saving. Wait until corn kernels are completely mature (shriveled, dented, or round), then strip the kernels from the cob and store them in a cool, dry place.

Corn Varieties

Variety	Days to Maturity	Description	Catalog Source*
Yellow			
Iochief	86–93	Yellow ears, 9- to 10-inches, 2 ears per stalk	5, 6, 7; 10, 12, 13, 17, 28, 30, 32, 33, 34, 36, 45, 58
White			
Silver Queen	92–94	White, 8 to 9 inches, 8-feet stalks	2, 6, 8, 10, 12, 13, 17, 18, 25, 29, 30, 32, 33, 34, 36, 40, 45, 47, 54, 55, 56, 58
Bicolor			
Butter and Sugar	80	Yellow and white, extra sweet, 8 inches	2, 8, 10, 12, 26, 45, 48, 54, 55
Honey and Cream	78	Yellow and white, 6½ to 7½ inches	2, 6, 8, 14, 17, 32, 56
Extra Sweet			
Early Extra Sweet	85	Early, All-America Selection, supersweet	6, 11, 12, 13, 26, 30, 32, 36, 48, 51, 54, 55

(continued)

Variety	Days to Maturity	Description	Catalog Source*
Extra Sweet—Continued			
Golden Kandy Korn	89	Yellow, 8 inches, 8½-foot stalks	5, 6, 7, 12, 13, 14, 26, 28, 30, 32, 33, 34, 35, 46, 48, 52, 54, 55, 56, 57, 58
How Sweet It Is	87	White, 8 inches, 7-foot stalk	5, 6, 12, 17, 18, 26, 28, 30, 32, 34, 35, 36, 48, 51, 54, 55, 56
Extra Sweet Bicolor			
Summer Flavor Brand 77BC		Bicolor, 8 inches, 6-foot stalk, narrow ears	54
Space Savers			
Baby Asian		Small ears, medium-sized plants, harvest ears when silks first appear	31
Butter Improved	55–60	Dwarf, half-size plants, very early maturing, stalk 2 to 2½ feet, 4-inch ears, ultrasweet	51
Fischer's Earliest	60	Yellow, dwarf plants, 5 to 6 inches, sweet	14
Golden Midget	58–65	Yellow, stalks 2 to 3 feet, 4-inch ears, yellow	1, 2, 5, 12, 17, 28, 35, 44, 52, 57
Ornamental			
Indian Ornamental	110	Large decorative ears, array of colors	2, 5, 7, 10, 12, 13, 17, 18, 29, 33, 40, 44, 48, 52, 54, 55, 56, 58
Popcorn			
Black Popcorn	100	Old-fashioned favorite, black kernels make white popcorn	31

Variety	Days to Maturity	Description	Catalog Source*
Cutie Pops	100	Multicolored minia-ture popcorn, baby, 4 inches	48
Pretty Pops	95	Multicolored, stalk 6 feet, 5-inch ears	36
Strawberry Ornamental	100	Mahogany red, 3- to 4-foot stalks, 1½- to 2-inch ears	2, 6, 12, 13, 17, 22, 26, 28, 33, 35, 36, 44, 48

*Listings correspond to seed companies listed under Sources of Seeds and Supplies.

CUCUMBERS

Cucumbers can be found in every shape imaginable: smooth, warty, crooked or straight, balloon-shaped, cigar-shaped, and everything in between. There are pickling varieties, slicing varieties, even burpless varieties. Slicing cukes are generally slender and 6 to 8 inches long, while pickling varieties have shorter, blockier fruits. You can use many varieties for both pickling and slicing.

Planting. Cucumbers are a warm-weather crop, so plant after the last frost. Start plants inside in individual peat pots, or buy cucumber seedlings from a nursery. You can transplant them several weeks before the last frost if they are under hotcaps, glass, or polyethylene plastic.

Grow full-size vines 6 to 12 inches apart on the Vegetable Factory back support. Bush varieties do well on a 3- to 4- foot cucumber post. You can also grow six plants in a wire cage that is 20 inches in diameter and 3 to 4 feet tall. When the plants reach the top of the fence, cage, or cucumber post, pinch off the fuzzy growing tip to make them spread out laterally. The minimum soil temperature is 60° F. Cucumbers are heavy feeders, so apply 2 tablespoons of Vegetable Factory organic nutrient mix per plant once a month during the growing season, or supplement with fish emulsion every three or four weeks according to the instructions on the bottle.

Container planting. Plant two or three full-sized cucumbers in a container that holds at least 5 gallons. Cover seed with 1 inch of soil and keep moist. Bush varieties do well in 2 to 3 gallons of soil. Place a small trellis at the back of the container to support the bush vines.

Companion planting. Plant cucumbers near beans, cabbage, corn, peas, radishes, and squash. Keep away from aromatic herbs.

Problems:

● *The cucumbers are bitter.* Some gardeners believe this is due to uneven watering. Others blame it on temperature fluctuations. Put down two or three inches of organic material to reduce moisture. If you're having trouble getting a good-tasting cucumber, try the 'Marketmore 76'.

● *Early flowers don't produce fruit.* Female flowers (which produce the cucumbers) may not have appeared. The first few flowers are male. Or there may be too few insects to carry the pollen from the male flowers to the female. Where bees are in short supply, few cucumbers are produced.

● *Plants stop producing.* If old cucumbers aren't picked off, the vine will stop production. Pick cucumbers from the vines when they reach edible size.

● *Diseases and pests.* Bacterial wilt: spread by cucumber beetle. Mosaic: keep perennial weeds away from the garden. Leaf spot: rotate crops in the garden. Striped cucumber beetle: control by heavy mulching.

Harvesting. Pick when green, firm, and a moderate size. The spines should just be beginning to soften. They are past their prime when dull, puffy, and yellowing.

Cucumber Varieties

Variety	Days to Maturity	Description	Catalog Source*
Picklers			
Liberty	56	Dark green, high-yielding, warted, tolerant of most diseases	5, 6, 8, 12, 17, 26, 28, 29, 35, 36, 40, 51, 54, 55, 58
National Pickling	53	Dark green, 5 to 7½ inches, blunt end, all-around good pickler	8, 13, 14, 17, 25, 26, 30, 32, 52, 55, 57, 58
Slicers			
Early Surecrop	58	8½ to 9 inches long, All-America Selection	7, 8, 13, 17, 26, 29, 40, 52, 55, 58
Marketmore 76	68	Glossy, deep green, uniform, straight, disease-resistant	1, 7, 10, 12, 14, 18, 26, 29, 33, 34, 45, 48, 54, 56
Spacesavers (Bush-Type)			
Bush Champion	55	Bright green fruit, 9 to 11 inches, vines short, compact, mosaic-resistant	6, 28, 35

Variety	Days to Maturity	Description	Catalog Source*
Bush Crop	55	Dwarf bush plants, good for containers, 6 to 8 inches	7, 13, 17, 26, 32, 33, 34, 45, 55
Bush Pickle	52	Light green fruit, compact vines 20 to 24 inches long, use small (4½ inches) fruit as sweet pickles, larger as dills	6, 13, 17, 26, 29, 32, 33, 34, 36, 45
Pot Luck	55	Green, grows well in container, 7 inches, straight	2, 5, 8, 11, 17, 26, 29, 30, 33, 34, 35, 52, 56, 58
Space Master	56	Dark green, 8 inches, mosaic-resistant	2, 6, 8, 13, 25, 30, 32, 40, 48, 57

Novelties

Variety	Days to Maturity	Description	Catalog Source*
Armenian Yard Long	70	Unusual fluting, fruits to 4 feet long, 3 to 4 inches around	5, 6, 13, 17, 28, 31, 34, 40, 43, 56
Lemon	64	Yellow, 3 inches, round	1, 6, 8, 10, 13, 14, 17, 26, 28, 31, 35, 40, 43, 46, 52
White Wonder	65	Ivory white when mature, 8 to 10 inches	5, 17, 58

*Listings correspond to seed companies listed under Sources of Seeds and Supplies.

EGGPLANT

Most eggplant varieties have purple fruit, but there are also green, yellow, pink, and white varieties: Several midget varieties are available.

Planting. Eggplant is a warm-weather crop. Plant seeds inside or buy seedlings from a nursery. Transplant 24 to 30 inches apart in the garden at least one week after the last frost. When plants are 6 inches tall, pinch off the growing tip to encourage the formation of side branches. Be sure to keep picking the fruits as soon as they are ready to eat, so that the plants will continue to bear. The minimum soil temperature is 60° F. Because eggplant is a heavy feeder, give each plant ½ cup of Vegetable Factory organic nutrient mix once a month, or feed every three or four weeks with fish emulsion according to the instructions on the bottle.

Container planting. Eggplant needs at least 5 to 10 gallons of soil per plant.

Companion planting. Plant with beans, peppers, potatoes, and tomatoes.

Problems:

● *Plants produce blossoms but no fruit.* The blossoms of many eggplant varieties drop when the temperature falls below 58° or goes much above 70° F. Plant early eggplant varieties that aren't affected by these temperatures—'Early Beauty Hybrid', 'Early Royal Hybrid', and 'Small-Fruited Number 1'.

● *The plants are stunted.* This happens if the temperature dips below 40° F while the seedllings are young. Set the plants out when the air temperature is above 65° F. Protect the plants with plastic jugs or other protective devices.

● *Diseases and pests.* Verticillium wilt: control through crop rotation. Colorado potato beetle: handpick and destroy egg clusters. Flea beetles: dust with wood ash or agricultural lime.

Harvesting: Pick when the fruits are half grown—just before the color dulls. Be sure to keep picking so the plants will continue to bear.

Seed-saving. Pick fruit when very ripe. Wash seeds from pulp. Dry and save.

Eggplant Varieties

Variety	Days to Maturity	Description	Catalog Source*
Oval			
Black Beauty	78	Globular, dark purple	2, 5, 6, 7, 8, 10, 11, 13, 17, 22, 24, 26, 28, 29, 30, 32, 33, 34, 36, 40, 43, 45, 48, 54, 55, 56, 57
Long Cylindrical			
Dusky	65	Long, cylindrical, early	5, 6, 7, 8, 12, 13, 14, 18, 28, 29, 32, 33, 35, 36, 45, 48, 50, 52, 54
Ichiban	65	Long, cylindrical, purple, 12 inches	28
Small			
Early Black Egg	65	Egg-shaped, 5 inches, tender	47, 50
Hito	65	Dozens of dark, shiny purple fruit the size of pecans	31

Variety	Days to Maturity	Description	Catalog Source*
Ronde de Valence	75	Small, round, dark purple, pick when the size of large navel oranges	31

Other Colors

Asian Bride	75	Strong, compact plants, lavender fruits with white stripes, 8 to 10 inches, slim	31
Easter Egg	65	Plants 32 inches high, pick fruits when shiny white, egg-shaped	24, 54
Long White	65	White, 9 inches, slim	44

Gourmet, European

Imperial	63	Glossy, purple-black, 10 inches, French variety	48, 54

*Listings correspond to seed companies listed under Sources of Seeds and Supplies.

KALE

Kale is a cool-weather crop. The borecole or Scotch type has blue or dark green leaves that are tightly curled. The Siberian type has smoother gray-green to blue-green leaves and a spreading habit.

Planting. If your summers are cool, plant either in spring (two to four weeks after the last frost) or fall. Sow seeds ½ inch deep and 3 to 4 inches apart. Thin plants to 8 inches apart. Kale can be started indoors, then transplanted to the garden. Some gardeners start a late crop of kale about 2 inches apart under protective devices, then transfer the seedlings to open beds two to four weeks after the last frost. Cold weather doesn't seem to bother mature kale plants. In fact, the vegetable is even crisper and more flavorful after being touched by a light frost. The minimum soil temperature is 40° F. Apply 1 tablespoon of Vegetable Factory organic nutrient mix per plant once a month, or supplement every three or four weeks with fish emulsion according to the instructions on the bottle.

Container planting. Plant kale in containers that hold at least 5 gallons. Sow three or four seeds to a container and thin to 16 inches apart. Give additional feedings during the season.

Companion planting. Plant with all other cabbage family vegetables.

Problems:

Kale has few problems, but it doesn't like heat and won't do well in temperatures of much over 75° F.

● *Growth practically stops, leaves lack crisp, fresh look.* This often happens when the temperature hits the high 80s. Plant kale in mid- or late summer for a fall crop.

● *Diseases and pests:* Cabbage looper: use *Bacillus thuringiensis.*

Harvesting. Harvest the younger, larger leaves individually. After a few weeks, pull up the entire plant—old kale becomes tough and stringy.

Seed-saving. Let some plants winter over in the garden. Cut the stalks when the seedpods are dry and brittle. Dry the pods on trays, then separate out the seed.

Kale Varieties

Variety	Days to Maturity	Description	Catalog Source*
Scotch Type			
Dwarf Blue Curled Vates	55	Bluish-green, leaves finely curled, low compact plants, withstands temperatures below freezing	1, 6, 8,10, 13, 18, 26, 28, 29, 30, 32, 33, 43, 45, 47, 52, 54, 56
Siberian Type			
Dwarf Siberian	65	Grayish-green, plumelike, 12 to 16 inches, sprawling growth, extremely hardy	6, 8, 14, 28, 30, 34, 50

*Listings correspond to seed companies listed under Sources of Seeds and Supplies.

LETTUCE

Lettuce is by far the most popular of all leafy vegetables. There are four basic types—head lettuce, butterhead, looseleaf, and romaine. Head lettuce (also called crisphead and iceberg) produces fairly solid heads that require 80 to 95 days to mature. Semiheading types, called butterhead or bibb, have outer leaves that do not wrap tightly together but rather develop an open, fairly flat rosette surrounding the inner leaves. Looseleaf lettuce forms a very loose head that separates into individual leaves.

Romaine (or cos) develops distinctly upright, cylindrical head, as opposed to the rounded form of head lettuce. The inner leaves become blanched naturally.

Some horticulturists also recognize a fifth group, stem lettuce or celtuce. An edible thickened stem shoots up from the base of the plant.

Planting. Lettuce can be planted four to six weeks before the average frost-free date in your area. (To get a jump on the season, start lettuce in simple protective devices such as cloches, or coldframes.) Sow seed in the bed and cover it with ½ inch of soil. Thin head lettuce to stand 10 inches apart and leaf lettuce to stand 6 inches apart. It is best to plant some leaf lettuce every two weeks until early summer. For midsummer growing, try to provide some shade. Leaf lettuce is an excellent vegetable to plant among slower-maturing vegetables.

After lettuce plants have reached 2 to 3 inches in height, spread a 2-inch mulch of compost or rotted horse manure over the beds to keep the soil cool and the plants growing well. In hot-summer areas, you can grow lettuce most of the summer by placing a slat frame or bamboo shade over the bed. The minimum soil temperature is 35° F. Lettuce is a heavy feeder. Feed with ¼ cup of Vegetable Factory organic nutrient mix per square foot every five or six weeks, or supplement every three or four weeks with fish emulsion according to the instructions on the bottle.

Container planting. Plant head lettuce 10 inches apart, leaf lettuce 4 to 5 inches apart. With romaine or looseleaf lettuce you have a choice. If you expect to gradually pick the outer leaves over a period of time, plant them 6 inches apart. If you intend to harvest the entire plant at once, plant 4 inches apart. All lettuce seeds should be covered with ¼ to ½ inch of potting soil.

Companion planting. Plant with carrot, cucumber, radish, or strawberry.

Problems:

● *Lettuce flowers and goes to seed before it is ready to eat.* This is caused by long hot summer days and warm nights. Plant in early spring before the weather warms up, or plant in late summer for a fall crop.

● *Head lettuce fails to form good heads.* Plants have been crowded too close together. Thin head lettuce to stand 12 inches apart.

● *Looseleaf varieties grow small, bitter outside leaves.* The plants are crowded too close together. Thin looseleaf lettuce to stand 6 inches apart.

● *Romaine doesn't form hearts.* Romaine seed is planted too deep. Sow seeds on bed and cover with ¼ inch of soil.

● *Diseases and pests.* Rots: keep the garden free of refuse; plant in well-drained soil. Slugs: place a shallow dish of beer in the garden.

Harvesting. Start harvesting head lettuce as soon as it is crisp and headed.

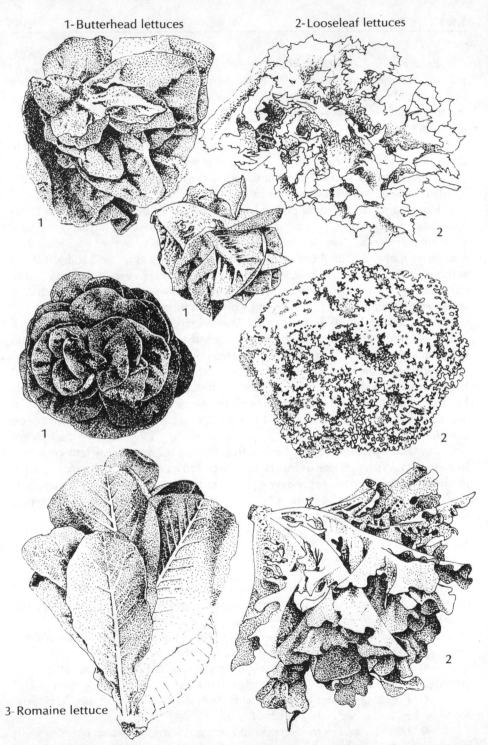

1- Butterhead lettuces

2- Looseleaf lettuces

1

1

1

2

2

3- Romaine lettuce

2

For variety, try growing butterhead, loose-leaf, and romaine lettuces. There are many new varieties available each year.

Stretch your leaf-lettuce crop by harvesting a few leaves at a time. With butterhead varieties, cut off the entire plant when it is large enough to use. The romaines are usually harvested as entire heads, but a few outer leaves can be taken earlier.

Seed-saving. Let a few plants go to seed. Cut stalks when seed is fully ripe. Let the stalks dry until flowers shatter easily. Winnow the seeds to remove the chaff.

Lettuce Varieties

Variety	Days to Maturity	Description	Catalog Source*
Butterhead			
Buttercrunch	68	Smooth, green leaves, heat-tolerant, All-America Selection	1, 2, 5, 6, 7, 8, 10, 11, 12, 13, 14, 18, 26, 28, 29, 30, 32, 33, 34, 35, 36, 40, 45, 48, 50, 51, 52, 55, 56, 57, 58
Mantila	60	Heat-tolerant, French butterhead type, crunchy, green leaves	46
Merveille des Quatre Saisons	60	Ruby red-tipped leaves, French butterhead type	19, 28, 31, 50
Summer Bibb	77	Thick leaves, creamy and firm interior, vigorous, slow to bolt	14, 18, 30, 34, 54
Head (Crisphead, Iceberg)			
Great Lakes	85	Large, erect leaves, bright green and fringed, high-quality heads, slow to bolt, All-America Selection	2, 6, 8, 10, 12, 13, 28, 32, 33, 35, 51, 52, 55, 58
Iceberg	85	Wavy, light green tinged with brown, hearts crisp, does well spring and summer, slow to bolt	2, 5, 10, 12, 13, 17, 24, 29, 30, 32, 33, 43, 51, 55, 56, 57, 58
Ithaca	72	Firm heads, some heat-resistance	13, 14, 17, 18, 25, 34, 45, 48, 52, 57

(continued)

Variety	Days to Maturity	Description	Catalog Source*
Leaf			
Grand Rapids	45	Leaves frilled, deeply cut, light green, heat-resistant	6, 10, 11, 12, 13, 18, 28, 29, 30, 32, 33, 34, 44, 54, 55, 58
Oakleaf	45	Leaves resemble oak leaves, tender, longstanding	1, 2, 5, 8, 10, 12, 13, 25, 29, 30, 31, 32, 35, 40, 44, 45, 47, 55, 57
Red Oakleaf	45	Red, leaves resemble oak leaves	31
Red Sails	45	Heavy, crinkled, deep red leaves	2, 6, 7, 8, 18, 20, 25, 26, 28, 29, 30, 32, 33, 35, 36, 40, 45, 48, 50, 52, 54, 55, 57
Ruby	50	Intense red, frilled leaves, All-America Selection	6, 8, 10, 17, 22, 24, 26, 28, 29, 30, 32, 34, 40, 43, 44, 48, 56, 57
Romaine			
Paris White	83	Elongated, 10 to 12 inches, light green head	6, 7, 10, 12, 13, 17, 26, 30, 32, 35, 36, 44, 48, 50, 57
Parris Island Cos	76	Large, oval, 8- to 9-inch dark green head, mild flavor	8, 18, 25, 28, 29, 30, 32, 33, 34, 44, 45, 48, 52, 54, 56
Baby, Spacesavers			
Little Jim Mini Romaine		English variety, thick, crunchy leaves, 5 to 6 inches, full, heavy heads	46
Summer Baby Bibb	60	Tiny bibb, 5 to 6 inches, teardrop-shaped leaves	46
Tom Thumb	65	Tennis-ball-size, medium green, crumpled leaves, Buttercrunch type	8, 10, 12, 17, 28, 29, 32, 35, 36, 44, 47, 51, 52

*Listings correspond to seed companies listed under Sources of Seeds and Supplies.

MELONS

Melons can have white, pink, orange, or green flesh. The early-maturing varieties are popularly known as cantaloupes, but most varieties are really muskmelons. Most cantaloupes are heavily netted with orange flesh. Long-season melons (casabas, crenshaws, honeydews, and Persians) require up to 115 days and a hot dry season to mature. Casaba has white flesh and golden skin that is wrinkled when mature; crenshaw has dark green skin that becomes yellow in parts on maturity; honeydew has a smooth, hard, creamy-white rind and a light green flesh; and Persian has dark green skin and deep orange flesh.

Planting. Grow cantaloupes and other melons on a 4-foot-tall frame in your garden or in wire cages 2 feet wide and 4 feet tall. Either method produces a good quantity of fruit. Melons are a warm-weather crop. Plant seeds outdoors about the date of the last frost, 1 inch deep and 6 to 12 inches apart. The minimum soil temperature is 60° F. Melons are heavy feeders. Apply 2 tablespoons of Vegetable Factory organic nutrient mix per plant each month, or supplement every three or four weeks with fish emulsion according to the directions on the bottle.

Container planting. You can grow two melon plants in a 5-gallon container. Feed according to the directions above. To get a jump on the season, plant seeds indoors in individual peat pots six to eight weeks before you expect to move them outside. You can plant seedlings outside after the weather has warmed up. You can also plant early maturing varieties in short-summer areas.

Companion planting. Plant near corn, peas, and radishes. Keep away from potatoes.

Problems:

● *Dark, dry, leathery areas on the blossom end of the fruit.* This is sometimes due to a sudden change in soil moisture. It can be a problem in areas where rains are followed by a dry spell. Maintain an even supply of moisture in the soil. Place 2 to 3 inches of organic material on top of the soil to hold down moisture loss.

● *Cantaloupes taste like mush or are extremely bitter.* This again is the result of uneven watering, although some gardeners wrongly blame it on the cross-pollination of cantaloupes with cucumbers. Handle this problem by maintaining an even supply of moisture in the soil.

● *Cantaloupes fail to ripen.* Most cantaloupes require a minimum of 75 days when the temperature is above 70° F to ripen. In short-season areas, grow early varieties like 'Alaska', 'Early Northern Queen', and 'Far North'.

● *Diseases and pests.* Downy mildew: rotate melons with other crops, or plant resistant varieties such as 'Early Market' and 'Edisto'. Fusarium wilt: spread by the striped cucumber beetle; control with heavy mulching. Pickleworm: control with *Bacillus thuringiensis*.

Harvesting. Cantaloupes are ready to eat when the stem pulls off easily, usually with only a slight touch. The skin also begins to look like a corky net, and the stem cracks all the way around. The blossom end of Persian and crenshaw melons should smell fruity and sweet when ripe. Honeydew and casaba melons are ripe when the rinds have turned completely yellow.

Seed-saving. Scoop out seeds from fully ripe melons. Wash and dry them. Store in a cool, dry place.

Melon Varieties

Variety	Days to Maturity	Description	Catalog Source*
Cantaloupes			
Delicious 51	85	Thick salmon flesh, 6½ inches, light to medium netting, resistant to fusarium wilt	2, 7, 18, 26, 29, 30, 32, 34, 45, 47, 48, 57
Hale's Best Jumbo	85	Thick, deep salmon flesh, oblong, 4½ pounds	5, 7, 10, 18, 28, 29, 32, 40, 43, 44, 54, 55, 56, 58
Iroquois	90	Deep orange, 8 inches, coarse netting, sweet, prolific, resistant to powdery mildew	8, 10, 12, 13, 17, 26, 30, 34, 45, 48, 50, 56
Spacesaver Cantaloupes (Muskmelons)			
Bush Musketeer	90	Orange, 5 to 6 inches, 3 to 4 pounds, round, netted, bush type, can easily be grown in pots and containers	8, 13, 17, 29, 32, 36, 47, 48, 51, 55
Bush Star Hybrid	88	Salmon, 5 inches, 2 to 2½ pounds, medium netting, good variety for containers and pickle poles	13, 29, 30, 34, 40
Honeybush	82	Salmon, 2 to 3 pounds, bush type, small seed cavity, tolerant of fusarium wilt	6, 28

Variety	Days to Maturity	Description	Catalog Source*
Minnesota Midget	65	Salmon, 4 inches, round melons, 3-foot vines	5, 6, 12, 17, 32, 36, 44, 51

Other Colors

Variety	Days to Maturity	Description	Catalog Source*
Marble White	95	Creamy white flesh, pure white smooth rind, Japanese variety, short productive vines	31
Rocky Ford Green Flesh	84–92	Green, 5 inches, oblong, 2½ pounds, solid netting, rust resistance	7, 10, 13, 33, 35, 40, 43, 55, 56, 58

Odd Shape

Variety	Days to Maturity	Description	Catalog Source*
Ananas	110	Pale yellow-green rind turns orange-beige when ripe, oblong, tolerant of crown blight	31, 40, 56, 57
Banana	95	Salmon-pink flesh, yellow rind, 18 to 24 inches, 7 pounds, resembles giant banana, no netting	5, 10, 13, 26, 28, 32, 33, 40, 43, 44, 56, 58

Other Melons

Variety	Days to Maturity	Description	Catalog Source*
Crenshaw	90–110	Salmon flesh, dark green rind turns yellow when ripe, 6 to 8 inches, round, 5 pounds	7, 10, 17, 31, 32, 43, 44
Earlydew	86	Emerald green flesh, smooth, ivory skin, 5 to 6 inches, 2 to 3 pounds, short-season	5, 8, 12, 13, 25, 26, 29, 30, 34, 35, 45, 48, 55, 56

(continued)

Variety	Days to Maturity	Description	Catalog Source*
Other Melons—Continued			
		variety, honeydew type	
Golden Beauty Casaba	110	Golden, wrinkled skin, nearly white flesh, casaba type	7, 18, 28, 40, 43
Golden Crenshaw	110	Pale orange flesh, mottled green and yellow rind, 6 to 7 pounds, crenshaw type	18, 34
Jaune des Canaries	105	Pale green to whitish-yellow flesh, 8 inches, egg-shaped, 8 to 9 pounds	18
Medium Persian	95	Deep orange flesh, small cavity, 7 to 8 pounds, heavily netted, Persian type	18, 35, 40, 44

*Listings correspond to seed companies listed under Sources of Seeds and Supplies.

MUSTARD GREENS

Mustard reaches maturity rapidly (in just 35 to 40 days) and therefore can be used for intercropping in big containers between larger, slower-growing plants.

Planting. Plant outside two to four weeks before the last frost. Sow seeds ½ inch deep and about 3 inches apart. Thin to stand 6 inches apart. You can make several plantings throughout the season. Seeds can also be started inside and transplanted to the garden. The minimum soil temperature is 40° F. Feed mustard with ¼ cup of Vegetable Factory organic nutrient mix per square foot of planting.

Container planting. Plant in any container wider than 4 inches. Sow seeds 4 inches apart.

Companion planting. Plant with carrots, celery, cucumbers, potatoes, spinach, and Swiss chard. Keep mustard away from strawberries and tomatoes.

Problems:

● *The plants start to flower as soon as it turns warm.* Mustard is a cool-weather crop. Once flowering starts, nothing helps, not even snapping off the tops. Wait until cooler weather and put in new plants.

● *Leaves develop a peppery tang.* The flavor becomes especially strong in older leaves when temperatures rise above 85° F. Grow mustard in the spring and fall when the temperature is below 65°. Cool weather improves the flavor.

● *Diseases and pests.* Blackleg: spread by cutworms and cabbage maggots; keep the garden and surrounding area free of weeds, and plant debris; plant mustard on a four-year rotation; control cutworms with a 2- to 3-inch cardboard collar around each plant, pushed 1 inch into the soil. Downy mildew: avoid overhead watering. Cabbage looper: control with *Bacillus thuringiensis*.

Harvesting. Snap off the lower leaves as needed. Leave the growing tip to produce replacements.

Seed-saving. Cut stalks when the seedpods are dry and brittle. Dry the pods on trays. Thresh the seeds.

Mustard Varieties

Variety	Days to Maturity	Description	Catalog Source*
Plain			
Florida Broadleaf	43	Medium green, broadleaved, smooth	7, 8, 10, 14, 28, 30, 33, 34, 40, 43, 44, 48, 54, 55, 56, 58
Slowbolt	40	Dark green, smooth, narrow, cream-colored ribs	34, 42
Curled			
Green Wave	45–55	Dark green, edges finely cut	8, 10, 11, 17, 20, 25, 28, 32, 33, 34, 42, 45, 48, 50
Southern Giant Curled	45	Longstanding, curled	7, 10, 26, 29, 30, 33, 34, 40, 44, 52, 54, 55, 56, 58

*Listings correspond to seed companies listed under Sources of Seeds and Supplies.

OKRA

Okra pods grow on erect, bushy plants with tropical-looking leaves. In most cases, okra takes up too much space to be a good Vegetable Factory plant. You might, however, want to try the compact bush varieties. The two best are 'Annie Oakley' and 'Blondy'.

Planting. Soak the seeds in water for 24 hours before planting. Plant the compact varieties 12 to 14 inches apart and ½ inch deep after the soil has warmed to 75° F. Apply 2 tablespoons of Vegetable Factory organic nutrient mix per plant monthly, or supplement every four weeks with fish emulsion according to the directions on the bottle.

Container planting. Grow the compact varieties in 3-gallon or larger containers. Give one or two supplemental feedings during the growing season.

Companion planting. Plant okra near beans and tomatoes.

Problems:

● *Seeds don't germinate.* The seeds rot if planted at soil temperatures of less than 70° F. Wait until the soil warms up before planting.

● *Woody or tough pods.* Failure to pick pods regularly. Pick plant clean of pods over 1½ to 2 inches long.

● *Diseases and pests.* Powdery mildew: rotate okra with other crops. Corn earworms: spot them by the holes in the okra pods; handpick earworms and destroy any worms in damaged pods; you can often avoid this pest by planting in midseason.

Harvesting. Pick pods four to six days after the flower opens. Harvest the ripened pods every two or three days. Pods left on the plant will become tough and stringy and will shorten the picking season.

Seed-saving. Let some pods ripen and dry toward the end of the season. Pick the seeds.

Okra Varieties

Variety	Days to Maturity	Description	Catalog Source*
Annie Oakley	48–52	Compact plant, grows to 3 feet; pick pods at ¾ to 2 inches	6, 7, 13, 17, 25, 29, 30, 40, 42, 52, 54
Blondy	50	Compact plants grow to 3 feet; creamy lime green 3-inch spineless pods	8, 13, 26, 30, 32, 36, 54

*Listings correspond to seed companies listed under Sources of Seeds and Supplies.

ONIONS, GARLIC, LEEKS, AND SHALLOTS

The onion family includes onions, garlic, leeks, and shallots. Onions themselves come in all shapes and sizes: round, flat, top-shaped, and spindle-shaped, and in red, yellow-brown, and white. They give you more food per square foot than almost any other vegetable.

Planting. Onions can be grown from seeds, seedlings, or sets (small bulbs). Since they are frost-hardy, you can start them from seed or sets in your Vegetable Factory beds as soon as the soil can be worked (four to six weeks before the last frost date). Sow seeds across the bed, and cover with ¼ inch of soil.

Plant the small bulbs (sets) about 1 inch deep and an inch apart. When seedlings first appear, thin until the onions stand about 1 inch apart (the sets are already at this spacing). About a month later, thin to 3 or 4 inches apart, and dig the soil back to expose the tops and sides of the bulbs. This helps stimulate bulb formation. In areas with mild winters, you can plant onions all year long. Onions need cooler weather for top growth and warmer weather for bulb growth.

Be sure to plant extra onions to be harvested as green onions in about 20 to 30 days. You can interplant them with larger, slower-maturing vegetables, or tuck them into odd places. Onions need a minimum soil temperature of 35° F. They are light feeders. Apply ¼ cup of Vegetable Factory organic nutrient mix per square foot in mid-season.

Container planting. Seeds should be planted about 1 inch apart on top of the soil. Cover with ¼ inch of soil and keep moist. They will grow fine as green onions on 1-inch spacings. For bulbs, thin to 3 inches apart. To grow onions to maturity, containers should be 12 inches deep. Use thinned plants as green onions.

Companion planting. Plant near beets, broccoli, cabbage, carrots, cauliflower, summer savory, and tomatoes. Keep away from peas and beans.

Problems:

- *The onions stay small.* Either you didn't thin them enough, or you didn't keep the soil moist while bulbs were forming.

- *The onions went to seed and produced flabby, hollow bulbs.* The onions were planted from sets (small bulbs) in late fall or winter. Keep the flower bud picked off, or harvest as soon as you detect flower stalks.

- *The onion bulbs split and look as if they will form two bulbs.* This results from uneven watering. Place 2 to 3 inches of organic material on top of the bed to retain moisture. Water your onions for several hours at a time, then don't water again until the soil has just about dried out in the top layers.

- *Diseases and pests.* Damping-off (seedlings rot at soil line): do not overwater as the plants start to come up. Neck rot: keep maturing bulbs dry. Thrips: eliminate weeds (their winter home) around the garden and yard.

Harvesting. When the tops of the onion plants begin to turn yellow, flatten them to the ground to prevent the flow of sap and to divert all growing energy to the bulbs. When all the tops are dead, dig up the bulbs and let them dry on top of the ground for a few days. Then store in a dry, frost-free place.

Seed-saving. Plant mature onion bulbs in the spring, or keep a few onion plants in the ground over winter. When the black seeds in the flower heads become exposed, cut the flower stalks and dry the heads on paper. Rub the seed from heads.

Garlic

Pull apart a garlic bulb, and plant in the individual cloves an inch deep and about 3 inches apart in the spring. Small cloves produce small garlic bulbs, so plant fairly large cloves. Place them in odd spots around the bed, wherever you have room. Bulbs should be mature in about three months. Lift the bulbs when the leaves start to yellow, and place them on a flat metal or plastic tray to dry. Store in a dry place.

Leeks

Leeks do not bulb but produce delicious thickened stems. Plant from seed in late winter or very early spring. Sow across the bed and cover with ¼ inch of soil. Thin to about 3 inches apart. To obtain long, white stems, plant in trenches 4 to 6 inches deep, about 3 inches apart. Now fill the trench gradually as the leeks develop. Don't brush soil on the leafstalks. If orange dusty spots (rust) appear on the leaves, destroy the plants. Dig up the leeks as you need them from September to April.

Shallots

Shallots are much larger than onion sets but require the same treatment. Plant shallot cloves 1 inch deep and about 1 inch apart. Later, thin them to stand 2 to 4 inches apart. Each shallot will produce four to eight shallot bulbs. Lift the bulbs once the leaves have yellowed and are beginning to die down.

Onion, Garlic, Leek, and Shallot Varieties

Variety	Days to Maturity	Description	Catalog Source*
Onions			
Thick, Flat			
Granex White	150	White skin, mild flavor, crisp, grown in southern United States	40, 56
Granex Yellow	130	Yellow skin, white flesh	6, 18, 36, 40

Variety	Days to Maturity	Description	Catalog Source*
Globe			
Benny's Red	112	Bright red skin, large, deep globe, pink to white flesh, pungent	7, 18, 34, 48, 50, 54
Early Yellow Globe	95	Deep yellow skin, clear white flesh, mild	1, 8, 10, 12, 18, 25, 26, 30, 45, 47, 48, 50
Southport Red Globe	100	Deep red skin, medium-sized, round, white flesh tinged with pink, strong flavor	1, 10, 12, 13, 17, 18, 26, 45, 48, 52, 57
Southport White Globe	110	Clear white skin, medium large, mild flavor	7, 10, 18, 26, 29, 30, 44
Yellow Sweet Spanish	105	Yellow skin, globe-shaped, large	5, 6, 10, 12, 13, 14, 17, 18, 26, 29, 32, 33, 34, 40, 52, 54, 58
Spindle-Shaped			
Italian Red	105	Torpedo-shaped, sweet	13, 17, 28, 51
Flattened			
Crystal White Wax	95	White skin, medium flat, mild taste	6, 10, 12, 13, 17, 34, 40, 43, 44
Ebenezer	105	Yellow-brown skin, white flesh, 3 inches, mild	9, 17, 36, 47
Red Burgundy	95	Huge bulbs, thick, flattened	3, 12, 13, 30, 32, 33, 56
Red Wethersfield	103	Red skin, white flesh, large and flat, pungent	2, 8, 10, 11, 44
Top-Shaped (Grano type)			
New Mexico Yellow	130	Light yellow skin, white flesh	31, 56

(continued)

Variety	Days to Maturity	Description	Catalog Source*
Garlic			
California White	110	White, 1½ inches in diameter	13, 16
Elephant Garlic	105	Huge, 4 to 5 inches in diameter, not a real garlic, but much in demand	5, 6, 12, 13, 14, 17, 26, 35, 36, 44, 47, 52
Leeks			
American Flag	120	Sweet, 8 to 9 inches long, 1 inch in diameter	1, 5, 10, 12, 29, 30, 32, 33, 34, 35, 48, 52, 55, 56
De Carentan	110	Sweet, long stems, fine-textured, grows rapidly, French variety	46
French Summer Kilma	75	Sweet, dark blue-green leaves, long slender stems, European variety	31, 44, 56
Tivi		Sweet, long, straight, medium green tops, Danish variety	18
Shallots			
Dutch Yellow	110	Mild Flavor	47, 51
French	110	Used in French cuisine	25, 35, 47, 57
Giant Red	105	Mildly spicy	51

*Listings correspond to seed companies listed under Sources of Seeds and Supplies.

PEAS

English (or garden) peas tend to take a lot of space for the crop produced. I recommend only 'Sugar Snap'–type peas and snow peas for Vegetable Factory gardens. They have edible pods that are eaten when immature and produce a tremendous crop for the space used.

Planting. Start your peas in the spring as soon as the ground can be worked. Plant them 2 inches deep and 2 or 3 inches apart. You should place an inoculant in the soil—active rhizobia bacteria that improve plant growth through the formation of nitrogen-fixing nodules on the roots. Inoculants can be purchased from most garden centers or from seed catalogs. Train tall varieties up the entire width of the Vegetable Factory back support. Plant either dwarf or semi-dwarf types in zone B and train up a short trellis; or plant them 2 or 3 inches apart in a wire cage that is 2 to 4 feet tall.

Take peas out when the vines dry up and replace them with squash, beans, or other vine crops. Follow this in the fall with a final crop of peas. The minimum soil temperature is 40° F. No supplemental feeding is needed.

Container planting. Plant peas in 5-gallon or larger containers. Plant 2 inches apart, cover with 2 inches of soil, and keep moist. Set up construction wire in a circle and train peas up the wire.

Companion planting: Plant with beans, carrots, corn, cucumbers, potatoes, radishes, and turnips. Keep away from garlic, leeks, onions, and shallots.

Problems:

● *Vines are green and bushy but produce few peas.* Pinch back the growing tips.

● *The pods are hard.* They stayed on the vines too long. Pick edible-podded peas when they are immature.

● *The blossoms don't produce pods.* Pollen isn't being transferred from the male parts of the flower to the female. Shake the vines. Peas are self-pollinating, but they sometimes need a little help at blossom stage.

● *Diseases and pests.* Fusarium wilt: plant resistant varieties. Root rot: avoid overwatering. Aphids: spray with a jet of water, use an insecticidal soap.

Harvesting: Pick edible-podded peas when pods are 2 to 3 inches long and the peas are undeveloped.

Seed-saving. Do not save the seeds of 'Sugar Snap'-type or snow peas.

Pea Varieties

Variety	Days to Maturity	Description	Catalog Source*
Short Vines (to 3 feet)			
Dwarf Gray Sugar (snow pea)	62–65	Light green, curved pods 2½ to 3 inches, pick when slender	1, 8, 10, 11, 12, 13, 17, 30, 32, 33, 34, 36, 40, 43, 44, 55, 57, 58
Oregon Sugar Pod	68	Curved green pods	1, 20, 24, 29, 44, 45, 51, 52, 54

(continued)

Variety	Days to Maturity	Description	Catalog Source*
Short Vines (to 3 feet) — Continued			
Sugar Ann	55	Long, blunt-ended, meaty pods, 3¼ inches	1, 5, 11, 12, 17, 18, 25, 29, 30, 32, 33, 35, 36, 40, 47, 48, 50, 51, 54, 55, 57
Sugar Bon	56	Sweet pods, 2 to 3 inches, compact vines	6, 8, 13, 33, 36, 40, 54, 56
Sugar Daddy	74	Stringless snap pea, compact vines, easy to pick	6, 8, 13, 17, 18, 26, 28, 29, 33, 35, 36, 40, 45, 48, 54
Tall Vines (3 to 6 feet)			
Snappy	63	Fleshy pods, 4 to 4½ inches, resistant to powdery mildew	6
Sugar Snap	70	Round, green, 2 to 3 inches, thick and fleshy, wilt-resistant	1, 2, 5, 6, 7, 8, 10, 11, 13, 18, 20, 25, 26, 28, 29, 30, 31, 32, 33, 34, 35, 36, 40, 43, 44, 45, 47, 48, 50, 52, 54, 55, 56, 57, 58

*Listings correspond to seed companies listed under Sources of Seeds and Supplies.

PEPPERS

Peppers are classed in two groups: sweet and hot. Sweet varieties include the big bells, pimiento, cherry, and slender sweet varieties. The pungent types include 'Anaheim,' 'Fresno,' 'Hungarian Yellow Wax,' jalapeño, passilla, and serrano.

Planting. Peppers are a warm-weather crop. Start from seed indoors or purchase plants from a nursery. Set transplants out in the garden 12 to 24 inches apart about the date of the last frost. They can be put out earlier under hotcaps, glass, or polyethylene. Set wire cages around pepper plants to keep them from being crowded by other vegetables. The minimum soil temperature is 60° F. Apply 1 tablespoon Vegetable Factory organic nutrient mix per plant every four weeks. Supplement with fish emulsion about every three or four weeks according to the instructions on the bottle.

Container planting. Plant one pepper plant to a 2-gallon or larger container.

Companion planting. Plant near basil, carrots, eggplant, onions, parsley, and tomatoes. Keep peppers away from kohlrabi.

Problems:

● *The blossoms fall off without producing fruit.* This happens when the temperature drops much below 60° or rises much about 75° F. Plant early varieties like 'Early Giant,' 'Neapolitan,' and 'Melrose.'

● *Plants produce few blossoms and few fruits.* If the plants start blooming and producing when they are too small, you may have purchased small nursery-grown seedlings that have already started to bloom.

● *Diseases and pests.* Bacterial spot: rotate crops. Mosaic: eliminate the host weed, nightshade. Aphids: spray aphids with a hose or with an insecticidal soap.

Harvesting. Most people prefer to pick sweet peppers when they are firm, crisp, and still green. Cut them off the vine with a sharp knife. If left on the plant to turn red, the flesh is much sweeter. Hot peppers should ripen fully on the vine to attain their full flavor.

Seed-saving. When fruit is fully ripe (showing some red), scrape out the seeds, dry them, and store in a cool, dry place.

Pepper Varieties

Variety	Days to Maturity	Description	Catalog Source*
Sweet Bell			
Bell Boy	70	Glossy, blocky, All-America Selection	6, 8, 12, 13, 17, 26, 28, 29, 30, 32, 33, 34, 45, 48, 55, 56
California Wonder	75	Blocky, good stuffing pepper	2, 5, 6, 7, 8, 10, 11, 12, 13, 14, 17, 24, 29, 30, 32, 33, 35, 40, 48, 52, 55, 56, 58
Canape	60	Green to red, 3 lobes	18, 35
Emerald Giant	74	Thick-walled, mosaic-tolerant	7, 10, 30, 33, 34, 52
Yolo Wonder	76	Thick-walled, blocky, 4 to 4½ inches	10, 17, 24, 34, 40, 48
Yellow-Orange			
Cal Wonder Golden	75	Golden, medium thick-walled	6, 30, 37, 55
Gold Crest	62	Turns golden yellow, sweet	25, 37

(continued)

Variety	Days to Maturity	Description	Catalog Source*
Yellow-Orange — Continued			
Gypsy Hybrid	65	Tapered fruit, crisp, sweet, yellow fruits turn orange and red, compact plants, All-America Selection	5, 6, 8, 12, 13, 14, 17, 18, 20, 26, 29, 30, 32, 34, 35, 36, 40, 48, 50, 51, 52, 54, 57
Pimento			
Canada Cheese	75	Miniature red pimento, good for pickling	48
Pimento Perfection	70	Smooth, heart-shaped, thick walls, sweet, flavorful	1, 3, 8, 18, 21, 28, 30, 31, 35, 37, 40, 43, 47, 55
Long Sweet			
Long Sweet Banana	75	Fruit 6 inches, 1½ inches wide	1, 6, 7, 8, 10, 17, 18, 28, 29, 30, 32, 34, 35, 36, 40, 47, 48, 54, 55, 57, 58
Spacesavers			
Park's Pot Hybrid	45	Crisp, plants 10 to 12 inches, good for hanging baskets, pots	36
Park's Tequila Sunrise	45	Edible ornamental fruits, deep green turning to golden orange, plants 12 to 14 inches	36
Pickling			
Sweet Cherry	75	Round, 1 to 1½ inches, use red or green, can be eaten young	5, 6, 7, 10, 13, 17, 18, 29, 30, 34, 35, 44, 48, 50
Super Sweet Cherry	75	Round, 1¾ inches, crack tolerant	48, 54

Variety	Days to Maturity	Description	Catalog Source*
Other Colors			
Chocolate Bell	75	Tan to dark brown, Dutch variety	48
Mildly Hot			
Anaheim	80	Long, tapered fruit, 6 to 8 inches, plants 2 feet high	1, 10, 13, 20, 22, 28, 40, 44, 46, 50, 56
Pepperoncini	70	Fiery red, 5 inches, southern Italian variety	21, 30, 31, 35, 37, 40, 44, 48
Medium Hot			
Ancho 101 (Pasilla)	75	Heart-shaped, rich flavor with touch of bitterness	17, 21, 31, 37, 46
Caloro TMR	75	Yellow-orange, waxy, long	21, 37
Hungarian Yellow Wax	65	Light yellow to red, 6 inches, tapering, good for pickling	5, 6, 7, 8, 11, 13, 18, 21, 30, 31, 32, 34, 35, 37, 38, 40
Large Red Cherry	75	Medium hot, 1½ inches in diameter, red when mature	6, 8, 10, 17, 18, 28, 29, 30, 32, 33, 34, 35, 48
Thai Hot	75	Tiny 1½-inch pepper, upright fruit, medium hot	28, 31
Hot			
Fresno	78	Tapers to point, 1½ to 2½ inches long, 1 inch in diameter, very pungent	17, 28, 40
Jalapeño	78	Tapers to blunt tip, hot, 3½ by 1½ inches, cylindrical	7, 8, 10, 13, 17, 28, 29, 30, 32, 34, 35, 40, 43, 44, 47, 48, 55

(continued)

Variety	Days to Maturity	Description	Catalog Source*
Hot — Continued			
Santa Fe Grande	75	Hot, yellow wax, 3½ inches long, 1½ inches in diameter, conical	7, 17, 34, 56
Serrano	75	Short and cylindrical, dark green to red	13, 17, 21, 31, 34, 36, 42, 46, 56

*Listings correspond to seed companies listed under Sources of Seeds and Supplies.

POTATOES

Don't rule out potatoes just because they take a lot of space. With a little care, they can be one of the most productive vegetables in the Vegetable Factory garden. You have a choice of red, white, russet, or blue, and round, oval, or oblong.

Planting. Buy seed potatoes and cut each into three or four pieces about 1½ inches square. Every piece must have one or two eyes. Plant the pieces cut-side-down 4 inches deep and about 4 inches apart in a circle 2 or 3 feet in diameter. Make sure this circle is located in zone B. The minimum soil temperature is 45° F. Apply 1 tablespoon Vegetable Factory organic nutrient mix per plant about every six weeks, or supplement in mid-season with fish emulsion according to the instructions on the bottle.

Around the circle, place a 3-foot-tall wire cage, 2 or 3 feet in diameter. When the plants reach 6 inches tall, start filling this circle with ripe compost or the special soil mix from Chapter 2, Vegetable Factory Soil. Leave about 3 inches of plant poking out. When the plants again reach 6 inches, repeat this procedure. Keep doing so until you have almost filled the cage. Your potatoes will be produced from top to bottom in the pile. You can start harvesting small potatoes within a couple of months. Thin plants to 10 inches and let them grow to maturity.

Container planting. Place eight plants in a half whiskey-barrel filled with planting mix (page 89), or plant four or five plants to a 5-gallon container. Place a 2-foot-tall wire cage on top of the container. Follow the procedure outlined under "Planting" above. You will be able to harvest small potatoes in about two months.

Companion planting. Plant potatoes with beans, broccoli, cabbage, cauliflower, corn, eggplant, marigolds, and peas. Keep them away from pumpkins and tomatoes.

Problems:

● *Potatoes become knobby.* This is caused by an unsteady water supply. Water potatoes deeply, then don't water again until the soil dries to a depth of 2 or

3 inches. Check with a trowel. 'Green Mountain' and 'Russet Burbank' tend to be particularly knobby.

● *Cavities occur near the center of the potato (hollow heart).* This is caused by rapid and uneven growth of potato tubers. To control it, cut down a bit on watering. Varieties prone to hollow heart include 'Chippewa', 'Katahdin', 'Irish Cobbler', and 'Russet Rural'.

● *Potatoes turn green (sunburn).* This is caused by the exposure to the sun during or after digging. Keep the tubers covered with soil. Store them in complete darkness.

● *Diseases and pests.* Blackleg: control by planting sound tubers. Scab: avoid through crop rotation. Colorado potato beetle: handpick, spray with pyrethrum.

Harvesting. Pull up entire plants, one plant at a time. They will pull out easily from the soft compost or soil. There will be potatoes along the entire root.

Seed-saving. Potatoes (except for the novelty 'Explorer') are not grown from seed. To grow your own seed potatoes, start with disease-free potatoes. Store in a cool dry place until you are ready to plant.

Potato Varieties

Variety	Days to Maturity	Description	Catalog Source*
Red			
Norland	110	Oblong, smooth, extra early	5, 11, 12, 13, 14, 17, 26, 32, 52
Red Pontiac	100	Round, big, heavy yields	5, 6, 11, 12, 29, 32, 36
Russet			
Norgold Russet	105	Oblong, golden netting	5, 12, 13, 17, 33
Russett Burbank	110	Oblong, netted	13, 14, 32, 36
White			
Irish Cobbler	100	Round, white, early	17, 29
Kennebec	115	Roundish, smooth skin	5, 6, 11, 13, 26, 29, 32, 33, 52

(continued)

Variety	Days to Maturity	Description	Catalog Source*
Yellow			
Fingerlings	100	Yellow skin, yellow flesh, 1 inch, boil with jackets on	26
Yellow Finnish		Yellow color	44, 52
Novelty			
All Blue Potato	100	Blue skin and flesh	17, 44
Explorer	120	Grow these potatoes from seeds	9, 23, 39

*Listings correspond to seed companies listed under Sources of Seeds and Supplies.

PUMPKINS

You can easily grow pumpkins in the Vegetable Factory garden if you stick to the smaller-fruited varieties. The new bush types with 2- to 3-inch pumpkins can be grown easily up a cucumber pole.

Planting. Plant pumpkinseeds outdoors about the date of the late frost, 1 to 1½ inches deep and 18 inches apart. Or start them indoors in individual peat pots, transplanting outdoors after the last frost date, or earlier if you use protective devices. The minimum soil temperature is 60° F. Pumpkins are heavy feeders. Apply 2 tablespoons of Vegetable Factory organic nutrient mix per plant every four weeks.

Container planting. Plant two or three of the bush type in 5 gallons of soil. You can plant one in a hanging container.

Companion planting. Plant near radishes or nasturtiums.

Problems:

● *Few flowers form fruit, even when both male and female flowers are present.* There aren't enough bees to pollinate the pumpkins. Recent research shows that the average size of pumpkins increases when pumpkins are pollinated by numerous bees. You can plant pollen-rich flowers to encourage bees.

● *Diseases and pests.* Powdery mildew: rotate pumpkins with other crops; restrict overhead watering. Squash bugs: keep the garden and yard free of trash where bugs can hibernate; pick eggs and insects off plants.

Harvesting. Cut pumpkins free of the vine after vines have died or just before a hard frost. Cure them in the sun or in a warm (85 to 90° F) room for 10 to 14 days. Stored pumpkins keep for months at 55 to 60° F in 60 to 70 percent humidity.

Seed-saving. Scoop out the seeds and pulp. Dry the seeds, separate from the pulp, and store.

Pumpkin Varieties

Variety	Days to Maturity	Description	Catalog Source*
Small			
Autumn Gold Hybrid	90	Golden orange, 7 to 10 pounds, vigorous vines	6, 7, 8, 13, 17, 25, 26, 30, 35, 36, 40, 48, 52, 54, 55, 57
Jack O' Lantern	100	Medium orange, 8 to 9 inches, firm flesh	1, 2, 5, 6, 7, 8, 10, 11, 12, 13, 14, 17, 28, 29, 30, 32, 33, 34, 43, 45, 48, 52, 54
Small Sugar Pie	100	New England pie pumpkin, fruits round, 7 inches	1, 2, 5, 7, 8, 11, 12, 20, 25, 28, 29, 32, 33, 34, 35, 40, 43, 44, 45, 47, 48, 52, 55, 56, 57, 58
Space Savers			
Bush Funnyface	90	10 to 15 pounds, good pie variety, small vines	5, 13, 28, 29, 30, 34, 40, 45, 54, 55, 56
Bush Spirit	100	Oval, 10 to 15 pounds, bush types, can be grown up a back support or on a cucumber pole	5, 6, 8, 13, 26, 29, 30, 32, 34, 35, 40, 48, 50, 55
Jack Be Little	90	Miniature pumpkin, 2 to 3 inches, deep orange, vigorous grower, good for decorations	12, 25, 26, 29, 30, 32, 33, 34, 36, 40, 44, 45, 52, 54, 56
Mini Jack	100	Miniature pumpkin, 3 to 6 inches, bright orange, mainly for decorations	43
Munchkin	110	Miniature pumpkin, 3 to 4 inches, deep orange, meaty interior, use as container for soup	18, 28, 46
Sweetie Pie	110	Miniature pumpkin, 1¾ to 3 inches, deeply ribbed, flattened	48

*Listings correspond to seed companies listed under Sources of Seeds and Supplies.

RADISHES

There are three main types of radish: round to oval, the long-rooted varieties, and winter species.

Planting. Sow radish seeds ½ inch deep and ½ inch apart. Radishes start to form bulbs in about two weeks. Before that time, thin them to stand 1 or 2 inches apart. It's best to start your plantings four to six weeks before the last frost. Since they mature quickly (in just about 21 to 30 days), plant them alongside larger, slower-maturing vegetables, or use them to follow a harvested crop. The minimum soil temperature is 40° F. No supplemental fertilizer needed.

Container planting. You can easily grow radishes in just 4 to 8 inches of soil. Plant seeds 1 inch apart, then add ½ inch of soil on top.

Companion planting. Plant with cucumbers, lettuce, melons, nasturtiums, peas, and other root crops.

Problems:

● *Radishes are too hot.* The soil dried out. Keep the soil moist during the growing season.

● *Radishes are pithy.* Summer-grown radishes turn pithy rapidly. Give them some shade.

● *Plants have leaves, but bulbs fail to form.* Radishes are planted too close together. Thin radishes to stand 2 inches apart.

● *Diseases and pests.* Root maggots: control with wood ashes.

Harvesting. Pick radishes when they're still fairly small and young. Older radishes tend to split or to become pithy or spongy.

Seed-saving. Leave a few plants to produce flowers and seedpods. Harvest the mature pods when they are brown and brittle. When thoroughly dry, thresh the pods. Screen them and remove the seeds.

Radish Varieties

Variety	Days to Maturity	Description	Catalog Source*
Long-Rooted			
White Icicle	27	White, 6 inches long, 1 inch wide	14, 17, 18, 30, 34, 45, 48, 58
Round to Oval			
Cherry Belle	22	Round, 3 to 4 inches wide, bright red, All-America Selection	1, 2, 5, 6, 7, 8, 10, 11, 12, 13, 17, 18, 24, 28, 29, 30, 32, 33, 35, 40, 44, 47, 48, 52, 55, 56, 57, 58

Variety	Days to Maturity	Description	Catalog Source*
Easter Egg	25	Multicolored, red to purple, oval, 1½ inches wide	6, 8, 11, 13, 17, 20, 25, 26, 30, 32, 35, 36, 40, 52, 55, 57, 58
French Breakfast	23	Red top, white bottom, oblong, 1¾ inches wide	2, 6, 8, 10, 12, 13, 14, 17, 26, 28, 29, 30, 32, 33, 35, 40, 43, 45, 47, 48, 50, 51, 52, 55

Winter

Variety	Days to Maturity	Description	Catalog Source*
China Rose	52	Deep rose, 6 to 7 inches long, 2½ inches wide, white flesh	17, 26, 29, 32, 33, 34, 40, 44, 45, 55
Round Black Spanish	55	Black, round, white flesh	6, 17, 22, 32, 33, 45, 48, 57

*Listings correspond to seed companies listed under Sources of Seeds and Supplies.

SALAD GREENS

Here are some special favorites of gourmet cooks: corn salad, cress, dandelion, and endive.

Corn Salad

Corn salad, also known as lamb's lettuce, has a bland taste and pale green, spatulate, 3-inch-long leaves.

Planting. Plant corn salad in the fall as a winter crop, ½ inch deep and 4 to 6 inches apart. (It is frost-hardy.) Two or three plants provide enough leaves for one person.

Harvesting. All the special salad greens, except endive and escarole, are harvested in the same manner as spinach and leaf lettuce—a few leaves at a time.

Cress—Garden and Upland

Garden cress, or peppergrass, has finely curled, parsleylike leaves. It is an annual, reaching maturity in about 35 days. Use it to fill odd spaces between larger plants. This is a cool-season plant that withstands some frost. Upland cress is a dwarf plant with slender stalks and notched leaves. It grows densely and reaches 5 to 6 inches tall.

Planting. Sow seeds of garden cress in the spring or fall across the bed. Cover with a ½-inch layer of compost. Thin plants to stand 2 or 3 inches apart. Start using as soon as the leaves form, in about ten days. Sow seeds of upland cress over a 1-square-foot area, then thin to stand 6 inches apart.

Dandelion

If you've never tried dandelion in your salads, you're in for a treat. This is a hardy plant.

Planting. Sow seeds in place and thin to about 8 inches apart. Plant at about the same time as lettuce, or sow in July or August for a fall crop. You can start seeds inside four to six weeks before you intend to plant outside.

Endive and Escarole

Escarole is broadleaved and slightly crumpled or twisted. Endive is a frilly green, highly cut and curled. These are cool-weather, frost-hardy crops.

Planting. Both produce best when planted in the fall. Sow seeds ½ inch deep and about 3 inches apart. Or start seeds inside and transfer the plants to the garden.

Harvesting. Two or three weeks before you intend to harvest, draw the outer leaves over the heart and center leaves. Tie the bunched leaves together with a string.

Salad Greens Varieties

Variety	Days to Maturity	Description	Catalog Source*
Corn Salad			
Big Seed	60	Round, large leaves, mild flavor	22, 35, 50
Large Round-Leaved	60	Large leaves	29, 33, 57
Cress			
Garden Cress (pepper-grass)	45	Finely curled, parsleylike leaves, fast-growing annual	1, 2, 8, 10, 14, 24, 25, 26, 35, 44, 45, 46, 48, 51, 54, 57
Upland Broadleaf Cress	49	Dense growth, 5 to 6 inches high, 10 to 12 inches wide	8, 10, 18, 22, 29, 44, 55, 58

Variety	Days to Maturity	Description	Catalog Source*
Dandelion			
Montmagny	95	Thick-leaved, full heart, use in stir-fry, soup, or salad	31
Thick Leaved	95	Stocky, broad leaves	6, 28, 48
Endive (Chicory)			
Salad King	85	Frilly, toothed, dark green leaves, 24-inch spread	5, 7, 8, 10, 18, 25, 33, 34, 48
Escarole			
Broadleafed Batavian	90	Finely cut, green, broad leaves	2, 6, 10, 18, 33, 35, 55, 57

*Listings correspond to seed companies listed under Sources of Seeds and Supplies.

SPINACH

You can grow savoyed (crinkled), semi-savoyed, and smooth-leaved varieties of spinach. Some types are partially heat-tolerant others have a verietal resistance to disease.

Planting. Spinach is frost-hardy. Plant outside four to six weeks before the last average frost-free date. It grows best from seeds set directly in the ground. Sow the seeds in early spring and again in late summer, planting about ½ inch deep and 2 inches apart. Thin the seedlings to stand 4 inches apart. The minimum soil temperature is 35° F. Spinach is a heavy feeder, so apply about ¼ cup of bloodmeal or other high-nitrogen fertilizer per square foot once a month.

The biggest problem with spinach is its tendency to flower (bolt). You can counteract this by selecting bolt-resistant varieties. In my own area, where we have cold, early springs but can often expect temperatures in the 80s and 90s in April and May, I have all but given up on spring spinach. Fortunately, it nearly always does well in the fall. If you face similar problems, try a heat-tolerant spinach substitute, such as Malabar or New Zealand spinach.

Container planting. Spinach can be grown in 4-inch and larger pots. Sow seeds about 2 inches apart. Cover with ½ inch of soil. Thin seedlings in large containers to about 5 inches apart. Make at least two plantings ten days apart. Feed spinach with fish emulsion every second week according to the instructions on the bottle.

Companion planting. Plant near cauliflower, celery, eggplant, and strawberries.
Problems:

● *Spinach rushes into flower, and leaves don't reach eating size.* This often happens during the first few weeks of growth, when the temperature rises from the 40s to the 80s. Plant varieties that resist early flowering such as 'Bloomsdale Long Standing' and 'America'. Or sow spinach in late summer, so plants mature in the cool days of fall.

● *Diseases and pests.* Blight: remove and destroy perennial weeds in or near the garden. Spinach leafminer: remove the white eggs laid on the underside of leaves; if leafminers have started to infest the leaves, cut away the affected portions with scissors.

Harvesting. Harvest spinach much the same way you would leaf lettuce, a few leaves at a time. Harvest the outer leaves when they are at least 3 inches long. The inner leaves will become the next crop.

Seed-saving. Let a few plants go to seed. Cut stalks when most of the seeds have ripened and dried. Strip the stalks, remove the chaff, and store seeds in a cool, dry place.

Spinach Varieties

Variety	Days to Maturity	Description	Catalog Source*
Savoyed Upright			
America	50	Crumpled, dark green, glossy, bolt-resistant	7, 8, 17, 29, 32, 45, 52, 54
Bloomsdale Long Standing	45	Thick, crinkled, dark green, glossy leaves, slow to bolt ·	1, 2, 6, 7, 10, 12, 13, 14, 17, 20, 22, 25, 26, 30, 35
King of Denmark	46	Rounded, slightly crumpled, dark green, hardy	2, 32, 44
Melody	42	Large plants, semi-crinkled, resistant to mosaic and powdery mildew	5, 6, 8, 12, 18, 20, 30, 31, 32, 34, 35, 36, 40, 45, 48, 51, 54, 57
Smooth, Erect			
Nobel Giant	46	Thick, pointed, dark green, enormous leaves	7, 10, 13, 43, 44, 52

Variety	Days to Maturity	Description	Catalog Source*
Spinach Substitutes			
Malabar Spinach	70	Bright green, glossy leaves, fast-growing, can be trained on fence	16, 35, 36, 51
New Zealand Spinach	70	Small, brittle, green leaves, heat-resistant plants	6, 8, 10, 11, 13, 30, 32, 33, 34, 35, 40, 45, 48, 52, 55, 56

*Listings correspond to seed companies listed under Sources of Seeds and Supplies.

SQUASH

Summer squash (pattypan, straightneck, crookneck, and zucchini) grows on bushy, rather compact plants. The fruits are reasonably small with fairly thin skins. Grow these in a wire cage in a Vegetable Factory garden. This keeps them from spreading out and allows other vegetables to be grown nearby without being crowded out.

Winter squash (acorn, buttercup, butternut, delicious, gold nugget, and spaghetti) has thick skins and huge vines. Grow these up the support at the north end of the garden. Every year, more bush varieties of winter squash are introduced by plant breeders. These don't produce as many fruits as the vine types, but they are useful for planting on cucumber poles, or in a wire cage, in zone B. You do not need to support the fruit of the smaller winter squash. Although 'Banana' and hubbard squash can be grown in a Vegetable Factory garden, you need to support the fruit with chickenwire slings. To keep the vines from getting too big, pinch out the growing tips once they reach the top of the supports.

Planting. Plant seeds of summer squash 1 inch deep and 12 inches apart; plant seeds of winter squash 1 inch deep and 24 inches apart. Squash can be started from seed in peat pots and transplanted outside after the last frost. The minimum soil temperature is 60° F. Squash is a heavy feeder. Give each plant 2 tablespoons of Vegetable Factory organic nutrient mix every month or supplement with fish emulsion every three or four weeks according to the instructions on the bottle.

Container planting. Two summer squash can be grown in a 5-gallon or larger container; the larger the container the better, with no more than two plants per

All varieties of winter squash grow well in Vegetable Factory gardens. The smaller-fruited varieties are especially productive. From left to right are: (top) 'Acorn', 'Butternut'; (center) 'Banana', 'Hubbard'; (bottom) 'Buttercup', 'Delicious'. (Not to scale.)

container. Grow two summer squash (zucchini, straightneck, crookneck, or pattypan) per half whiskey barrel. Summer squash is extremely easy to grow, but don't set it outside until the nighttime temperatures stay above 55° F. You can also grow bush winter squash in containers. Provide some sort of a trellis at one side of the container to support the vines.

Companion planting. Plant near corn, nasturtiums, and radishes.

Problems:

● *The first small squash always rot.* Squash produces female flowers before the male flowers are available to pollinate them. This unpollinated fruit will simply rot. Before very long, male flowers will show up, and shortly after that the female flowers will begin to produce mature squash.

● *Some seeds fail to come up.* Soak seeds in tepid water for 24 hours. Dry seeds on a paper towel before planting.

● *Dark brown, leathery areas appear on the blossom end of the squash fruit (blossom-end rot).* This is caused primarily by uneven soil moisture. If the soil is intermittently wet, then dries out for too long, it promotes blossom-end rot. Keep soil moist. Water deeply, then don't water again until the soil is dry to a depth of 4 to 8 inches.

● *Diseases and pests.* Bacterial wilt: remove affected plants and control cucumber beetles. Mosaic: control aphids; destroy weeds in and around the garden. Cucumber beetle: control by rotating crops; mulch heavily; plant in late spring; rotenone is effective. Squash bug: pick eggs and insects off plants; remove trash in and near garden. Squash vine borer: inject stems with *Bacillus thuringiensis*.

Harvesting. Pick summer squash when fruits are small or moderate size and the rind is easily dented with your thumbnail. Pick winter squash when the rind is thick enough so it is not penetrated by a thumbnail. Pick pattypan squash when small and greenish. Pick yellow varieties when they are pale yellow.

Seed-saving. Pick winter squash at the edible stage. Let summer squash get big and hard. Remove seeds from pulp, wash them carefully, and spread them out on screens to dry.

Squash Varieties

Variety	Days to Maturity	Description	Catalog Source*
Summer Squash			
Patty Pan			
Early White Bush	54	Pale green to creamy white, deep scalloped edges, milkwhite flesh	6, 7, 10, 14, 29, 30, 32, 33, 35, 40, 47, 52, 55, 56, 58
Golden Bush	60	Yellow, flat, disk-shaped, scallop variety	44
Scallopini	50	Bright green, cross between scallop and zucchini	5, 14, 24, 26, 28, 35, 40, 45, 48, 50
Sunburst	50	Bright yellow scalloped fruit, marked with green at both ends, 3 inches	6, 8, 18, 25, 26, 28, 31, 32, 35, 36, 40, 45, 46, 54

(continued)

Variety	Days to Maturity	Description	Catalog Source*
Summer Squash — Continued			
Crookneck			
Butter Swan	50	Light yellow, bushy, compact plants, 3 to 4 feet, 6- to 8-inch fruits, swan-shaped	36
Daytona	41	Yellow skin, creamy yellow flesh	17
Early Golden Summer Crookneck	48	Yellow, changes to deep golden orange	1, 2, 6, 10, 13, 20, 29, 30, 36, 40, 47, 55, 56, 57, 58
Straightneck			
Early Prolific Straightneck	50	Creamy yellow, heavy yields, bush-type plant	2, 7, 8, 10, 13, 17, 18, 29, 30, 34, 50, 55, 56
Goldbar	50	Yellow, compact open bush	8, 26, 30, 32, 33, 34, 40, 54, 55, 56, 58
Park's Creamy Hybrid	48	Yellow, dwarf plant, 18 inches, fruit 6 to 8 inches	36
Zucchini			
Ambassador	53	Dark green, early	8, 30, 32, 33, 34, 36, 54
Black	55	Black, bush-type plant, greenish-white flesh	2, 5, 7, 10, 14, 17, 20, 25, 29, 30, 32, 33, 34, 44, 55, 58
Blondy	40	Creamy green, harvest from 2 to 8 inches	51
Burpee Golden	54	Bright, glossy golden yellow, distinctive	6, 10
Goldrush	52	Glossy golden, 4 to 8 inches long, small open plant	7, 8, 11, 17, 25, 29, 30, 32, 33, 34, 35, 36, 40, 45, 48, 51, 52, 54, 55, 56, 57

Variety	Days to Maturity	Description	Catalog Source*
Green Cocozella	60	Dark green stripes, Italian variety	2, 8, 13, 17, 20, 25, 35, 44, 51, 55, 56, 57
Romano	60	Blossoms stay open a long time, cook the blossoms or the fruit	31

Round Zucchini

Variety	Days to Maturity	Description	Catalog Source*
Gourmet Globe	55	Fruit can be sliced for salads	28, 32, 36, 46, 51, 55
Ronde de Nice	45	Pale green, European variety, harvest anytime after reaching 1 inch	31

Spacesavers

Variety	Days to Maturity	Description	Catalog Source*
Green Magic	48	Dark green, thick-skinned, 18-inch plant	36

Winter Squash

Acorn

Variety	Days to Maturity	Description	Catalog Source*
Jersey Golden Acorn	55–80	Yellow, semi-bush, eat as summer squash or winter squash	6, 7, 8, 13, 17, 20, 25, 28, 30, 31, 34, 35, 36, 40, 45, 47, 48, 54, 57
Table King	75	Dark, glossy green, acorn-shaped fruits, 5 to 6 inches, golden yellow flesh, bush type	6, 12, 18, 29, 32, 45, 48, 54
Table Queen	85	Light yellow flesh, 4½ to 5 inches, trailing vines	1, 2, 5, 7, 10, 11, 12, 14, 17, 18, 26, 28, 30, 32, 33

(continued)

Variety	Days to Maturity	Description	Catalog Source*
Winter Squash — Continued			
Buttercup			
Buttercup	100	Dark green rind with silvery white stripes, 4 to 5 pounds, thick orange flesh	2, 5, 6, 7, 8, 10, 11, 12, 13, 17, 18, 25, 26, 28, 30, 32, 34, 35, 44, 45, 48, 50, 52, 54, 57
Kindred	80	Bright yellow, deep orange flesh, bush type	30, 48
Moregold	90	Bright orange, orange flesh, vigorous vines	26, 44
Butternut			
Bush Butternut	85	10 to 12 inches, thick orange flesh, bush type	52
Waltham Butternut	85	Small seed cavity, bottle-shaped, All-America Selection	1, 5, 6, 7, 10, 12, 13, 17, 18, 25, 26, 28, 29, 30, 32, 34, 45, 47, 48, 56, 57, 58
Delicious			
Golden Delicious	103	Bright orange, heart-shaped	2, 17, 18, 30, 48
Hubbard			
Baby Hubbard	100	Green, small fruit, 5 to 6 pounds, yellow-orange flesh	48
Other			
Delicata Squash	100	Ivory with green stripes, oblong, limited vine-spread	15, 30, 35, 44, 48

Variety	Days to Maturity	Description	Catalog Source*
Golden Nugget	96	Bright orange, softball-size fruit, orange flesh, bush plant	48
Spaghetti	100	Yellow, oblong squash, flesh looks like spaghetti	1, 2, 6, 7, 8, 10, 11, 13, 18, 20, 25, 26, 28, 29, 30, 32, 33, 34, 35, 40, 44, 45, 47, 48, 50, 51, 52, 55, 56, 57

*Listings correspond to seed companies listed under Sources of Seeds and Supplies.

SWISS CHARD

Few vegetables can match Swiss chard for its vigorous growth and productivity. You can cook the delicious, big, crinkly leaves and white stalks. Cook the leaves like spinach and the stalks like asparagus. Plants take strong summer heat, yet will mature within 60 days where summers are cool.

Planting. Sow seeds ½ inch deep and about 4 inches apart. When the seedlings come up, thin to stand 5 to 8 inches apart. Chard is so prolific that two to five plants will probably provide all you need over a season. Plant together in an odd corner. The minimum soil temperature is 40° F. Chard is a light feeder. Feed with fish emulsion in mid-season according to the directions on the bottle.

Container planting. Sow seeds 1 inch apart and cover with ½ inch of soil. Thin plants to 8 inches. Eat the thinned plants. Grow in containers at least 12 inches wide.

Companion planting. Plant near bush beans, kohlrabi, and onions. Keep away from pole beans.

Problems:

● *Chard blue mold.* Caused by humid cool weather; avoid crowding; use a two- or three-year rotation with other crops.

Harvesting: Harvest the outer leaves when they are at least 6 inches long and let the inner leaves become your next crop.

Seed-saving: Let a few plants winter over in the garden. In the spring, cut the seed stalks after the seed balls are dry. Strip the seed from the stalks and winnow the chaff.

Swiss Chard Varieties

Variety	Days to Maturity	Description	Catalog Source*
Fordhook Giant	60	Crumpled leaves, white stalks	1, 2, 8, 11, 14, 20, 25, 28, 32, 33, 34, 43, 44, 45, 48, 50, 56
Lucullus	60	Yellow-green leaves, white stalks	1, 2, 5, 11, 12, 17, 26, 29, 30, 32, 36, 40, 44, 47, 51, 55
Rhubarb Chard	60	Dark green leaves, red stalks	1, 2, 6, 8, 10, 14, 17, 18, 26, 28, 29, 30, 40, 44, 47, 48, 50, 51, 52, 54

*Listings correspond to seed companies listed under Sources of Seeds and Supplies.

TOMATOES

Tomatoes are probably the most productive vegetable you can grow in a Vegetable Factory garden. There are two types of tomato vines, indeterminate and determinate. The terminal buds of indeterminate tomato vines do not set fruit, and the vine grows without stopping until killed by frost. Examples are 'Burpee Big Boy', 'Super Fantastic', 'Ace', and 'Sweet 100'. The terminal buds of determinate vines set fruit. The plant is self-stopping. All the blossoms and fruit develop on the plant at about the same time. Indeterminate vines produce a great many more tomatoes than determinate vines do.

Planting. Plant only one to four tomato plants per Vegetable Factory garden, on 18-inch spacings. The problem here is space; one to four plants allows you to grow a garden complete with a number of other vegetables; more than this, and about all you have is a tomato garden.

The easiest way to train an indeterminate tomato vine is to put it in a tomato cage, roughly 18 to 24 inches wide and 4 to 6 feet tall, and let it go its own way. All evidence shows that these plants left alone in this type of structure outproduce pruned vines, sometimes by a ratio of two to one. Some gardeners pinch out the sideshoots, and train only the long central stem up a string. I don't recommend this method since I have found that it cuts down total tomato production. The minimum soil temperature is 50° F. The tomato is a heavy feeder; give each plant 2 tablespoons of Vegetable Factory organic nutrient mix once a month.

Container planting. A number of determinate varieties are especially suited for small containers. The smallest is 'Tiny Tim', a 15-inch plant with cherry-sized fruits. It can be fruited successfully on a windowsill in a 4-inch pot. 'Small Fry' and 'Burpee Pixie Hybrid' are slightly larger, with clusters of small fruits. They should be staked in a 6- to 8-inch pot or placed in a hanging basket.

Companion planting. Plant with asparagus, basil, broccoli, carrots, cauliflower, mustard, onions, parsley, rosemary, and sage.

Many tomato varieties do well in containers. A few varieties can be grown in 4-inch pots. Shown are (left to right): (top) 'Patio', 'Pixie'; (bottom) 'Tiny Tim', 'Toy Boy'.

Problems:

● *Flowers but no fruits.* It's probably too cold. Tomatoes will pollinate above nighttime temperatures at 55° F; below this, try shaking the flowers with an electric toothbrush, or wait until the weather warms up.

● *The ends of the tomatoes rot (blossom-end rot).* This is usually caused by a sudden moisture shortage in the soil. Make sure your soil never dries out completely during the growing season. Some experts believe this is also due to a calcium shortage in the soil.

● *Yellowish patches on the fruit (sunscald) turn into large grayish-white spots.* This is caused by too much direct exposure to the sun at temperatures between 90 and 100° F. To avoid the problem, grow tomato varieties with heavy leaf cover like 'Vineripe', 'Star Fire', 'Marglobe', and 'Early Girl'.

● *Tomato fruits are malformed, with ugly scars between the segments (catfacing).* Cool weather at the time of blossoming may cause the blossoms to stick to the small fruits and create tearing and distortion. To avoid this, pull blossoms off when the fruit is small. 'Big Set' and 'Burpee's VF' resist catfacing.

● *Diseases and pests.* Mosaic: remove weeds in and around garden; use pyrethrum to control aphids, which spread the disease. Tomato hornworm: control with *Bacillus thuringiensis;* handpick off plants. Colorado potato beetle: pick the adults, and crush the yellow eggs found on the undersides of the leaves.

Harvesting. Pick when the color is good all over. Size is no indication of maturity. Before frost, cut the plants and hang them upside down until they ripen. Tomatoes should be stored where it is cool and dark. You can pick the green tomatoes off the plants in the fall, and place them on a tray or shallow pan in the dark at about 50° F. They will ripen over time.

Seed-saving. Pick the ripest, best-looking fruit. Scoop out seeds and pulp, and place them in an open pan to ferment for a few days at room temperature. Remove the mold from the top, rinse with water, and store the seeds.

Tomato Varieties

Variety	Days to Maturity	Description	Catalog Source*
Early			
Early Girl	56	Bears both early and late, 4 to 5 ounces, indeterminate	2, 5, 6, 10, 13, 17, 26, 28, 30, 32, 33, 35, 36, 40, 52, 55
Fireball	64	Compact plant, 4 to 5 ounces, determinate	2, 10, 30, 48, 52, 57

Variety	Days to Maturity	Description	Catalog Source*
Spring Giant	65	All-America Selection, 4 to 5 ounces, VFN (wilt- and nematode- resistant), determinate	12, 26, 32, 40, 43, 52, 57

Large Fruit

Variety	Days to Maturity	Description	Catalog Source*
Beefsteak	90	Large, firm meat, indeterminate	2, 5, 10, 24, 28, 30, 33, 34, 44, 55
Burpee Big Early	62	Medium early, up to 1 pound, indeterminate	6, 29, 30, 33, 34

Midseason

Variety	Days to Maturity	Description	Catalog Source*
Ace 55	75	Medium large, meaty, bears heavily, VF (wilt- resistant)	6, 28, 29, 33, 56, 58
Glamour	75	Solid, crack-resistant, indeterminate	5, 10, 18, 30, 44, 45, 48, 57
Marglobe	75	Smooth, vigorous, determinate	2, 5, 6, 8, 10, 13, 25, 30, 33, 34, 56, 58

Pink

Variety	Days to Maturity	Description	Catalog Source*
Ponderosa	82	Purplish-pink, 1 pound, indeterminate	2, 29, 34, 35, 40, 48, 56, 57

Yellow, White

Variety	Days to Maturity	Description	Catalog Source*
Jubilee	75	Deep orange to yellow, globe	2, 10, 13, 24, 25, 32, 52, 55, 56, 57
White Beauty	84	Ivory skin, large	5, 17, 44, 47

Small-Fruited Indeterminate

Variety	Days to Maturity	Description	Catalog Source*
Currant	75	Pea-size tomatoes, good for salads	44

(continued)

Variety	Days to Maturity	Description	Catalog Source*
Small-Fruited Indeterminate—Continued			
Gardener's Delight	50	Bite-size, productive	6, 25, 44, 51
Large Red Cherry	70	Half-dollar size, indeterminate, sweet and mild	1, 5, 12, 17, 28, 29, 30, 34, 35, 50, 56
Sunburst	76	Deep orange, Ping-Pong–ball size, fruit resists cracking	6
Sweet 100	65	Cherry-sized, red, grows in clusters, will produce until fall	2, 6, 8, 11, 17, 18, 28, 31, 33, 34, 36, 40, 45, 48, 52, 54, 55, 57
Sweetie	65	Cherry-sized tomatoes grow in clusters, large vine	5, 12, 13, 35, 44, 50
Yellow Pear	70	Bright yellow, pear-shaped, small	1, 2, 5, 6, 10, 11, 13, 17, 18, 20, 22, 28, 30, 32, 33, 34, 35, 40, 44, 46, 47, 48, 55, 57
Yellow Plum	70	Plum-shaped, small	1, 5, 10, 17, 18, 28, 29, 30, 31, 34, 44, 48
Special Container Varieties (Small Fruit)			
Basket Pak	55	1½ inches, round, bears in clusters, sweet, cascading branches	6
Burpee Pixie Hybrid	52	Grows 14 to 18 inches, 1¾ inches, scarlet	1, 2, 6, 20, 28, 51
Golden Pygmy	52	Marble-size, plant 18 inches	31
Patio Hybrid	70	Plant 30 inches, almost round, should be staked	8, 28, 29, 30, 32, 34, 35, 45, 48, 55, 57, 58
Presto Hybrid	55	24 inches tall, fruit 1½ inches	18

Variety	Days to Maturity	Description	Catalog Source*
Small Fry	52	Marble-size, red, 1 inch, grows in heavy clusters, heavy cropper	5, 8, 29, 30, 32, 34, 40, 45, 48, 50, 55
Tiny Tim	55	Plant 15 inches, ¾ inch, scarlet	2, 5, 6, 8, 25, 26, 29, 30, 32, 34, 35, 40, 44, 47, 48, 57

*Listings correspond to seed companies listed under Sources of Seeds and Supplies.

TURNIPS AND RUTABAGAS

Turnips grow to about 2 inches across and have white flesh and purple tops. You can cook turnip leaves as edible greens. Rutabagas grow to 4 or 5 inches across, and have white or yellow flesh and purple tops.

Planting. Sow turnip seeds ¼ inch deep and 1 inch apart. Place near larger, slower-maturing crops. They tend to sprout in clumps that require thinning. Thin every few days for the first two to four weeks until plants stand 3 inches apart. Since the crop is frost-hardy, it can be started in the garden four to six weeks before the last average frost. Plant again in late July or August for an early fall harvest. The minimum soil temperature is 40° F. Give turnips and rutabagas ⅛ cup of Vegetable Factory organic nutrient mix per square foot of soil at midseason.

Sow rutabaga seeds ½ inch deep, or cover with ½ inch of soil; space them 3 inches apart. Thin them to stand 6 inches apart.

Container planting. Sow seeds of both vegetables 1 inch apart, then thin turnips to 2 inches apart and rutabagas to 6 inches.

Companion planting. Plant them near peas. Keep them away from mustard and potatoes.

Problems:
● *Diseases and pests.* Powdery mildew: avoid overhead watering. Yellow verbena leafminer: handpick infested leaves.

Harvesting. Harvest turnip roots when they are 2 to 4 inches in diameter. For turnip greens, harvest the leaves when they are young and tender. Dig rutabagas when the roots are 3 or 4 inches in diameter.

Seed-saving. Both vegetables will cross with other turnip and rutabaga varieties, Chinese cabbage and oriental mustard, so isolate varieties you want to set seed. Let those roots you want to use for seed production overwinter in a cool place, then replant them, or leave roots in the ground to overwinter. Mulch heavily. Plants will flower in the summer. Cut stalks when seedpods turn brown. Dry pods and separate out chaff.

Turnip and Rutabaga Varieties

Variety	Days to Maturity	Description	Catalog Source*
Turnip			
Golden Ball	60	Yellow, yellow flesh	1, 28, 32, 35, 57
Just Right	40	White skin, globe-shaped	5, 10, 17, 18, 30, 32, 55, 56, 58
Purple Top White Globe	55	Bright purple tops, uniform	1, 2, 5, 6, 7, 8, 10, 11, 12, 13, 14, 17, 18, 20, 24, 25, 26, 28, 29, 30, 32, 33, 34, 40, 43, 44, 45, 47, 48, 50, 52, 54, 55, 56, 57, 58
Shogoin	30	20 inches, grown for greens	1, 28, 32, 35, 57
Tokyo Cross Hybrid	35	Pure white, semi-globe, All-America Selection	12, 13, 26, 28, 29, 30, 36, 48, 51, 54, 55, 57
Rutabaga			
American Purple Top	90	Purple tops, darker yellow globe, light yellow flesh	2, 7, 10, 13, 17, 18, 26, 28, 30, 32, 33, 35, 40, 43, 44, 52, 54, 56, 58
Laurentian Neckless	90	Purple tops, globe-shaped, yellow flesh	1, 10, 12, 25, 26, 29, 32, 34, 44, 48, 57

*Listings correspond to seed companies listed under Sources of Seeds and Supplies.

WATERMELONS

Watermelons do well in Vegetable Factory gardens, provided you stick to the smaller-fruited varieties. Icebox varieties produce 5- to 10-pound, 6- to 8-inch round melons on full-size vines. Bush types produce small melons on 3- to 5-foot vines.

Grow the vining types up the Vegetable Factory back support. Grow the bush types in a cage in zone B that is 20 inches wide and 4 feet high. Plant four vines to a cage.

Planting. Plant watermelon seeds outdoors around the date of the last frost, 1 inch deep and 12 inches apart. Melons can be started indoors in individual peat pots and transplanted outdoors about the date of the last frost. Since the watermelon fruits are heavy, plant only the smaller-fruiting varieties, and support the

melons with a chickenwire cradle. Place the chickenwire around the fruit, and wire
the cradle to the cage or support wire. The minimum soil temperature is 60° F.
Watermelons are heavy feeders, so apply 2 tablespoons of Vegetable Factory
organic nutrient per plant once a month, or supplement with fish emulsion every
three or four weeks according to the directions on the bottle.

Container planting. Plant one bush-type watermelon in a 5-gallon container.

Companion planting. Plant near beans, corn, peas, and radishes. Keep them
away from potatoes.

Problems:

● *Melons fail to ripen before frost.* The melons haven't had a long enough
season. Most require at least 75 days. In short-season areas, grow "early" varieties.

● *Diseases and pests.* Fusarium wilt: spread by cucumber beetle; control
by deep mulching, rotating plants.

Harvesting. When watermelons are ripe, they give off a dull, hollow sound
when thumped with a knuckle. A sharp sound means they're still green. Look at
the discolored spots on the melons where they touched the ground. If the melons
are ready, these spots will have turned from white to pale yellow.

Seed-saving. Remove seeds from fully ripe melons. Wash and dry them. Store
in a cool, dry place.

Watermelon Varieties

Variety	Days to Maturity	Description	Catalog Source*
Icebox Types			
New Hampshire Midget	68	Striped dark green rind, 4 to 6 pounds, 7 inches, red flesh, black seeds	2, 10, 12, 30, 44, 57
Sugar Baby	73–90	Dark green rind, 10 pounds, 8 inches, round, dark red flesh, not many seeds	1, 2, 5, 6, 7, 8, 11, 13, 17, 18, 24, 25, 26, 28, 29, 30, 32, 33, 34, 36, 40, 45, 48, 50, 54, 55, 56, 57, 58
Round			
Crimson Sweet	80	To 25 pounds, round, dark red	1, 5, 6, 7, 12, 13, 17, 18, 26, 28, 29, 30, 33, 34, 40, 48, 50, 54, 55, 56, 58

(continued)

Variety	Days to Maturity	Description	Catalog Source*
Round — Continued			
Early Northern Sweet	78	Striped, green, 10 to 12 pounds, dark red flesh	12
Spacesavers			
Bush Baby	80	Green-striped skin, dwarf determinate, 8-pound fruit, pink flesh	36
Bush Charleston Gray	90	Bush type, vines 3 to 5 feet, oblong, blocky, 17-pound, dark red flesh, resistant to fusarium wilt and anthracnose	30, 32, 36, 54, 55
Bush	95	Light green rind	13, 17, 18, 29, 32
Jubilee		Dark stripes, small, oblong, blocky fruit, resistant to fusarium wilt and anthracnose	30, 36, 54, 55, 58
Sugar Jade	80	Jade-green skin, 16 pounds, aroma of wine, compact vines	51
Yellow, Pink Flesh			
Moon and Stars (pink flesh)	80	Stars on dark green rind, pink flesh, Amish heirloom	47
Moon and Stars (yellow flesh)	80	Rinds have yellow moons with small yellow stars, yellow flesh, heirloom variety	44, 47

*Listings correspond to seed companies listed under Sources of Seeds and Supplies.

CHAPTER 10

SPECIAL GARDENS

THE SMALL SIZE OF A VEGETABLE FACTORY GARDEN makes it ideal for growing a single specialty such as baby, gourmet, or oriental vegetables, unusual vegetables for adventurous cooks, or a specialty herb garden. In this chapter, we'll take a look at vegetables and herbs for these special gardens and examine a few of their requirements.

BABY AND GOURMET VEGETABLES

The baby vegetable boom is sweeping the nation. In Washington D.C., New York, Chicago, Los Angeles, Seattle, and many other metropolitan areas, people are discovering baby beans, carrots, and zucchini, and marble-size beets and tomatoes. Most of these are expensive if purchased in a gourmet food store, costing as much as six times the price of regular vegetables. And in many areas, baby vegetables are extremely hard to find.

They are, however, easy to grow in a Vegetable Factory garden. Some of these, such as "Baby Nantes' carrots and 'Baby Asian' corn, are true genetic miniatures that bear small fruit. Others, such as 'Golden Wax' beans, are standard varieties that become baby vegetables when picked very young. To get the best results with these, you need to grow varieties that develop flavor and variety at an early stage.

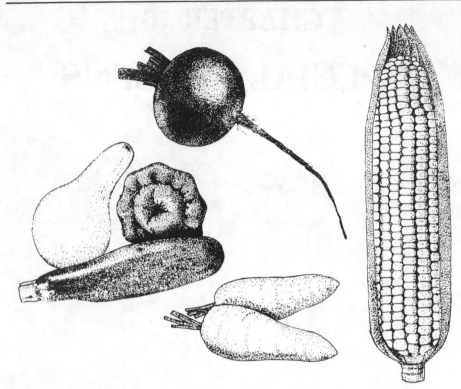

These lilliputians sometimes sell for six times as much as regular vegetables. Some are true baby varieties, others are regular-sized vegetables picked when immature. Shown are baby corn, squash, beets, and carrots.

Genetic Miniatures

Genetic miniature varieties are bred for their size. They reach harvest size slightly faster than standard varieties, and all mature at about the same time. Let's look at some of them.

Beets. Plant breeders have developed some flavorful beets that are only an inch across when mature. The best ones to plant include 'Badger's Baby', 'Fire Chief', 'Little Ball', and 'Spinel'. These mature in about 50 days. To capture the full flavor, pick within a week or two after the beets reach maturity. Plant at about two-week intervals to keep baby beets coming all season long.

Cabbage. Try stuffing these small baby cabbages such as 'Baby Early' (red) and 'Badger Babyhead' (green). Plant about 6 inches apart.

Carrots. There are several baby carrot varieties that are crisp and tender at 2 to 3 inches long. Some of the best are 'Little Finger', 'Minicor', and 'Tiny Sweet'. Plant on same spacing as full-sized carrots.

Corn. Midget varieties include 'Baby Asian', 'Butter Improved', and 'Golden Midget'. All can be harvested when the ears are 3 inches long. Plant 8 inches apart in 4-square-foot blocks.

Eggplant. 'Hito' produces dozens of dark, shiny purple fruit the size of pecans. Most other eggplant miniatures are standard varieties picked before they reach maturity.

Lettuce. Midget varieties can be picked to serve as an individual salad. 'Tom Thumb' produces heads the size of tennis balls. 'Summer Baby Bibb' grows 5 to 6 inches in diameter, with teardrop-shaped leaves, and 'Little Jim Mini Romaine' produces a 5- to 6-inch-tall head. Because these plants don't need as much room as full-sized lettuce, you can plant them about 4 inches apart.

Melons. Both cantaloupes and watermelons have been bred to produce baby fruits. 'Minnesota Midget' is a softball-sized cantaloupe that grows on 3-foot vines. Among baby watermelons that grow well in small gardens and containers are 'Bush Baby' and 'Bush Jubilee'.

Peppers. Several small pickling varieties produce bite-sized peppers. 'Sweet Cherry' forms miniature 1-inch globes. 'Canape' is delicious when picked 1 to 2 inches long.

Babies from Full-sized Varieties

To obtain babies for the table, these varieties must be picked small. Once flowering starts, you need to check the plants daily and pick the quantities you need. Here are the ones to plant.

Beans. Full-flavored snap beans such as 'Blue Lake', 'Kentucky Wonder', 'Slenderette', and 'Venture' produce tasty baby beans. Check every day or two when the beans start to develop, and pick when the pods are 3 to 4 inches long.

Corn. Full-sized varieties such as 'Early Sunglow', 'Early Extra-Sweet', and 'Kandy Korn' should be picked early, when the silks first show. If you intend to harvest corn as baby ears, plant in 4-square-foot blocks 6 to 8 inches apart.

Eggplant. The thin-skinned, long Japanese eggplant (see Chapter 9 for varieties) can be picked when the fruit are only 2 to 4 inches long. 'Easter Egg' can be picked for eating when the fruits are young, white, and egg-size.

Okra. 'Annie Oakley' is a compact plant that can be squeezed into an odd corner. The pods should be picked when they are ¾ to 2 inches long. At this stage they are firm and crunchy, with little of the gelatinous quality of full-size okra.

Squash. There are not any true genetic baby squash. Most summer squash (zucchini, long- and shortneck, and pattypan) are delectable when harvested as babies. For a mildly sweet flavor, pick the newly formed fruits one to three days after the flowers open. Especially good ones are 'Scallopini', (dark green), 'Sunburst' (green and gold), 'Gourmet Globe' (round), 'Gold Rush' (a golden zucchini), and 'Aristocrat' (a green zucchini).

EUROPEAN GOURMET VEGETABLES

In the last few years, European vegetables have become popular with American gardeners looking for something different. In Europe, many regions have their own varieties. The French varieties are particularly popular in the United States.

French green beans are described as either gourmet types *(filets)* or commercial types *(mangetout)*. Filets are as slim as a pencil and especially tasty. Try either 'Fin de Bagnols' or 'Aramis'.

Some of the tastiest carrot varieties *(carottes)* are 'Baby Nantes' and the round French forcing type, 'Paramex'. Be sure to consider the European cucumber *(concombre)*, 'Sweet Slice Hybrid'; eggplant *(cornichon)*, 'Ichiban'; 'Agusta' lettuce *(laitues)*, onion *(oignon)*, 'Yello Virtus'; pumpkin *(potiron)*, variety 'Jack-Be-Little' (decoration only); 'Flamboyant' radish *(radis)*; 'Sweet Spanish' pepper *(poivron)*; and 'Giant Viroflay' spinach *(epinard)*. See Chapter 9 for other European varieties.

ORIENTAL VEGETABLES

Gardeners everywhere are growing and cooking oriental vegetables with names like *dai gai choy, choy sum, bok choy, siew choy,* and *gai lohn.* These varieties, the oriental relatives of mustard, broccoli, and cabbage, are available in the supermarket. But if you want to cook with the full range of oriental vegetables, you will have to grow your own. At one time these seeds could be purchased only from one or two specialty seed sources. Today you will find oriental vegetables in catalogs of almost all of the major seed firms.

Burdock *(gobo).* This Japanese specialty is used in many oriental dishes. The plant has long stalks, broad leaves, and sharp burrs. Plant burdock seeds ¼ inch deep and 2 to 3 inches apart. Keep the soil moist during the entire germination period. The root is edible: scrape, scald, and boil it.

Chinese broccoli or Chinese kale *(gai lohn).* The dark green leaves and stems look and taste like broccoli, but the stalks are tougher and need to be peeled before cooking. It matures in 70 days. Plant seeds ½ inch deep and 3 inches apart. Thin seedlings to stand 6 inches apart when 2 inches tall.

Chinese or celery cabbage *(siew choy).* This plant produces a compact leafy head. There are two types: *michihli* is the tall one, and *wong bok* is often short and barrel-shaped. A number of varieties of each type are available from the seed catalogs. Sow seeds directly in the beds about 4 inches apart, or start them in peat pots. Thin or transplant seedlings to stand 12 to 15 inches apart. When the plants are 5 to 8 inches tall, tie their leaves loosely to help form heads. Harvest when firmly headed.

Chinese celery *(heun kunn).* This slow-growing plant forms an 8-inch-wide clump of leafy celery-like stalks. It is fragrant, aromatic, and delicious. Sow seeds in March in peat pots. Plant outdoors in late April or early May. Space the plants 8 inches apart.

   Chinese chives *(gow choy)*. This member of the onion family forms handsome clumps of slender, flat, awl-shaped leaves. The flavor has a hint of garlic and blends with many salads and mixed meat dishes. Sow seeds directly in the ground about 10 inches apart. You can slip plants into odd spaces. Cut the tops when they are 5 to 6 inches high, and continue cutting throughout the season as new growth appears.

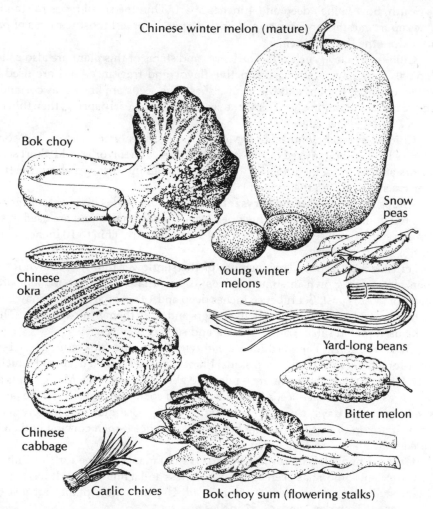

Chinese winter melon (mature)

Bok choy

Snow peas

Chinese okra

Young winter melons

Yard-long beans

Bitter melon

Chinese cabbage

Garlic chives

Bok choy sum (flowering stalks)

An increasing number of gardeners are growing at least a few oriental vegetables. Many are now sold in supermarkets, but if you want a complete selection, you must grow your own.

Chinese mustard cabbage *(pak choi).* *Pak choi* is the general name for loose-leaf, nonheading Chinese cabbage. Even the slightly heading varieties do not form a tight head. Individual varieties include *bok choy* and *hung chin.* The heart of bok choy is tender when cooked; this green, loose-leafed, white-stalked cabbage has a stronger flavor than the regular Chinese cabbage. *Choy sum* or flowering white cabbage is a small variety of bok choy; the tiny yellow flowers in the center of the cabbage are harvested when barely open. Fry them lightly in oil.

Plant pak choi in early spring to midsummer in cooler areas, and in the fall in the South. Sow ¼ inch deep and 4 inches apart. Thin the small types to stand 6 inches apart and the large types to 10 inches apart. Harvest most varieties of pak choi before the flowers open.

Chinese parsley *(yuen sai).* The leaves and stems of this plant are also called cilantro. They have a strong distinctive flavor and fragrance, and are used to garnish oriental, Indian, and Mexican dishes. The seeds are known as coriander and are used as a cooking herb. Sow the seeds in place in early spring, then thin the plants 7 to 10 inches apart.

Chinese spinach *(hinn choy).* Most varieties have green leaves, but some varieties have mahogany red or red-streaked leaves. The flavor is mild. Start seeds indoors and set out 4 inches apart in April. It comes into its own about the time other greens are losing their vigor.

Chopsuey green, garland chrysanthemum *(shungiku).* This vegetable grows 3 feet tall if allowed to flower. The lobed leaves are aromatic, and are used in stir fries and soup. Sow seeds ¼ inch deep and 6 inches apart. Thin to 10 inches apart. Harvest before flowering.

Jerusalem artichoke. This member of the sunflower family is grown for its tubers. It is also grown in some gardens as an ornamental flower. Plant after danger of frost is past. Set tubers 6 inches deep and 1 foot apart. Plants may grow to a height of 8 feet. In the late fall, dig tubers and store them in a cool place. They can be used raw in salads, or be pickled and served as relish.

Oriental beans. The yard-long *asparagus bean* vine *(dok gouk)* has 1- to 2-foot-long pods with thick, crisp skins. Plant the seeds ¾ inch deep and 6 inches apart. Harvest when the beans are tender and about 1½ feet long. *Mung beans* are popular as sprouts. Place seeds in a quart jar and soak overnight. Turn the jar on its side for three days, rinsing the beans regularly. Use mung bean sprouts in salads. If grown to maturity, mung beans will produce 3-inch curving pods with white seeds. Plant 4 to 6 inches apart.

Oriental bunching onion *(he she ko)* is the Japanese name for the Chinese *chung the.* This onion has been bred for crispness and a mild flavor. It has a green tubular stalk and a long, slender white head. Use the whole plant, not just the bulb. Plant ½ inch deep and 2 to 3 inches apart.

Oriental cucumber. These are longer, thinner, and crisper than conventional cucumbers. The plants can easily be grown on the back supports of a Vegetable Factory garden. Plant 6 to 12 inches apart when all danger of frost is past.

Oriental eggplant. The long, narrow fruits are harvested at about two-thirds of maximum size. They are usually steamed or cooked in mixed vegetable dishes. Start the plants in peat pots indoors, and move them outdoors after all danger of frost is past. Place them 12 to 18 inches apart. There are both Chinese and Japanese varieties.

Oriental melons. The oriental melons are more like squash than like melons. There are four you might like to try—bitter, fuzzy, winter, and sponge gourd. Oriental melons are warm-weather vegetables. After all danger of frost is past, plant them outside 12 inches apart on the Vegetable Factory back supports.

Bitter melon (foo gwah) has lobed leaves and pearly green fruits. The mature fruits turn golden yellow and split up the side to reveal red seeds. Harvest when melons are 4 to 8 inches long. In India, the mature fruits are sliced and used in curries.

Fuzzy melon (moh gwah) matures to about a foot in diameter, but cooks like the immature zucchini-sized melons best. They can be peeled, sliced, and cooked in butter and water, or stuffed for baking as you would zucchini.

Chinese winter melon (doong gwah) grows to about the size of a pumpkin and looks like a watermelon with firm white flesh. Grow them up a fence or trellis. Harvest after the melons reach pumpkin-size, or use the little ones in soup or cooked like any other vegetable. You can try serving soup in a hollowed-out melon.

Sponge gourd (see gwah) is also known as *Chinese okra*. The gourds are between 6 and 12 inches long and have a delicate sweet taste. Harvest when young (6 to 7 inches long). Be sure to remove the ridges before using. Stir-fry with chunks of chicken or shrimp; cut into chunks to simmer in soup; or deep-fry for tempura. As the sponge gourds mature, their ridges turn brown and their flesh becomes spongy. If you want to use them as sponges, leave the gourds on the vine until they are entirely brown. Crush the skin lightly, and soak the gourds in boiling water until soft enough to peel easily.

Oriental (or Chinese) leaf mustard. This green is known as *gai choy* if narrow-leafed, and *dai gai choy* if broadleafed. It has a strong taste, with a touch of bitterness that increases as the plant matures. The plants are 1 to 3 feet tall and resemble pak choi. Some varieties produce heads or semi-heads in cold weather. Sow seeds ¼ inch deep and 4 inches apart. When the seedlings are 2 to 3 inches tall, thin them to stand 8 inches apart. Harvest from 4 inches tall up, until they are tough and bitter.

Edible-podded peas. Snow peas and 'Sugar-Snap' types are considered to be oriental peas *(hor lon dough)*. These are covered in Chapter 9.

Oriental radish. This vegetable is called *daikon* if Japanese and *lo bok* if Chinese. Oriental radishes have a large, crisp, swollen root. There are many variations in root size, shape, and color of skin and flesh. The weight of the root ranges from 2 to 8 pounds, and the length from 2 to 20 inches. Plant the smaller ones 2 to 3 inches apart, and the larger ones 4 to 6 inches apart.

Oriental Vegetable Varieties

Variety	Days to Maturity	Description	Catalog Sources*
Burdock (Gobo)			
Takingoama	150	Long, slender 32-inch roots	1, 25, 49
Chinese Broccoli (Kale)			
White Flower Kale	70	Smooth, pointed leaves, white flowers	49
Yellow Flower Kale	70	Dwarf plants, yellow flowers	49
Chinese Cabbage (Heading)			
Michihli type			
Early Top	55	Cylindrical, 3- to 4-pound heads	25, 49
Jade Pagoda	72	Compact, uniform, 16-inches, deep green heads	8, 18, 34, 36, 40, 48, 54
Michihli	70	Dark green, resembles celery, 18 by 4 inches, 4 to 6 pounds	1, 2, 5, 6, 7, 8, 10, 11, 12, 14, 29, 32, 33, 34, 40, 43, 45, 48, 55, 57, 58
Tip Top	65	Cylindrical, 4- to 5-pound heads	49
Winter Giant	85	Cylindrical, 10-pound heads	49
Wong Bok type			
Spring A-1	65	Oval, 3-pound heads	25, 27, 34, 35, 49, 50
Spring Triumph	70	Barrel-shaped, 5- to 7-pound heads	49
Tropical	50	Oval, 3- to 4-pound heads	27, 54
Wong Bok	65	Barrel-shaped, 5- to 6-pound heads	8, 10, 35, 44, 49, 53, 44
Chinese Cabbage (Nonheading Varieties)			
Bok Choy	45	Loose green heads	8, 17, 35, 44, 48, 49
Chin Kang	45	Erect green heads	49
Hung Chin	35	Loose, white or green heads	49

Variety	Days to Maturity	Description	Catalog Sources*
Mei Qing Choi (baby pak choi)	45	Compact, pale green heads	18, 21, 46, 48, 51
Prize Choy	50	Compact, spoon-shaped, dark green leaves	20, 45
Round Leafed Santung	35	Erect green heads	49
Spoon Cabbage	45	Erect green heads	49
White Stalked	50	Upright heads	49

Chinese Celery

Variety	Days to Maturity	Description	Catalog Sources*
Chinese Golden	90	Light green leaves, long hollow stalks	49

Chinese Chives (Leek)

Variety	Days to Maturity	Description	Catalog Sources*
Broad Leaf	110	Broadleaf leek	31, 35, 53, 49
Chinese Leek Flower	110	Young stalks and flower buds can be eaten	49

Chinese Parsley

Variety	Days to Maturity	Description	Catalog Sources*
Chinese Parsley	45	Young shoots have a strong flavor	49

Chinese Spinach

Variety	Days to Maturity	Description	Catalog Sources*
Oriental Spinach	45	Leaves smooth, dark green, heat-tolerant	49

Chop Suey Greens (Garland Chrysanthemum, Shungiku)

Variety	Days to Maturity	Description	Catalog Sources*
Large Leaf	35	Oblong, large, thick, smooth leaves	25, 27, 49, 53, 56
Small Leaf	35	Large dark green leaves, serrated with deep cuts	49

Jerusalem Artichoke

Variety	Days to Maturity	Description	Catalog Sources*
Dwarf Sunray	100	Crisp, 5 to 7 feet tall, flowers frequently	51

(continued)

Variety	Days to Maturity	Description	Catalog Sources*
Oriental Beans			
Asparagus beans			
Green Pod Black Seed	75	Seeds black when mature	49
Green Pod Red Seed	75	Pods light green, seeds red when mature	49
Mung beans			
Mung Bean Berkin	90	Pods light green, seeds white	1, 13, 17, 31, 32, 40, 44, 49, 51, 55, 57
Oriental Bunching Onions			
Evergreen Hardy Long White	70	Single stalks, extremely hardy	15, 25, 47
Long White Tokyo	68	Single stalks, leaves dark green	8, 18, 33, 34, 35, 48, 49, 54
Multi-stalk 9 (Iwatsuki)	70	Grows in clusters of 5 to 6 stalks	49
Oriental Cucumber			
Kyoto Three Feet	80	Long, slim fruit, to 19 inches long, 3 inches in diameter	28, 49, 51
Suyo Long	81	Dark green fruits, 15 inches long	25, 47, 49
Oriental Eggplant			
Hybrid Nagaoka	78	Dark purple fruits, 4 inches long, 2 inches in diameter	49
Taiwan Long (Chinese)	80	Glossy, purple-black, fruit, 7 inches long, 1½ inches in diameter	49
Oriental Leaf Mustard			
Common Leaf	40	Looseleaf	49
Green-In-Snow	50	Looseleaf	49, 50

Variety	Days to Maturity	Description	Catalog Sources*
Dai, Gai Choy (Indian Mustard)	65	Semiheading	4, 49
Leaf Heading	45	Semiheading	49
Tendergreen	50	Looseleaf	49

Oriental Melons

Bitter melon

Hong Kong Bitter Melon	80	Fruits 5 inches long, dark green	49
Large Bitter Melon	80	Fruits tapering, 5 inches long, 2 inches in diameter	49

Oriental pickling melon

Oriental Pickling Melon	73	Fruits 12 inches long, 3 inches in diameter, with deep green stripes	49
Chinese Fuzzy Gourd	90	Squashlike, fruits small, heavy	49

Sponge gourd (Chinese okra)

Ridged Luffa	90	2 feet long, 8 or 10 ridges	49
Smooth Short Luffa	90	Round tube type, 6 pounds	49

Winter melon

Long Green and White Gourd	90	Cylindrical, 20 pounds	49
Small Wax Gourd	85	White flesh, 5 pounds	49

Oriental Radishes

All Season	45	18 inches long, 2⅕ inches in diameter, white skin, white flesh	27

(continued)

Variety	Days to Maturity	Description	Catalog Sources*
Oriental Radishes — Continued			
Chinese Rose Winter	52	7 inches long, 2 inches in diameter, red roots, white flesh	49
Crimson and Long	90	11 inches long, 2 inches in diameter, red skin, white flesh	49
Green Skin and Red Flesh	55	5 inches long, 4 inches in diameter, green skin and red flesh	49
Mino Early	58	16 inches long, 2 inches in diameter, white skin, white roots	49
Mino Spring Cross	53	16 inches long, 2 inches in diameter, white skin, white flesh	49
Shantung Green	50	10 inches long, 2 inches in diameter, green skin, green flesh	49
Winter King	55	16 inches long, 2 inches in diameter, white skin, white flesh	49

*Listings correspond to seed companies listed under Sources of Seeds and Supplies.

UNUSUAL VEGETABLES FOR ADVENTUROUS COOKS

These vegetables aren't for every gardener, but if you'd like to try something different, grow a few or all of these.

Cardoon. This relative of the globe artichoke is a big ornamental with deeply cut leaves. Cardoon is grown for its young leafstalks, which are blanched. Plant the seeds in late April, spaced 18 inches apart. In September, tie the leaves together in a bunch with paper or burlap, and mound up the soil to blanch the leafstalks. Cut off the blanched plants below the crown, trim off the outside leaves. Cut the heart into sections and parboil for an hour. Dress with oil and wine vinegar and serve chilled. The stalks can be dipped in batter and deep-fried until crispy. (Catalog sources: 8, 10, 29, 35, 41, 44; see Sources of Seeds and Supplies for addresses.)

Curly Mallow. An old-time salad plant, mallow makes a distinctive garnish in place of parsley. The leaves are frilled and have a mild flavor. Plant 18 inches apart. (Catalog source: 35.)

Florence Fennel. Florence fennel is a variety of common fennel that is grown for its bulblike base. Plant in the spring, spaced 6 inches apart. Pull the plant from the ground when the bulbous base measures 3 to 6 inches long. Don't separate the overlapping leaf stalk until ready to use. The bulbous base can be eaten raw, sliced and served in an antipasto tray. Or you can cut the stalks into slices and boil them in salted water, then serve with butter. (Catalog sources: 1, 2, 6, 8, 17, 26, 29, 30, 32, 33, 35, 36, 44, 45, 48, 50, 51, 52, 54, 57, 58.)

Horseradish. This root has found its way into cuisines around the world. Start it from cuttings. Set the small end down 2 to 3 inches below the soil surface. Space 12 inches apart. When the leaves are about a foot high, pull the soil back from the cuttings and remove all but one or two of the crown sprouts. At the same time, rub off the small roots that have started from the sides of the cuttings. Don't disturb the branch roots at the base. Replace the soil. Harvest in October or November. Peel and grate the root, and blend with sour cream to accompany roast pork. (Catalog sources: 2, 5, 12, 13, 17, 26, 29, 30, 36.)

Nasturtium. Plant seeds ½ inch deep and 4 to 10 inches apart. This plant grows almost anywhere, anytime during the growing season. The flowers can be used like a chip for cheese dip. The chopped leaves spice up a salad. The unripened seed pods are often pickled in vinegar. (Catalog sources: commonly available.)

Parsnips. Parsnips have a nutty flavor. Seeds are slow to germinate, taking 5 to 25 days. Sow 12 to 20 seeds per square foot and cover with clear plastic. Remove the plastic after the seeds have germinated. Thin seedlings to stand 4 inches apart. The roots grow 12 to 18 inches over 100 days. Parsnips should be parboiled or steamed in their skins, then peeled and sliced lengthwise. Mashed cooked parsnips can be shaped into round cakes and fried. Add peeled parsnips to a roast. They can also be cooked with a brown sugar glaze. (Catalog sources: 8, 10, 13, 18, 30, 32, 43, 48.)

Radicchio. A salad green of Italian origin, radicchio is now popular in gourmet markets and restaurants because of its sharp flavor. The dark red heads look like small cabbages. Sow 8 inches apart in May or June. Harvest in the fall before frost. Plants may bolt if they are sown too early. This is a good green for tossed salads. (Catalog sources: 35.)

Roquette. Also known as garden rocket, this plant has a hot, spicy taste. Sow seeds 4 to 5 inches apart in early spring. In hot weather, roquette goes to seed and becomes bitter. Make several sowings throughout the growing season. It can be used very young, at the four-leaf stage. Both the leaves and flowers make good additions to salads. (Catalog sources: 17, 35, 41.)

Salsify. The flavor of the salsify root has earned it the name oyster plant. Sow seeds ½ inch deep and about 2 inches apart as soon as the ground can be worked. Cover seeds with clear plastic until they sprout. Salsify roots will be ready to harvest in the fall. Oyster plant is good both raw with dips and cooked with sauces such as hollandaise. (Catalog sources: 1, 2, 6, 7, 10, 11, 12, 13, 26, 28, 29, 30, 32, 33, 34, 35, 43, 45, 48, 51, 57, 58.)

Scorzonera. The skin or scorzonera is black (it is also known as black salsify), but the flesh is white. The roots are long and cylindrical. Plant seeds ½ inch deep and 2 inches apart. Dig up the roots in the fall, or leave them in the ground to overwinter. Cut the roots into rounds or small cubes, then place them in cold water with 1 tablespoon of vinegar to prevent discoloration. Drain and use like salsify. (Catalog sources: 10, 17, 31, 35, 51.)

Sorrel. Sorrel is a perennial green relished throughout Europe. The leaves grow 8 to 16 inches long. Because it has creeping roots, sorrel is frequently grown in containers. Plant seeds 4 to 6 inches apart in early spring. The leaves have a lemony taste and are used to make a soup. You can also use them to wrap fresh fish and vegetables, and wake up salads. (Catalog sources: 15, 29, 30, 35, 46, 50, 51.)

Tyfon Holland Greens. This new green is a cross between turnips and Chinese cabbage. It has a mild, pleasant flavor. Plant 3 to 4 inches apart, and make cuttings at 30- to 40-day intervals. Cut when young and tender. Use in salads, or serve boiled greens with butter. (Catalog source: 35.)

HERBS

Herbs can be an integral part of the Vegetable Factory garden. They repel certain insects and have a beneficial effect on other plants. In addition, their flavors and aromas make them valuable to creative cooks.

Squeeze herbs in wherever you have a little space, or plant them to form a narrow border around part of your garden. For the most part, they like full sun. You can grow them in the ground or in containers scattered around the garden. Don't be afraid to pinch the shoots of most herbs regularly—after pinching, they just get stronger.

The varieties available are almost unlimited: the mints alone offer apple mint, Corsican mint, English mint, orange bergamot mint, pineapple mint, and dozens more. You also have a choice of pink rosemary, Santa Barbara rosemary, Tuscan blue rosemary, wood rosemary, and many others.

Herbs are annuals, biennials, or perennials. Annuals complete their life cycle in one year, while biennials produce seed the second season. Perennials grow year after year without having to be replanted. Many catalog seed firms carry some herbs. See Sources of Seeds and Supplies, page 241.

Herbs

Herb	Description	How to Grow	How to Harvest	Use	Catalog Source*
Anise	Lower leaves oval, serrated edges, small white flowers, low-spreading plant, 20 to 24 inches tall	Annual. Sow in place, thin to 6 to 8 inches, full sun	Pick leaves before flowers appear, harvest seeds 1 month after flowers bloom	Seeds in cookies, candy, meat, soup; leaves for stews, salads, meats	1, 2, 8, 10, 17, 25, 29, 30, 33, 35, 47, 48, 51, 52, 57, 58

Herb	Description	How to Grow	How to Harvest	Use	Catalog Source*
Basil	Leafy, light green foliage, spikelets of tiny flowers, 20 to 24 inches tall	Annual. Sow in place, thin to 6 to 8 inches, full sun	Harvest leaves when flowering begins; cut plants 4 to 6 inches above ground	Use leaves in tomato dishes, spaghetti sauce, soups, stews	2, 6, 7, 8, 12, 13, 17, 32, 36, 54, 57
Borage	Coarse, rough gray-green leaves, light blue flowers in clusters, 12 to 36 inches tall	Annual. Sow seeds in place, space 12 inches apart	Harvest young leaves before flowers open	Leaves in salads; flowers in soups, stews	2, 6, 7, 8, 13, 25, 29, 30, 33, 35, 36, 48, 51, 55, 57, 58
Caraway	Carrotlike leaves, creamy white, carrotlike flowers, 12 to 24 inches tall	Biennial. Sow seeds in place, space 12 inches apart	Harvest leaves when mature; seeds will form second season	Seeds in breads, cheese, cakes, salads; leaves for salads	6, 7, 8, 14, 17, 25, 26, 29, 32, 33, 35, 48, 51, 57
Chervil	Fernlike foliage turns pink in fall, small white flowers, 12 to 24 inches tall	Annual. Sow seeds 6 inches apart, keep soil moist, partial shade	Harvest leaves when mature and before flowers open	Fresh or dried leaves in salads, sauces, soups, poultry dishes	2, 8, 10, 25, 29, 35, 48, 50, 52, 57
Chives	Onionlike leaves, lavender flowers, 10 inches tall	Perennial. Grow from seeds or divide clumps, space 6 inches apart	Clip leaves close to ground	Salads, soups, eggs, sauces	1, 6, 7, 8, 11, 12, 17, 26, 29, 30, 32, 34, 35, 36, 45, 46, 48, 51, 52, 54, 57, 48

(continued)

Herb	Description	How to Grow	How to Harvest	Use	Catalog Source*
Coriander	Large, coarse plant, small flowers in clusters, to 36 inches tall	Annual. Sow seeds in place in early spring, thin to 6 to 7 inches apart	Pick leaves when plants are 4 to 6 inches tall, harvest seeds when they begin to turn brown	Fresh leaves in guacamole, shellfish; crushed seeds in pastries, sauces, curries, shellfish platters	1, 6, 8, 10, 11, 14, 18, 25, 29, 33, 34, 35, 48, 51, 54, 55, 58
Dill	Tall plants with light green, feathery flowers in open heads, 24 to 40 inches tall	Annual. Sow seeds in place in spring, thin to 12 inches apart	Pick leaves when flowers open, gather seeds when brown	Use slightly bitter seeds in pickles, salads, sauces, meats	2, 5, 7, 8, 10, 12, 14, 18, 26, 29, 33, 34, 35, 36, 40, 51, 54, 56
Marjoram	Small oval leaves, knot-like clusters of flowers, 12 to 24 inches tall	Perennial. Sow in place, or start inside and transplant when danger of frost is past	Pick leaves before flowers bloom	Leaves complement salads, eggs, pork, veal	2, 6, 7, 8, 10, 13, 25, 26, 29, 30, 35, 46, 47, 48, 55, 57
Mint (peppermint)	Bushy plant with purple flowers, 18 inches tall	Perennial. Start from root divisions or cuttings, space 8 to 10 inches apart	Cut sprigs or leaves frequently	In tea, jelly, sauces, summer drinks	8, 11, 18, 25, 29, 32, 35, 36, 48, 51, 55, 57

Herb	Description	How to Grow	How to Harvest	Use	Catalog Source*
Mint (spearmint)	Reddish stems, crinkled leaves, lavender flowers in spikes, 12 to 24 inches tall	Perennial. Start from root divisions or cuttings, space 8 to 10 inches apart	Cut sprigs or leaves frequently	Garnish on fresh fruits, in ices, summer drinks	6, 8, 13, 17, 26, 30, 35, 40, 45, 48, 50, 51, 57, 58
Oregano	Shrublike plant with dark leaves, pink flowers, 24 inches tall	Perennial. Start seeds indoors, or divide established plants	Gather leaves as needed	Dried or fresh in tomato sauces, beans, soups, roasts	2, 6, 8, 10, 11, 13, 17, 18, 25, 29, 30, 32, 33, 35, 36, 45, 48, 55
Parsley	Dark green, curled or plain leaves, 5 to 6 inches tall	Biennial. Soak seeds in warm water for 24 hours before planting, thin to 6 to 8 inches apart	Pick good-sized green leaves as needed	As garnish	6, 10, 25, 29, 30, 35, 44, 47, 48, 51, 54, 57
Rosemary	Needlelike, glossy green leaves, lavender-blue flowers 18 inches to 3 feet tall	Perennial. Propagate from slips or seeds	Gather leaves and sprigs as needed	Fresh or dried in lamb, pork, veal, sauces, soup	2, 6, 8, 10, 13, 26, 29, 30, 33, 35, 36, 48, 52, 55, 57, 58

(continued)

Herb	Description	How to Grow	How to Harvest	Use	Catalog Source*
Sage	Shrublike plant with gray leaves, purple flowers, 18 inches tall	Perennial. Start from seeds or stem cuttings, or divide plants; space 30 inches apart	Harvest leaves before flowering; cut flowering stems before blooms are gone	Fresh or dried in stuffings, rabbit, chicken, fish, other meats	2, 6, 8, 13, 17, 25, 26, 30, 32, 35, 36, 40, 45, 48, 51, 54, 55, 58
Summer Savory	Small gray-green leaves with purple and white flowers, 18 inches tall	Annual. Sow seeds in place after danger of frost is past, space 6 to 9 inches apart	Gather leaves anytime	In soups, salads, dressings, poultry dishes	2, 6, 7, 8, 10, 11, 17, 18, 26, 29, 30, 32, 33, 35, 48, 51, 55, 58
Tarragon (French)	Dark green leaves, clustered white flowers, 24 inches tall	Perennial. Start from root pieces, space 12 inches apart	Gather leaves before flower buds show	In fish, poultry, eggs, vegetables	2, 13, 17, 35, 36, 51, 58
Thyme	Small gray-green leaves, flowers in spikes, 8 to 10 inches tall	Perennial. Start from seeds or cuttings, space 10 to 12 inches apart	Clip off tops of plants in full leafy growth	In soups, salads, omelettes, vegetables	2, 6, 8, 10, 11, 13, 17, 26, 29, 30, 32, 33, 35, 45, 48, 54, 55

*Listings correspond to seed companies listed under Sources of Seeds and Supplies.

APPENDIXES

Appendix A

Average Date of Last Hard Freeze in Spring, First Hard Freeze in Fall

State	Last Spring Frost	First Fall Frost
Alaska		
Interior	June 15	Aug. 15
Coast	May 30	Sept. 30
Alabama		
North	Mar. 25	Oct. 30
South	Mar. 8	Nov. 15
Arizona		
North	Apr. 23	Oct. 19
South	Mar. 1	Dec. 1
Arkansas		
North	Apr. 7	Oct. 23
South	Mar. 25	Nov. 3
California		
Central Valley	Mar. 1	Nov. 15
Imperial Valley	Jan. 30	Dec. 20
North Coast	Feb. 28	Dec. 1
South Coast	Jan. 30	Dec. 15
Mountain	Apr. 20	Sept. 1
Colorado		
West	May 30	Sept. 15
Northeast	May 10	Sept. 30
Southeast	Apr. 30	Oct. 10
Connecticut	Apr. 28	Oct. 10
Delaware	Apr. 15	Oct. 20
Florida		
North	Feb. 20	Nov. 30
Central	Jan. 30	Dec. 20
South	No frost	

(continued)

State	Last Spring Frost	First Fall Frost
Hawaii	No frost	
Georgia		
North	Mar. 30	Nov. 10
South	Mar. 10	Nov. 20
Idaho	May 30	Sept. 25
Illinois		
North	Apr. 30	Oct. 10
South	Apr. 10	Oct. 20
Indiana		
North	Apr. 30	Oct. 10
South	Apr. 20	Oct. 20
Iowa		
North	May 1	Oct. 1
South	Apr. 30	Oct. 10
Kansas		
Northwest	Apr. 30	Oct. 10
Southeast	Apr. 10	Oct. 20
Kentucky	Apr. 20	Oct. 20
Louisiana		
North	Mar. 20	Nov. 20
South	Feb. 8	Dec. 10
Maine		
North	May 30	Sept. 20
South	May 10	Oct. 10
Maryland	Apr. 20	Oct. 20
Massachusetts	Apr. 25	Oct. 25
Michigan		
Upper Peninsula	May 30	Sept. 20
North	May 20	Sept. 25
South	May 10	Oct. 10

State	Last Spring Frost	First Fall Frost
Minnesota		
North	May 30	Sept. 10
South	May 10	Sept. 30
Mississippi		
North	Mar. 30	Oct. 30
South	Mar. 10	Oct. 20
Missouri	Apr. 20	Oct. 20
Montana	May 20	Sept. 20
Nebraska		
East	Apr. 30	Oct. 10
West	May 10	Sept. 30
Nevada		
North	May 30	Sept. 5
South	Apr. 15	Nov. 10
New Hampshire	May 20	Sept. 20
New Jersey	Apr. 20	Oct. 20
New Mexico		
North	Apr. 30	Oct. 10
South	Apr. 1	Oct. 30
New York		
East	May 1	Oct. 10
West	May 10	Oct. 5
North	May 20	Sept. 30
North Carolina		
Northeast	Apr. 10	Nov. 1
Southeast	Mar. 30	Nov. 30
North Dakota	May 20	Sept. 20
Ohio		
North	May 10	Sept. 20
South	Apr. 20	Sept. 30
Oklahoma	Apr. 1	Oct. 30

(continued)

Average Date of Last Hard Freeze in Spring, First Hard Freeze in Fall — *Continued*

State	Last Spring Frost	First Fall Frost
Oregon		
West	Apr. 20	Oct. 30
East	May 30	Sept. 10
Pennsylvania		
West	Apr. 20	Oct. 20
East	May 10	Sept. 20
Rhode Island	Apr. 20	Oct. 20
South Carolina		
Southeast	Mar. 10	Nov. 10
Northwest	Mar. 20	Nov. 20
South Dakota	May 10	Sept. 30
Tennessee	Apr. 10	Oct. 30
Texas		
Northwest	Apr. 20	Oct. 30
Northeast	Mar. 20	Nov. 20
South	Feb. 5	Dec. 10
Utah		
North	May 30	Sept. 30
South	Apr. 30	Apr. 10
Vermont	May 20	Sept. 30
Virginia		
North	Apr. 20	Oct. 10
South	Apr. 10	Oct. 20
Washington		
West	Apr. 20	Oct. 30
East	May 20	Sept. 30
West Virginia	May 5	Oct. 10
Wisconsin		
North	May 20	Sept. 20
South	May 10	Oct. 10
Wyoming		
West	June 20	Aug. 20
East	May 30	Sept. 30

Appendix B

Earliest Dates, and Range of Dates, for Safe Spring Planting of Vegetables in the Open

Crop	Planting Dates for Localities in Which Average Date of Last Freeze Is —						
	Jan. 30	Feb. 8	Feb. 18	Feb. 28	Mar. 10	Mar. 20	Mar. 30
Asparagus*	—	—	—	—	Jan. 1-Mar. 1	Feb. 1-Mar. 10	Feb. 15-Mar. 20
Beans, lima	Feb. 1-Apr. 15	Feb. 10-May 1	Mar. 1-May 1	Mar. 15-June 1	Mar. 20-June 1	Apr. 1-June 15	Apr. 15-June 20
Beans, snap	Feb. 1-Apr. 1	Feb. 1-May 1	Mar. 1-May 1	Mar. 10-May 15	Mar. 15-May 25	Mar. 15-May 25	Apr. 1-June 1
Beet	Jan. 1-Mar. 15	Jan. 10-Mar. 15	Jan. 20-Apr. 1	Feb. 1-Apr. 15	Feb. 15-June 1	Feb. 15-May 15	Apr. 1-June 1
Broccoli, sprouting*	Jan. 1-30	Jan. 1-30	Jan 15-Feb. 15	Feb. 1-Mar. 1	Feb. 15-Mar. 15	Feb. 15-Mar. 15	Mar. 1-20
Brussels sprouts*	Jan. 1-30	Jan. 1-30	Jan. 15-Feb. 15	Feb. 1-Mar. 1	Feb. 15-Mar. 15	Feb. 15-Mar. 15	Mar. 1-20
Cabbage*	Jan. 1-15	Jan. 1-Feb. 10	Jan. 1-Feb. 25	Jan 15-Feb. 25	Jan. 25-Mar. 1	Feb. 1-Mar. 1	Feb. 15-Mar. 10
Cabbage, Chinese	(†)	(†)	(†)	(†)	(†)	(†)	(†)
Carrot	Jan. 1-Mar. 1	Jan. 1-Mar. 1	Jan. 15-Mar. 1	Feb. 1-Mar. 1	Feb. 10-Mar. 1	Feb. 15-Mar. 20	Mar. 1-Apr. 10
Cauliflower*	Jan. 1-Feb. 1	Jan. 1-Feb. 1	Jan. 10-Feb. 10	Jan. 20-Feb. 20	Feb. 1-Mar. 1	Feb. 10-Mar. 10	Feb. 20-Mar. 20
Celery and celeriac	Jan. 1-Feb. 1	Jan. 10-Feb. 10	Jan. 20-Feb. 20	Feb. 1-Mar. 1	Feb. 20-Mar. 1	Mar. 1-Apr. 1	Mar. 15-Apr. 15
Chervil and chives	Jan. 1-Feb. 1	Jan. 1-Feb. 1	Jan 1-Feb. 1	Jan. 15-Feb. 15	Feb. 1-Mar. 1	Feb. 10-Mar. 10	Feb. 15-Mar. 15
Chicory, witloof	—	—	—	—	June 1-July 1	June 1-July 1	June 1-July 1
Collards*	Jan. 1-Feb. 15	Jan. 1-Feb. 15	Jan. 1-Mar. 15	Jan. 15-Mar. 15	Feb. 1-Apr. 1	Feb. 15-May 1	Mar. 1-June 1
Corn salad	Jan. 1-Feb. 15	Jan. 1-Feb. 15	Jan. 1-Mar. 15	Jan. 1-Mar. 15	Jan. 1-Apr. 1	Jan. 1-May 15	Jan. 15-Mar. 15
Corn, sweet	Feb. 1-Mar. 15	Feb. 10-Apr. 1	Feb. 20-Apr. 15	Mar. 1-Apr. 15	Mar. 10-Apr. 15	Mar. 15-May 1	Mar. 25-May 15
Cress, upland	Jan. 1-Feb. 1	Jan. 1-Feb. 15	Jan. 15-Feb. 15	Jan. 15-Feb. 15	Feb. 10-Mar. 15	Feb. 20-Mar. 15	Mar. 1-Apr. 1
Cucumber	Feb. 15-Mar. 15	Feb. 15-Apr. 15	Feb. 15-Apr. 15	Mar. 1-Apr. 15	Mar. 15-Apr. 15	Apr. 1-May 1	Apr. 10-May 15
Eggplant*	Feb. 1-Mar. 1	Feb. 10-Mar. 15	Feb. 20-Apr. 1	Mar. 10-Apr. 15	Mar. 15-Apr. 15	Apr. 1-May 1	Apr. 15-May 15
Endive	Jan. 1-Mar. 1	Jan. 1-Mar. 1	Jan. 1-Mar. 1	Feb. 1-Mar. 1	Feb. 15-Mar. 15	Mar. 1-Apr. 1	Mar. 10-Apr. 10
Fennel, Florence	Jan. 1-Mar. 1	Jan. 1-Mar. 1	Jan. 15-Mar. 1	Feb. 1-Mar. 1	Feb. 15-Mar. 15	Mar. 1-Apr. 1	Mar. 10-Apr. 10
Garlic	(†)	(†)	(†)	(†)	(†)	Feb. 1-Mar. 1	Feb. 10-Mar. 10
Horseradish*	—	—	—	—	—	—	Mar. 1-Apr. 1
Kale	Jan. 1-Feb. 1	Jan. 10-Feb. 1	Jan. 20-Feb. 10	Feb. 1-20	Feb. 10-Mar. 1	Feb. 20-Mar. 10	Mar. 1-20
Kohlrabi	Jan. 1-Feb. 1	Jan. 10-Feb. 1	Jan. 20-Feb. 10	Feb. 1-20	Feb. 10-Mar. 1	Feb. 20-Mar. 10	Mar. 1-Apr. 1
Leek	Jan. 1-Feb. 1	Jan. 1-Feb. 1	Jan. 1-Feb. 1	Jan. 15-Feb. 15	Jan. 25-Mar. 1	Feb. 1-Mar. 1	Feb. 15-Mar. 15
Lettuce, head*	Jan. 1-Feb. 1	Jan. 1-Feb. 1	Jan. 1-Feb. 1	Jan. 15-Feb. 15	Feb. 1-20	Feb. 15-Mar. 10	Mar. 1-20
Lettuce, leaf	Jan. 1-Feb. 1	Jan. 1-Feb. 1	Jan. 1-Mar. 15	Jan. 1-Mar. 15	Jan. 15-Apr. 1	Feb. 1-Apr. 1	Feb. 15-Apr. 15
Muskmelon	Feb. 15-Mar. 15	Feb. 15-Apr. 15	Feb. 15-Apr. 15	Mar. 1-Apr. 15	Mar. 15-Apr. 15	Apr. 1-May 1	Apr. 10-May 15
Mustard	Jan. 1-Mar. 1	Jan. 1-Mar. 1	Jan. 1-Mar. 1	Feb. 1-Mar. 1	Feb. 10-Mar. 1	Feb. 20-Apr. 1	Mar. 1-Apr. 1
Okra	Feb. 15-Apr. 1	Feb. 15-Apr. 15	Mar. 1-June 1	Mar. 10-June 1	Mar. 20-June 1	Apr. 1-June 15	Apr. 10-June 15
Onion*	Jan. 1-15	Jan. 1-15	Jan. 1-15	Jan. 1-Feb. 15	Jan. 15-Feb. 15	Feb. 15-Mar. 15	Feb. 15-Mar. 15
Onion, seed	Jan. 1-15	Jan. 1-15	Jan. 1-15	Jan. 1-Feb. 15	Jan. 15-Feb. 15	Feb. 10-Mar. 10	Feb. 20-Mar. 15
Onion, sets	Jan. 1-15	Jan. 1-15	Jan. 1-15	Jan. 1-Mar. 1	Jan. 15-Mar. 1	Feb. 1-Mar. 1	Feb. 15-Mar. 15
Parsley	Jan. 1-30	Jan. 1-30	Jan. 1-30	Jan. 1-Mar. 1	Jan. 15-Mar. 1	Feb. 1-Mar. 20	Mar. 1-Apr. 1
Parsnip	—	—	Jan. 1-Feb. 1	Jan. 15-Feb. 15	Jan. 15-Mar. 1	Feb. 1-Mar. 1	Feb. 15-Mar. 15
Peas, black-eye	Feb. 15-May 1	Feb. 15-May 15	Mar. 1-June 15	Mar. 10-June 20	Mar. 15-July 1	Apr. 1-July 1	Apr. 15-July 1
Peas, garden	Jan. 1-Feb. 15	Jan. 1-Feb. 15	Jan. 1-Mar. 1	Jan. 15-Mar. 1	Jan. 15-Mar. 15	Feb. 1-Mar. 15	Feb. 10-Mar. 20

(continued)

SOURCE: *Growing Vegetables in Home Gardens* (Washington, D.C.: U.S. Department of Agriculture).

Earliest Dates, and Range of Dates, for Safe Spring Planting of Vegetables in the Open—Continued

Crop	Planting Dates for Localities in Which Average Date of Last Freeze Is—						
	Jan. 30	Feb. 8	Feb. 18	Feb. 28	Mar. 10	Mar. 20	Mar. 30
Pepper*	Feb. 1-Apr. 1	Feb. 15-Apr. 15	Mar. 1-May 1	Mar. 15-May 1	Apr. 1-June 1	Apr. 10-June 1	Apr. 15-June 1
Potato	Jan. 1-Feb. 15	Jan. 1-Feb. 15	Jan. 15-Mar. 1	Jan. 15-Mar. 1	Feb. 1-Mar. 1	Feb. 15-Mar. 1	Feb. 20-Mar. 20
Radish	Jan. 1-Apr. 1	Jan. 1-Apr. 1	Jan. 1-Apr. 1	Jan. 1-Apr. 1	Jan. 1-Apr. 15	Jan. 20-May 1	Feb. 15-May 1
Rhubarb*	—	—	—	—	—	—	—
Rutabaga	Jan. 1-Feb. 1	Jan. 10-Feb. 10	Jan. 15-Feb. 20	Jan. 15-Mar. 1	Jan. 15-Mar. 1	Jan. 15-Mar. 1	Feb. 1-Mar. 1
Salsify	Jan. 1-Feb. 1	Jan. 1-Feb. 10	Jan. 15-Feb. 20	Jan. 15-Mar. 1	Feb. 1-Mar. 1	Jan. 15-Mar. 10	Mar. 1-15
Shallot	Jan. 1-Feb. 1	Jan. 1-Mar. 1	Jan. 15-Mar. 1	Jan. 1-Mar. 1	Jan. 15-Mar. 1	Feb. 1-Mar. 10	Feb. 15-Mar. 15
Sorrel	Jan. 1-Mar. 1	Jan. 1-Mar. 1	Jan. 15-Mar. 1	Jan. 15-Mar. 1	Feb. 1-Mar. 10	Feb. 10-Mar. 20	Feb. 20-Apr. 1
Soybean	Mar. 1-June 30	Mar. 1-June 30	Mar. 10-June 30	Mar. 20-June 30	Apr. 10-June 30	Apr. 10-June 30	Apr. 20-June 30
Spinach	Jan. 1-Feb. 15	Jan. 1-Feb. 15	Jan. 1-Mar. 1	Jan. 1-Mar. 1	Jan. 15-Mar. 10	Jan. 15-Mar. 15	Feb. 1-Mar. 20
Spinach, New Zealand	Feb. 1-Apr. 15	Feb. 1-Apr. 15	Mar. 1-Apr. 15	Mar. 15-May 15	Mar. 15-May 15	Apr. 1-May 15	Apr. 10-June 1
Squash, summer	Feb. 1-Apr. 15	Feb. 15-Apr. 15	Mar. 1-Apr. 15	Mar. 15-May 1	Mar. 20-May 15	Apr. 10-June 1	Apr. 10-June 1
Sweet potato	Feb. 15-May 15	Feb. 15-May 15	Mar. 1-May 15	Mar. 20-June 1	Apr. 1-May 20	Apr. 10-June 1	Apr. 20-June 1
Swiss chard	Jan. 1-Apr. 1	Jan. 10-Apr. 1	Jan. 20-Apr. 15	Feb. 1-May 1	Feb. 20-May 10	Mar. 1-May 20	Mar. 1-May 25
Tomato	Feb. 1-Apr. 1	Feb. 20-Apr. 10	Mar. 1-Apr. 20	Mar. 10-May 1	Mar. 20-May 10	Apr. 1-May 20	Apr. 10-June 1
Turnip	Jan. 1-Mar. 1	Jan. 1-Mar. 1	Jan. 10-Mar. 1	Jan. 20-Mar. 1	Feb. 1-Mar. 1	Feb. 10-Mar. 10	Feb. 20-Mar. 20
Watermelon	Feb. 15-Mar. 15	Feb. 15-Mar. 15	Mar. 15-Apr. 15	Mar. 15-May 15	Mar. 15-Apr. 15	Apr. 1-May 1	Apr. 10-May 15

Crop	Planting Dates for Localities in Which Average Date of Last Freeze Is—						
	Apr. 10	Apr. 20	Apr. 30	May 10	May 20	May 30	June 10
Asparagus*	Mar. 10-Apr. 10	Mar. 15-Apr. 15	Mar. 20-Apr. 15	Apr. 10-Apr. 30	Apr. 20-May 15	Apr. 20-May 15	May 15-June 1
Beans, lima	Apr. 1-June 30	May 1-June 20	May 15-June 15	May 25-June 15	—	—	—
Beans, snap	Apr. 10-June 30	Apr. 25-June 30	May 10-June 30	May 10-June 30	May 15-June 30	May 25-June 15	May 15-June 15
Beet	Mar. 10-June 1	Mar. 20-June 1	Apr. 1-June 15	Apr. 15-June 15	Apr. 25-June 15	May 1-June 15	May 20-June 10
Broccoli, sprouting*	Mar. 15-Apr. 15	Mar. 25-Apr. 20	Apr. 1-May 1	Apr. 15-June 1	May 1-June 15	May 10-June 15	May 20-June 10
Brussels sprouts*	Mar. 15-Apr. 15	Mar. 25-Apr. 20	Apr. 1-May 1	Apr. 15-June 1	May 1-June 15	May 10-June 15	May 20-June 10
Cabbage*	Mar. 1-Apr. 1	Mar. 10-Apr. 1	Mar. 15-Apr. 10	Apr. 1-May 15	May 1-June 15	May 10-June 15	May 20-June 1
Cabbage, Chinese	(†)	(†)	(†)	Apr. 1-May 15	May 1-June 15	May 10-June 15	May 20-June 1
Carrot	Mar. 10-Apr. 20	Apr. 1-May 15	Apr. 10-June 1	Apr. 20-June 15	May 1-June 1	May 10-June 1	May 20-June 1
Cauliflower*	Mar. 1-Mar. 20	Mar. 15-Apr. 20	Apr. 15-May 10	Apr. 15-May 15	May 10-June 15	May 20-June 1	June 1-15
Celery and celeriac	Apr. 1-Apr. 20	Apr. 10-May 1	Apr. 15-May 1	Apr. 20-June 15	May 10-June 15	May 20-June 1	June 1-15
Chervil and chives	Mar. 1-Apr. 1	Mar. 10-Apr. 10	Mar. 20-Apr. 20	Apr. 1-May 1	Apr. 15-May 15	May 1-June 1	May 15-June 1
Chicory, witloof	June 10-July 1	June 15-July 1	June 15-July 1	June 1-20	June 1-15	June 1-15	June 1-15
Collards*	Mar. 1-June 1	Mar. 10-June 1	Apr. 1-June 1	Apr. 15-June 1	May 1-June 1	May 10-June 15	May 20-June 1
Corn salad	Feb. 1-Apr. 1	Feb. 10-Apr. 1	Mar. 1-May 1	Apr. 1-June 1	Apr. 15-June 1	May 10-June 15	May 15-June 15
Corn, sweet	Apr. 10-June 1	Apr. 25-June 15	May 10-June 15	May 10-June 15	May 15-June 1	May 20-June 1	May 20-June 1
Cress, upland	Mar. 10-Apr. 15	Mar. 20-May 1	Apr. 10-May 10	Apr. 20-May 20	May 1-June 1	May 1-June 1	—
Cucumber	Apr. 20-June 1	May 1-June 15	May 15-June 15	May 20-June 15	June 1-15	June 1-15	May 15-June 15

Planting Dates for Localities in Which Average Date of Last Freeze Is—

Crop	Apr. 10	Apr. 20	Apr. 30	May 10	May 20	May 30	June 10
Eggplant*	May 1-June 1	May 10-June 1	May 15-June 10	May 20-June 15	June 1-15	—	—
Endive	Mar. 15-Apr. 15	Mar. 25-Apr. 15	Apr. 1-May 1	Apr. 15-May 15	Apr. 20-May 20	May 1-30	May 15-June 1
Fennel, Florence	Mar. 15-Apr. 15	Mar. 25-Apr. 15	Apr. 1-May 1	Apr. 15-May 15	Apr. 20-May 20	May 1-30	May 15-June 1
Garlic	Feb. 20-Mar. 20	Mar. 10-Apr. 1	Mar. 15-Apr. 15	Apr. 1-May 1	Apr. 15-May 15	May 1-30	May 15-June 1
Horseradish*	Mar. 10-Apr. 10	Mar. 20-Apr. 20	Apr. 1-30	Apr. 15-May 15	Apr. 20-May 20	May 1-30	May 15-June 1
Kale	Mar. 10-Apr. 1	Mar. 20-Apr. 10	Apr. 1-20	Apr. 10-May 1	Apr. 20-May 10	May 1-30	May 15-June 1
Kohlrabi	Mar. 10-Apr. 10	Mar. 20-May 1	Apr. 1-May 10	Apr. 10-May 15	Apr. 20-May 20	May 1-30	May 15-June 1
Leek	Mar. 1-Apr. 1	Mar. 15-Apr. 15	Apr. 1-May 1	Apr. 15-May 15	May 1-May 20	May 1-15	May 1-15
Lettuce, head*	Mar. 10-Apr. 1	Mar. 20-Apr. 10	Apr. 1-May 1	Apr. 15-May 15	May 1-May 30	May 10-June 30	May 20-June 30
Lettuce, leaf	Mar. 15-May 15	Mar. 20-May 1	Apr. 1-May 1	Apr. 15-May 15	May 1-June 30	May 10-June 30	May 20-June 30
Muskmelon	Apr. 20-June 1	May 1-June 15	May 15-June 15	June 1-June 15	June 1-15	—	—
Mustard	Mar. 10-Apr. 20	Mar. 20-May 1	Apr. 1-May 10	Apr. 15-May 15	May 1-June 30	May 10-June 30	May 20-June 30
Okra	Apr. 20-June 15	May 1-June 1	May 10-June 1	May 20-June 20	June 1-20	—	—
Onion*	Mar. 1-Apr. 1	Mar. 15-Apr. 10	Apr. 1-May 1	Apr. 10-May 1	Apr. 20-May 15	May 1-30	May 10-June 10
Onion, seed	Mar. 1-Apr. 1	Mar. 15-Apr. 1	Mar. 15-Apr. 15	Apr. 1-May 1	Apr. 20-May 15	May 1-30	May 10-June 10
Onion, sets	Mar. 1-Apr. 1	Mar. 15-May 1	Mar. 15-Apr. 15	Apr. 10-May 1	Apr. 20-May 15	May 1-30	May 10-June 10
Parsley	Mar. 10-Apr. 10	Mar. 20-Apr. 20	Apr. 1-May 1	Apr. 15-May 15	May 1-20	May 10-June 1	May 20-June 10
Parsnip	Mar. 10-Apr. 10	Mar. 20-Apr. 20	Apr. 1-May 1	Apr. 15-May 15	May 1-20	May 10-June 1	May 20-June 10
Peas, back-eye	May 1-July 1	May 10-June 15	May 15-June 1	—	—	—	—
Peas, garden	Feb. 20-Mar. 20	Mar. 10-Apr. 10	Mar. 20-May 1	Apr. 1-May 15	May 1-June 1	May 1-June 15	May 10-June 15
Pepper*	May 1-June 1	May 10-June 10	May 15-June 10	May 20-June 10	May 25-June 15	June 1-15	—
Potato	Mar. 10-Apr. 1	Mar. 15-Apr. 10	Mar. 20-May 10	Apr. 1-June 1	Apr. 15-June 1	May 1-June 15	May 15-June 1
Radish	Mar. 1-May 1	Mar. 15-May 1	Mar. 20-May 10	Apr. 1-June 1	Apr. 15-June 15	May 1-June 15	May 15-June 1
Rhubarb*	Mar. 1-Apr. 1	Mar. 15-Apr. 15	Mar. 20-Apr. 15	Apr. 15-May 1	Apr. 15-May 10	May 1-20	May 15-June 1
Rutabaga	—	May 10-June 20	May 15-June 15	May 1-June 1	May 1-20	May 10-20	May 20-June 1
Salsify	Mar. 10-Apr. 15	Mar. 20-May 1	Apr. 1-May 15	Apr. 15-June 1	May 1-June 1	May 10-June 1	May 20-June 1
Shallot	Mar. 1-Apr. 1	Mar. 15-Apr. 15	Apr. 1-May 1	Apr. 15-June 1	Apr. 20-June 1	May 1-June 1	May 1-June 1
Sorrel	Mar. 1-Apr. 15	Mar. 15-May 1	Apr. 1-May 15	Apr. 15-June 1	May 1-June 1	May 10-June 10	May 1-June 1
Soybean	May 1-June 30	May 10-June 20	May 15-June 15	May 25-June 10	May 20-June 15	May 20-June 10	May 20-June 10
Spinach	Feb. 15-Apr. 1	Mar. 1-Apr. 15	Mar. 20-Apr. 20	Apr. 1-June 15	Apr. 10-June 15	Apr. 20-June 15	May 1-June 15
Spinach, New Zealand	Apr. 20-June 1	May 1-June 15	May 15-June 15	May 10-June 15	May 20-June 15	June 1-15	—
Squash, summer	Apr. 20-June 1	May 1-June 15	May 1-30	May 10-June 10	May 20-June 15	June 1-20	June 10-20
Sweet potato	May 1-June 1	May 10-June 10	May 20-June 10	—	—	—	—
Swiss chard	Mar. 15-June 15	Apr. 1-June 15	Apr. 15-June 15	Apr. 20-June 15	May 10-June 15	May 20-June 15	June 1-June 15
Tomato	Mar. 1-Apr. 1	May 5-June 10	May 10-June 15	May 15-June 10	May 25-June 15	June 5-20	June 15-30
Turnip	Mar. 1-Apr. 1	Mar. 10-Apr. 1	Mar. 20-May 1	Apr. 1-June 1	Apr. 15-June 1	May 1-June 15	May 15-June 15
Watermelon	Apr. 20-June 1	May 1-June 15	May 15-June 15	June 1-June 15	June 15-July 1	—	—

*Transplants.
†Generally fall planted.

Appendix C

Latest Dates, and Range of Dates, for Safe Fall Planting of Vegetables in the Open

Crop	Planting Dates for Localities in Which Average Date of First Freeze Is—					
	Aug. 30	Sept. 10	Sept. 20	Sept. 30	Oct. 10	Oct. 20
Asparagus*	—	—	—	—	Oct. 20-Nov. 15	Nov. 1-Dec. 15
Beans, lima	—	—	—	June 1-15	June 1-15	June 15-30
Beans, snap	—	May 15-June 15	June 1-July 1	June 1-July 10	June 15-July 20	July 1-Aug. 1
Beet	May 15-June 15	May 15-June 15	June 1-July 1	June 1-July 10	June 15-July 25	July 1-Aug. 5
Broccoli, sprouting	May 1-June 1	May 1-June 1	May 1-June 15	June 1-30	June 15-July 15	July 1-Aug. 1
Brussels sprouts	May 1-June 1	May 1-June 1	May 1-June 15	June 1-30	June 15-July 15	July 1-Aug. 1
Cabbage*	May 1-June 1	May 1-June 1	May 1-June 15	June 1-July 10	June 1-July 15	July 1-20
Cabbage, Chinese	May 15-June 15	May 15-June 15	June 1-July 1	June 1-July 15	June 15-Aug. 1	June 15-Aug. 15
Carrot	May 15-June 15	May 15-June 15	June 1-July 1	June 1-July 10	June 1-July 20	July 1-Aug. 1
Cauliflower*	May 1-June 1	May 1-June 1	May 1-July 1	May 10-July 15	June 1-July 25	July 1-Aug. 5
Celery* and celeriac	May 1-June 1	May 1-June 15	May 15-July 1	June 1-July 5	June 1-July 15	June 1-Aug. 1
Chervil and chives	May 10-June 10	May 15-June 15	May 15-June 15	(†)	(†)	(†)
Chicory, witloof	May 15-June 15	May 15-June 15	May 15-June 15	June 1-July 1	July 1-Aug. 1	July 15-Aug. 15
Collards*	May 15-June 15	May 15-June 15	May 15-June 15	July 15-Sept. 1	Aug. 15-Sept. 15	Sept. 1-Oct. 15
Corn salad	May 15-July 1	May 15-July 1	June 1-Aug. 1	June 1-July 1	June 1-July 10	June 1-July 20
Corn, sweet	—	—	June 1-July 1	July 15-Sept. 1	Aug. 15-Sept. 15	Sept. 1-Oct. 15
Cress, upland	May 15-June 15	May 15-July 1	June 15-Aug. 1	June 1-July 1	June 1-July 1	June 1-July 1
Cucumber	—	—	June 1-15	May 20-June 10	May 15-June 15	June 1-July 15
Eggplant*	—	—	—	June 15-Aug. 1	May 15-June 15	July 15-Sept. 1
Endive	June 1-July 1	June 1-July 1	June 15-July 15	June 15-Aug. 1	July 1-Aug. 15	July 15-Sept. 1
Fennel, Florence	May 15-June 15	May 15-July 15	June 1-July 1	June 1-Aug. 1	June 15-July 15	June 15-Aug. 1
Garlic	(†)	(†)	(†)	(†)	(†)	(†)
Horseradish*	(†)	(†)	(†)	(†)	(†)	(†)
Kale	May 15-June 15	May 15-June 15	June 1-July 1	June 15-July 15	July 1-Aug. 1	July 15-Aug. 15
Kohlrabi	May 15-June 15	June 1-July 1	June 1-July 15	June 15-July 15	July 1-Aug. 1	July 15-Aug. 15
Leek	May 1-June 1	May 1-June 1	(†)	(†)	(†)	(†)
Lettuce, head*	May 15-July 15	May 15-July 15	June 1-July 15	June 15-Aug. 1	July 15-Aug. 15	July 15-Sept. 1
Lettuce, leaf	May 15-July 15	May 15-July 15	June 1-Aug. 1	June 1-Aug. 1	July 15-Sept. 1	June 15-July 20
Muskmelon	—	—	May 1-June 15	May 15-June 1	June 1-June 15	Aug. 1-Sept. 1
Mustard	May 15-July 15	May 15-July 15	June 1-Aug. 1	June 15-Aug. 1	June 15-Aug. 15	June 1-Aug. 1
Okra	—	—	June 1-20	June 1-July 1	June 1-July 15	June 1-Aug. 1
Onion*	May 1-June 10	May 1-June 10	(†)	(†)	(†)	(†)
Onion, seed	May 1-June 1	May 1-June 1	(†)	(†)	(†)	(†)
Onion, sets	May 1-June 1	May 1-June 1	(†)	(†)	(†)	(†)
Parsley	May 15-June 15	May 15-June 15	June 1-July 1	June 1-July 15	June 15-Aug. 1	July 15-Aug. 15
Parsnip	May 15-June 1	May 15-June 1	May 15-June 15	June 1-July 1	June 1-July 10	June 1-July 1
Peas, black-eye	—	—	—	—	June 1-July 1	June 1-July 1
Peas, garden	May 10-June 15	May 1-July 1	June 1-July 15	June 1-Aug. 1	(†)	(†)

234

Planting Dates for Localities in Which Average Date of First Freeze Is—

Crop	Aug. 30	Sept. 10	Sept. 20	Sept. 30	Oct. 10	Oct. 20
Pepper*	—	—	June 1-June 20	June 1-July 1	June 1-July 1	June 1-July 10
Potato	May 15-June 1	May 1-June 15	May 1-June 15	May 1-July 1	May 15-June 15	June 15-July 15
Radish	May 1-July 15	May 1-Aug. 1	June 1-Aug. 15	July 1-Sept. 1	July 15-Sept. 15	Aug. 1-Oct. 1
Rhubarb*	Sept. 1-Oct. 1	Sept. 15-Oct. 15	Sept. 15-Nov. 1	Oct. 1-Nov. 1	Oct. 15-Nov. 15	Oct. 15-Dec. 1
Rutabaga	May 15-June 15	May 1-June 15	June 1-July 1	June 1-July 1	June 15-July 15	July 10-20
Salsify	May 15-June 1	May 10-June 10	May 20-June 20	June 1-20	June 1-July 1	June 1-July 1
Shallot	(†)	(†)	(†)	(†)	(†)	(†)
Sorrel	May 15-June 15	May 1-June 15	June 1-July 1	June 1-July 15	July 1-Aug. 1	July 15-Aug. 15
Soybean	—	—	—	May 25-June 10	June 1-25	June 1-July 5
Spinach	May 15-July 1	June 1-July 15	June 1-Aug. 1	July 1-Aug. 15	Aug. 1-Sept. 1	Aug. 20-Sept.10
Spinach, New Zealand	—	—	—	May 15-July 1	June 1-July 15	June 1-Aug. 1
Squash, summer	June 10-20	June 1-20	May 15-July 1	June 1-July 1	June 1-July 15	June 1-July 20
Squash, winter	—	—	May 20-June 10	June 1-15	June 1-July 1	June 1-July 1
Sweet potato	—	—	—	—	May 20-June 10	June 1-15
Swiss chard	May 15-June 15	May 15-July 1	June 1-July 1	June 1-July 5	June 1-July 20	June 1-Aug. 1
Tomato	June 20-30	June 10-20	June 1-20	June 1-20	June 1-20	June 1-Aug. 1
Turnip	May 15-June 15	June 1-July 15	June 1-July 15	June 1-Aug. 1	July 1-Aug. 1	July 15-Aug. 15
Watermelon	—	June 1-July 1	May 1-June 15	May 15-June 1	June 1-June 15	June 15-July 20

Planting Dates for Localities in Which Average Date of First Freeze Is—

Crop	Oct. 30	Nov. 10	Nov. 20	Nov. 30	Dec. 10	Dec. 20
Asparagus*	Nov. 15-Jan. 1	Dec. 1-Jan. 1	—	—	—	—
Beans, lima	July 1-Aug. 1	July 1-Aug. 15	July 15-Sept. 1	Aug. 1-Sept. 15	Sept. 1-30	Sept. 1-Oct. 1
Beans, snap	July 1-Aug. 15	July 1-Sept. 1	July 1-Sept. 10	Aug. 15-Sept. 20	Sept. 1-30	Sept. 1-Nov. 1
Beet	Aug. 1-Sept. 1	Aug. 1-Oct. 1	Sept. 1-Dec. 1	Sept. 1-Dec. 15	Sept. 1-Dec. 31	Sept. 1-Dec. 31
Broccoli, sprouting	July 1-Aug. 15	Aug. 1-Sept. 1	Aug. 1-Sept. 15	Aug. 1-Oct. 1	Aug. 1-Nov. 1	Sept. 1-Dec. 31
Brussels sprouts	July 1-Aug. 15	Aug. 1-Sept. 1	Aug. 1-Sept. 15	Aug. 1-Oct. 1	Aug. 1-Nov. 1	Sept. 1-Dec. 31
Cabbage*	Aug. 1-Sept. 1	Sept. 1-15	Sept. 1-Dec. 1	Sept. 1-Dec. 31	Sept. 1-Dec. 31	Sept. 1-Dec. 31
Cabbage, Chinese	Aug. 1-Sept. 15	Aug. 15-Oct. 1	Sept. 1-Oct. 15	Sept. 1-Nov. 15	Sept. 1-Nov. 15	Sept. 15-Dec. 1
Carrot	July 1-Aug. 15	Aug. 1-Sept. 1	Sept. 1-Nov. 1	Sept. 15-Dec. 1	Sept. 15-Dec. 1	Sept. 15-Dec. 1
Cauliflower*	July 15-Aug. 15	Aug. 1-Sept. 1	Aug. 1-Sept. 15	Aug. 15-Oct. 10	Sept. 15-Oct. 20	Sept. 15-Nov. 1
Celery* and celeriac	June 15-Aug. 15	July 1-Aug. 15	Aug. 1-Sept. 1	Aug. 15-Oct. 31	Sept. 1-Dec. 1	Oct. 1-Dec. 31
Chard	June 1-Sept. 10	June 1-Sept. 15	July 15-Sept. 1	Aug. 1-Nov. 1	June 1-Dec. 1	June 1-Dec. 31
Chervil and chives	(†)	(†)	June 1-Oct. 1	June 1-Nov. 1	Nov. 1-Dec. 31	Nov. 1-Dec. 31
Chicory, witloof	July 10-Aug. 20	July 10-Aug. 20	July 20-Sept. 1	Aug. 15-Sept. 30	Aug. 15-Oct. 15	Aug. 15-Oct. 15
Collards*	Aug. 15-Oct. 1	Aug. 15-Oct. 1	Aug. 25-Nov. 1	Sept. 1-Dec. 1	Sept. 1-Dec. 31	Sept. 1-Dec. 31
Corn salad	Sept. 15-Nov. 1	Oct. 1-Dec. 1	Oct. 1-Dec. 1	Oct. 1-Dec. 1	Oct. 1-Dec. 31	Oct. 1-Dec. 31
Corn, sweet	June 1-Aug. 1	June 1-Aug. 15	June 1-Sept. 1	June 1-Sept. 1	—	—
Cress, upland	Sept. 15-Nov. 1	Sept. 15-Nov. 1	Oct. 1-Dec. 1	Oct. 1-Dec. 1	Oct. 1-Dec. 31	Oct. 1-Dec. 31
Cucumber	June 1-Aug. 15	June 1-Aug. 15	June 1-Aug. 15	June 1-Aug. 15	Aug. 15-Oct. 1	Aug. 15-Oct. 1
Eggplant*	June 1-July 1	June 1-July 15	June 1-Aug. 1	July 1-Sept. 1	Aug. 1-Sept. 1	Aug. 1-Sept. 30
Endive	July 15-Aug. 15	Aug. 1-Sept. 15	Sept. 1-Oct. 1	Sept. 1-Nov. 15	Sept. 1-Dec. 31	Sept. 1-Dec. 31

SOURCE: *Growing Vegetables in Home Gardens* (Washington, D.C.: U.S. Department of Agriculture).

(continued)

Latest Dates, and Range of Dates, for the Safe Fall Planting of Vegetables in the Open—Continued

Crop	Planting Dates for Localities in Which Average Date of First Freeze Is—					
	Oct. 30	Nov. 10	Nov. 20	Nov. 30	Dec. 10	Dec. 20
Fennel, Florence	July 1-Aug. 1	July 15-Aug. 15	Aug. 15-Sept. 15	Sept. 1-Nov. 15	Sept. 1-Dec. 1	Sept. 1-Dec. 1
Garlic	(†)	Aug. 1-Oct. 1	Aug. 15-Oct. 1	Sept. 1-Nov. 15	Sept. 15-Nov. 15	Sept. 15-Nov. 15
Horseradish*	(†)	(†)	(†)	(†)	(†)	(†)
Kale	July 15-Sept. 1	Aug. 1-Sept. 15	Aug. 15-Oct. 15	Sept. 1-Dec. 1	Sept. 1-Dec. 31	Sept. 1-Dec. 31
Kohlrabi	Aug. 1-Sept. 1	Aug. 15-Sept. 15	Sept. 1-Oct. 15	Sept. 1-Dec. 1	Sept. 15-Dec. 31	Sept. 1-Dec. 31
Leek	(†)	(†)	Sept. 1-Nov. 1	Sept. 1-Nov. 1	Sept. 1-Nov. 1	Sept. 15-Nov. 1
Lettuce, head*	Aug. 1-Sept. 15	Aug. 15-Oct. 15	Sept. 1-Nov. 1	Sept. 1-Dec. 1	Sept. 15-Dec. 31	Sept. 15-Dec. 31
Lettuce, leaf	Aug. 15-Oct. 1	Aug. 25-Oct. 1	Sept. 1-Nov. 1	Sept. 1-Dec. 1	Sept. 15-Dec. 31	Sept. 15-Dec. 31
Muskmelon	July 1-July 15	July 15-July 30	—	—	—	—
Mustard	Aug. 15-Oct. 15	Aug. 15-Nov. 1	Sept. 1-Dec. 1	Sept. 1-Dec. 1	Sept. 1-Dec. 1	Sept. 15-Dec. 1
Okra	June 1-Aug. 10	June 1-Aug. 20	June 1-Sept. 10	June 1-Sept. 20	Aug. 1-Oct. 1	Aug. 1-Oct. 1
Onion*	—	Sept. 1-Oct. 15	Oct. 1-Dec. 31	Oct. 1-Dec. 31	Oct. 1-Dec. 31	Oct. 1-Dec. 31
Onion, seed	—	—	Sept. 1-Nov. 1	Sept. 1-Nov. 1	Sept. 1-Nov. 1	Sept. 15-Nov. 1
Onion, sets	—	Oct. 1-Dec. 1	Nov. 1-Dec. 31	Nov. 1-Dec. 31	Nov. 1-Dec. 31	Nov. 1-Dec. 31
Parsley	Aug. 1-Sept. 15	Sept. 1-Nov. 15	Sept. 1-Dec. 31	Sept. 1-Dec. 31	Sept. 1-Dec. 31	Sept. 1-Dec. 31
Parsnip	(†)	(†)	Aug. 1-Sept. 1	Sept. 1-Dec. 1	Oct. 1-Dec. 1	Sept. 1-Dec. 1
Peas, garden	Aug. 1-Sept. 15	Sept. 1-Nov. 1	Oct. 1-Dec. 1	Oct. 1-Dec. 31	Oct. 1-Dec. 31	Oct. 1-Dec. 31
Peas, blackeye	June 1-Aug. 1	June 15-Aug. 15	July 1-Sept. 1	July 1-Sept. 10	July 1-Sept. 20	July 1-Sept. 20
Pepper*	June 1-July 20	June 1-Aug. 1	June 1-Aug. 15	June 15-Sept. 1	Aug. 15-Oct. 1	Aug. 15-Oct. 1
Potato	July 20-Aug. 10	July 25-Aug. 20	Aug. 10-Sept. 15	Aug. 1-Sept. 15	Aug. 1-Sept. 15	Aug. 1-Sept. 15
Radish	Aug. 15-Oct. 15	Sept. 1-Nov. 15	Sept. 1-Dec. 1	Sept. 1-Dec. 31	Oct. 1-Dec. 1	Oct. 1-Dec. 31
Rhubarb*	Nov. 1-Dec. 1	Oct. 15-Nov. 15	—	—	—	—
Rutabaga	July 15-Aug. 1	July 15-Aug. 15	Aug. 1-Sept. 15	Sept. 1-Nov. 15	Oct. 1-Nov. 15	Oct. 15-Nov. 15
Salsify	June 1-July 10	June 15-July 20	July 15-Aug. 15	Aug. 15-Sept. 30	Aug. 15-Oct. 15	Sept. 1-Oct. 31
Shallot	(†)	Aug. 1-Oct. 1	Aug. 15-Oct. 15	Aug. 15-Oct. 15	Sept. 15-Nov. 1	Sept. 15-Nov. 1
Sorrel	Aug. 1-Sept. 15	Aug. 15-Oct. 1	Sept. 1-Nov. 15	Sept. 1-Nov. 15	Sept. 1-Dec. 15	Sept. 1-Dec. 31
Soybean	June 1-July 15	June 1-July 25	June 1-July 30	June 1-July 30	June 1-July 30	June 1-July 30
Spinach	Sept. 1-Oct. 1	Sept. 15-Nov. 1	Oct. 1-Dec. 1	Oct. 1-Dec. 31	Oct. 1-Dec. 31	Oct. 1-Dec. 31
Spinach, New Zealand	June 1-Aug. 1	June 1-Aug. 15	—	—	—	—
Squash, summer	June 1-Aug. 1	June 1-Aug. 10	June 1-Aug. 15	June 1-Sept. 1	June 1-Sept. 15	June 1-Oct. 1
Squash, winter	June 10-July 10	June 20-July 20	July 1-Aug. 1	July 15-Aug. 15	Aug. 1-Sept. 1	Aug. 1-Sept. 1
Sweet potato	June 1-15	June 1-July 10	June 1-July 1	June 1-July 1	June 1-July 1	June 1-July 1
Tomato	June 1-July 1	June 1-July 15	June 1-Aug. 1	Aug. 1-Sept. 1	Aug. 15-Oct. 1	Sept. 1-Nov. 1
Turnip	Aug. 1-Sept. 15	Sept. 1-Nov. 15	Sept. 1-Nov. 15	Sept. 1-Nov. 15	Oct. 1-Dec. 1	Oct. 1-Dec. 31
Watermelon	July 1-July 15	July 15-July 30	—	—	—	—

*Transplants.
†Generally spring planted.

Appendix D

Vegetable Planting Guide

	Seed germination temperature range (°F)	Optimum growing temperature (°F)	Max./min. growing temperature (°F)	Planting method	Number of days for seed to germinate	Weeks to transplant	Days to maturity	Plant outside 4 to 6 weeks before last frost	Plant outside 2 to 4 weeks before last frost	Plant outside after last frost	Seed planting depth (in.)	Spacing between plants (in.)	Plants needed per person	Number of plants per square foot, or space needed per plant
Artichoke	50 to 85	65	45 to 75	*	7 to 15	4 to 6	na	x			½	36 to 48	1	3 to 4 sq ft. per plant
Asparagus	na	65	30 to 85	†	na	na	3 yr.	see text			1½	12 to 18	20	1 to 2
Beans — Dry, shell	65 to 75	85	60 to 90	‡	7 to 15	4 to 6	60 to 100			x	1 to 2	3 to 4	15 to 45	12 to 16
Beans — Fava	50 to 85	65	40 to 75	§	6 to 15	na	80 to 95		x		2½	3 to 5	15 to 30	9 to 12
Beans — Lima bush	65 to 85	85	60 to 90	‡	7 to 13	4 to 6	60 to 80			x	1½ to 2	6 to 8	15	4
Beans — Lima pole	65 to 85	85	60 to 90	‡	7 to 13	4 to 6	85 to 90			x	1½ to 2	8 to 10	12 to 15	2 to 3
Beans — Snap bush	65 to 85	85	60 to 90	‡	7 to 15	4 to 6	45 to 65			x	1 to 2	3 to 4	15 to 45	9 to 12
Beans — Snap pole	65 to 85	85	60 to 90	‡	7 to 15	4 to 6	60 to 70			x	1 to 2	6 to 8	12 to 15	4
Beans — Soybean	65 to 85	85	60 to 90	‡	6 to 14	4 to 6	60 to 100			x	1½ to 2	2 to 4	15 to 30	16 to 30
Beets	50 to 85	65	40 to 75	§	8 to 11	na	50 to 70		x		1½ to 1	3	40	36
Broccoli	50 to 85	65	40 to 75	†	4 to 10	5 to 7	60 to 90	x			½	12 to 16	2	1
Brussels sprouts	50 to 85	65	40 to 75	†	4 to 10	4 to 6	70 to 130	x			½	12 to 18	1 to 3	1 to 2
Cabbage	50 to 85	65	40 to 75	†	4 to 10	5 to 7	65 to 110	x			½	12 to 18	3 to 4	1 to 2
Cabbage, Chinese	50 to 85	65	40 to 75	‡	4 to 10	4 to 7	75 to 90			x	½	10 to 12	3 to 4	1 to 2

(continued)

SOURCE: Adapted from Growing Vegetables in Home Gardens (Washington, D.C.: U.S. Department of Agriculture).

Vegetable Planting Guide — *Continued*

	Seed germination temperature range (°F)	Optimum growing temperature (°F)	Max./min. growing temperature (°F)	Planting method	Number of days for seed to germinate	Weeks to transplant	Days to maturity	Plant outside 4 to 6 weeks before last frost	Plant outside 2 to 4 weeks before last frost	Plant outside after last frost	Seed planting depth (in.)	Spacing between plants (in.)	Plants needed per person	Number of plants per square foot, or space needed per plant
Cardoon	50 to 85	65	45 to 75	†	7 to 14	7 to 8	110 to 150		x		½	14 to 18	1	1 to 2
Carrot	50 to 85	65	45 to 75	§	12 to 25	na	60 to 80		x		¼	1 to 2	60 to 90	40 to 144
Cauliflower	50 to 85	65	45 to 75	†	5 to 10	5 to 7	60 to 75		x		½	12 to 18	2 to 3	1 to 2
Celeriac	50 to 65	65	45 to 75	†	10 to 20	10 to 12	90 to 120	x			½	4 to 8	20	4 to 9
Celery	50 to 65	65	45 to 75	†	10 to 20	10 to 12	90 to 120		x		⅛	6 to 8	2 to 3	4
Collards	50 to 85	60	40 to 75	‡	5 to 10	4 to 6	70 to 80		x		¼	12	3 to 5	1
Corn salad	50 to 85	65	45 to 75	§	6 to 10	na	45 to 55		x		½	4 to 6	2 to 3	5 to 9
Corn, sweet	65 to 85	80	50 to 90	‡	6 to 10	4	60 to 100			x	1 to 2	8	10 to 15	4
Cress, garden	50 to 85	60	45 to 75	§	5 to 10	na	30 to 45		x		¼	2 to 3	5 to 10	16 to 36
Cucumber	65 to 85	80	60 to 90	‡	5 to 11	4 to 5	50 to 70			x	1	6	2 to 3	4 to 5
Dandelion	50 to 85	60	40 to 75	‡	10 to 15	4 to 6	75 to 90	x			½	8	2 to 3	4
Eggplant	65 to 85	80	65 to 95	†	8 to 15	6 to 9	75 to 85			x	¼ to ½	24 to 30	1 to 2	4
Endive/ Escarole	50 to 85	60	45 to 75	‡	5 to 9	4 to 6	60 to 90	x			¼ to ½	8 to 9	4 to 8	2
Florence fennel	50 to 85	60	45 to 75	†	5 to 16	na	90		x		¼ to ½	6 to 8	1	4
Garlic	50 to 85	70	45 to 85	Sets	6 to 10	na	90	x			1 to 1½	3	5 to 8	16

	Seed germination temperature range (°F)	Optimum growing temperature (°F)	Max./min. growing temperature (°F)	Planting method	Number of days for seed to germinate	Weeks to transplant	Days to maturity	Plant outside 4 to 6 weeks before last frost	Plant outside 2 to 4 weeks before last frost	Plant outside after last frost	Seed planting depth (in.)	Spacing between plants (in.)	Plants needed per person	Number of plants per square foot, or space needed per plant
Horseradish	50 to 85	60	40 to 75	roots	na	na	6 to 8 mo.	see text			2	6 to 8	2 to 3	2 to 4
Kale	50 to 85	60	40 to 75	‡	3 to 10	4 to 6	60 to 80	x			½	8 to 10	2 to 4	4
Kohlrabi	50 to 85	60	40 to 75	‡	3 to 10	4 to 6	50 to 70	x			½	4 to 6	5 to 6	6 to 9
Leeks	50 to 85	70	45 to 85	‡	5 to 10	10 to 12	80 to 100	x			½ to 1	2 to 6	6 to 10	4 to 36
Lettuce head	50 to 65	65	45 to 75	‡‡	5 to 8	3 to 4	60 to 80	x			¼	8 to 12	3 to 4	2 to 4
Lettuce leaf	50 to 65	65	45 to 75	‡‡	5 to 8	3 to 4	45 to 60	x			¼	4 to 6	2 to 2	4 to 16
Muskmelon	55 to 85	75 to 90	60 to 90	‡	3 to 9	3 to 5	70 to 100			x	1	12	2 to 4	1
Mustard	50 to 75	45 to 75	60	‡	4 to 10	3 to 4	50		x		½	3 to 6	4 to 6	6 to 16
Okra	65 to 85	85	65 to 95	§	8 to 12	na	55 to 70			x	1	15 to 18	1 to 2	1 to 3
Onion seed / sets / plants	50 to 65	65	45 to 85	‡	6 to 10	6 to 8	95 to 150	x			½ / 1 to 2 / 2 to 3	3 to 4	20 to 50	16 to 36
Parsnips	50 to 85	65	40 to 75	§	20	na	100 to 125	x			½	3 to 4	15 to 20	9 to 16
Peas	50 to 65	65	45 to 75	‡	5 to 12	3 to 4	60 to 90	x			2	2 to 3	90	16 to 36
Peppers	65 to 85	75	65 to 80	†	12 to 18	6 to 8	60 to 80			x	½	12 to 24	1 to 2	1 to 4
Potato	50 to 85	65	45 to 75	*§	9 to 15	na	100 to 115		x		4 see text	4 to 10	10 to 20	9

(continued)

Vegetable Planting Guide — Continued

	Seed germination temperature range (°F)	Optimum growing temperature (°F)	Max./min. growing temperature (°F)	Planting method	Number of days for seed to germinate	Weeks to transplant	Days to maturity	Plant outside 4 to 6 weeks before last frost	Plant outside 2 to 4 weeks before last frost	Plant outside after last frost	Seed planting depth (in.)	Spacing between plants (in.)	Plants needed per person	Number of plants per square foot, or space needed per plant
Pumpkin	65 to 85	80	50 to 90	‡	6 to 12	6 to 8	70 to 120			x	1 to 1½	18	1	1 to 4
Radish	50 to 65	60	40 to 75	§	3 to 10	na	20 to 60	x			½	1 to 2	30 to 60	36 to 144
Rhubarb	50 to 85	65	30 to 85	*†	na	na	2 yr.		see text		3 to 4	12 to 36	1	1 to 8
Rutabaga	50 to 85	60	40 to 75	§	4 to 8	na	80 to 90	x			½	6 to 10	5 to 10	2 to 4
Salsify	50 to 65	65	45 to 85	§	7 to 14	na	115 to 145	x			½	2 to 3	15 to 20	16 to 36
Shallot	50 to 85	65	45 to 85	*§	—	na	90 to 110	x			1*	2 to 4	4 to 10	9 to 36
Spinach	50 to 65	60	40 to 75	§	5 to 12	na	40 to 65	x			½	3 to 6	5 to 10	6 to 16
Malabar	50 to 85	75	50 to 95	§	8 to 10	na	70			x	½	8	5 to 10	2 to 3
New Zealand	50 to 85	75	50 to 95	‡	7 to 10	4 to 6	70 to 80			x	½	12	5	1
Squash summer	65 to 85	75	50 to 90	‡	4 to 11	4 to 8	45 to 65			x	1	12	1 to 2 per type	1
Squash winter	65 to 85	75	50 to 90	‡	4 to 11	4 to 8	80 to 110			x	1	12 to 24	1 to 2 per type	1 or more
Sweet potato	65 to 85	85	65 to 95	*§	na	na	120			x	see text	12 to 18	2 to 3	1 or more
Swiss chard	50 to 85	60	40 to 75	§	8 to 10	na	55 to 70		x		½	6	10 to 15	6
Tomato	65 to 85	75	65 to 80	†	5 to 12	5 to 7	55 to 90			x	½	18	1 to 2	2 or more
Turnip	50 to 65	60	40 to 75	§	4 to 10	na	35 to 60	x			½	2 to 3	15 to 30	16 to 36
Watermelon	65 to 85	80	65 to 90	‡	3 to 14	4 to 6	80 to 100			x	1	12	1	1

*Start from root cuttings, slips, crowns, or tubers. †Transplant seedlings into the garden. ‡Transplant or direct seed. §Sow seed directly into the garden.
naNot applicable. see text.

SOURCES OF SEEDS AND SUPPLIES

SEED CATALOGS

1 Abundant Life Seed Foundation
P.O. Box 772
Port Townsend, WA 98368

Offers many open pollinated varieties, member-
ship in the foundation and an apprentice program.
Bulk seed available.

2 Allen, Sterling & Lothrop
191 U.S. Rte. 1
Falmouth, ME 04105
(207) 781-4142

Complete general list plus information on soil
improvement, Garden supplies, items for the
organic gardener.

3 Archia's Seed Store
P.O. Box 109
Sedalia, MO 65301

Varieties for Midwest gardeners. Good selection
of garden supplies.

4 The Banana Tree
715 Northhampton St.
Easton, PA 18042

A selection of Chinese vegetable seed, exotic
varieties, many banana varieties.

5 Burgess Seed and Plant Co.
Dept. 89
905 Four Seasons Rd.
Bloomington, IL 61701

A number of unusual items, garden supplies.

6 W. Atlee Burpee Co.
300 Park Ave.
Warminster, PA 18991

A good list of vegetables, garden supplies.

7 D. V. Burrell Seed Growers
Rocky Ford, CO 81067
(303) 254-3318

Primarily sells to commercial growers, but also
serves home gardeners, with garden supplies,
planting information.

8 Comstock, Ferre & Co.
P.O. Box 124
Wethersfield, CT 06109

Vegetable and herb list, planting instructions.

9 Dan's Garden Shop
5821 Woodwinds Circle
Frederick, MD 21701

Offers good planting information, many hybrid
varieties.

10 DeGiorgi Co.
1411 Third St.
Council Bluffs, IA 51502

Very complete vegetables list, some novelties,
planting instructions.

11 Early's Farm & Garden Centre
Box 3024
Saskatoon, Saskatchewan
S7K 3S9

Good small catalog, garden supplies.

12 Farmer Seed and Nursery
2207 E. Oakland Ave.
Bloomington, IL 61701

Complete catalog, many new varieties, special
selections, good choice of hardy varieties, many
aids for home gardeners.

13 Henry Field's Seed & Nursery Co.
Shenandoah, IA 51602

Large full-color catalog, good vegetable and herb list, gardening aids.

14 Fisher's Garden Store
P.O. Box 236
Belgrade, MT 59714

Small catalog, with a selection of vegetable seed for high altitudes and short growing seasons.

15 Garden City Seeds
P.O. Box 297
Victor, MT 59875

Open pollinated varieties for northern climates, information on companion planting, soil planting temperatures, culture.

16 Gleckler's Seedmen
Metamora, OH 43540

Small catalog of unusual seeds.

17 Gurney Seed and Nursery Co.
Yankton, SD 57079

Large catalog contains many varieties, good selection of garden supplies.

18 Harris Moran Seed Co.
Eastern Operations
3670 Buffalo Rd.
Rochester, NY 14624

Western Operations
1155 Harkins Rd.
Salinas, CA 93901

Intended for commercial vegetable growers. Excellent variety charts, good full-color illustrations. Seed sold only in fairly large quantities.

19 Herb Gathering
5742 Kenwood
Kansas City, MO 64110

French vegetables, herbs and a selection of flowers for drying.

20 High Altitude Gardens
P.O. Box 4238
Ketchum, ID 83340

Unusual catalog, tabloid size, well illustrated,
good selection, organic supplies, many aids for
the home gardener.

21 Horticultural Enterprises
P.O. Box 810082
Dallas, TX 75381

One sheet illustrated, containing 41 chili pepper
varieties.

22 J. L. Hudson, Seedsman
P.O. Box 1058
Redwood City, CA 94064

Complete catalog, many varieties of flowers and
vegetables, offers a great deal of information.

23 Ed Hume, Seeds
P.O. Box 1450
Kent, WA 98032

Untreated seeds, some varieties for short season
areas and Alaska.

24 Le Jardin du Gourmet
West Danville, VT 05873

Seeds from France, herbs, small 22-cent seed
packets.

25 Johnny's Selected Seeds
305 Foss Hill Rd.
Albion, ME 04910

Strictly organic gardening, good planting
instructions, germination guides.

26 Jung's Seeds & Nursery
335 S. High St.
Randolph, WI 53597

Large, full-color catalog, good selection of
vegetables, garden supplies.

27 Kitazawa Seed Co.
1748 Laine Ave.
Santa Clara, CA 95051

Small catalog of oriental seeds.

28 Lagomarsion Seeds
5675-A Power Inn Rd.
Sacramento, CA 95824

Small list, no descriptions, has some hard-to-find
varieties.

29 Orol Ledden and Sons
Sewell, NJ 08080

General catalog of seeds and garden supplies.

30 Letherman Seed Co.
1221 Tuscarawas St. E
Canton, OH 44707

Not a home gardener's catalog, but does sell
seeds in fairly small quantities, garden supplies.

31 Le Marche Seeds International
P.O. Box 190
Dixon, CA 95620

Highly creative catalog with a good list of
European and gourmet vegetables. Send for this
one if you don't order any of the others.

32 Earl May Seed & Nursery
Shenandoah, IA 51603

Offers seed collections, like snap peas, "Grandma's
choice" of cucumbers, many garden aids, gardening tips.

33 Meyer Seed Co.
600 S. Caroline St.
Baltimore, MD 21231

Good variety charts, herbs, garden supplies.

34 Midwest Seed Growers
505 Walnut St.
Kansas City, MO 64106

Vegetables listed alphabetically.

35 Nichols Garden Nursery
1190 N. Pacific Hwy.
Albany, OR 97321

Gourmet vegetable seeds from around the world,
herbs, garden aids, wine-making supplies

36 George W. Park Seed Co.
Greenwood, SC 29647

One of the best general catalogs, offers many
special varieties, herbs, garden supplies.

37 The Pepper Gal
10536 119th Ave. N
Largo, FL 34643

Good selection of peppers, no descriptions.

38 Piedmont Plant Co.
P.O. Box 424
Albany, GA 31703

Offers plants of a number of vegetables.

39 Pinetree Garden Seeds
New Gloucester, ME 04260

Mostly untreated seed, many vegetable varieties,
herbs, oriental, continental, and Latin American
vegetables, others from around the world.

40 Porter & Son, Seedsmen
P.O. Box 104
Stephenville, TX 76401

New varieties, many varieties suited to southern
climates, a good selection of garden supplies,
unusual varieties.

41 Redwood City Seed Co.
P.O. Box 361
Redwood City, CA 94064

Open pollinated varieties, also contains fruits,
nuts, berries and other plants such as sequoia.

42 Rispens, Martin & Sons
3332 Ridge Rd. (rear)
Lansing, IL 60438

Seeds for market gardeners.

43 Rosewell Seed Co.
    115–117 S. Main
    Roswell, NM 88201

    Special attention to varieties suited to the Southwest.

44 Seeds Blum
    Idaho City Stage
    Boise, ID 83706

    Interesting catalog offers heirloom varieties, special garden collections, garden-to-garden network.

45 Seedway Seed
    Hall, NY 14463

    Includes many new items each year.

46 Shepherd's Garden Seeds
    7389 W. Zayante Rd.
    Felton, CA 95018

    European vegetable varieties, herbs, excellent drawings, a baby vegetable collection.

47 Southern Exposure Seed Exchange
    P.O. Box 158
    North Garden, VA 22959

    Heirloom varieties suited to the mid-Atlantic region, planting calendar ($2.00).

48 Stokes Seeds
    Box 548
    Buffalo, NY 14240

    Over 500 varieties, European varieties, garden supplies, emphasis on short-season northern strains.

49 Sunrise Enterprises
    P.O. Box 1058
    Elmwood, CT 06110

    Very complete collection of oriental vegetables, some garden supplies.

50 Territorial Seed Co.
    P.O. Box 27
    Lorane, OR 97451

    Good selection of seeds that grow well in the maritime weather west of the Cascades in Oregon and Washington.

51 Thompson & Morgan
    P.O. Box 1308
    Jackson, NJ 08527

    Varieties from all over the world.

52 Tillinghast Seed Co.
    P.O. Box 4738
    La Conner, WA 98257

    Specializes in varieties suited to northwest climates.

53 Tsang and Ma International
    P.O. Box 294
    Belmont, CA 94002

    A fair collection of oriental seeds, plus everything
    you need for a Chinese kitchen.

54 Otis Twilley Seed Co.
    P.O. Box 65
    Trevose, PA 19047

    Catalog features varieties, selection for all states.

55 Wetsel Seed Co.
    P.O. Box 791
    Harrisonburg, VA 22801

    Good selection of vegetables, special varieties,
    garden supplies.

56 Wilhite Seed Co.
    P.O. Box 23
    Poolville, TX 76076

    Offers a small garden pack, many large prize-
    winning varieties, good watermelon selection.

57 William Dam Seeds
    Box 8400
    Dundas, Ontario
    L9H 6M1

    Many varieties, garden supplies.

58 Wyatt-Quarles Seed Co.
    P.O. Box 739
    Garner, NC 27529

    Good selection of vegetables for southern climates.

SUPPLIERS OF BENEFICIAL INSECTS

Allan's Aquarium and Exotic Birds
Yankton, SD 57079
Fly parasites, lacewings, ladybugs, praying mantids

Bio-Control Co.
Rte. 2, Box 2397
Auburn, CA 95603
Ladybugs, praying mantids

W. Atlee Burpee Co.
Warminster, PA 18974
Fly parasites, green lacewings, ladybugs, praying
mantis egg cases, trichogramma wasps

California Green Lacewings
P.O. Box 2495
Merced, CA 95340
Lacewings, trichogramma wasps

Connecticut Valley Biological Supply Co.
Valley Rd.
South Hampton, MA 01073
Damselfly nymphs, dragonfly nymphs

Eastern Biological Control Co.
Rte. 5, Box 379
Jacksoon, NJ 08527
Praying mantids

Gothard
P.O. Box 370
Canutillo, TX 79835
Praying mantids, trichogramma wasps, whitefly
parasites

Gurney Seed and Nursery Co.
Yankton, SD 57079
Mealybug destroyers, parasitic wasps, predatory
mites, whitefly parasites

Henry Field Seed and Nursery Co.
Shenandoah, IA
Ladybugs, green lacewings, praying mantids,
trichogramma wasps

King Labs
P.O. Box 69
Limerick, PA 19468
Green lacewings, praying mantids

Lakeland Nursery Sales
340 Poplar
Hanover, PA 17331
Ladybugs, praying mantids

Natural Pest Controls
8864 Little Creek Dr.
Orangevale, CA 95662
Green lacewings, ladybugs, mealybug destroyers,
parasitic wasps, predatory mites, whitefly parasites

Nature's Control
P.O. Box 35
Medford, OR 97501
Green lacewings, ladybugs, mealybug destroyers,
parasitic wasps, predatory mites

Organic Pest Management
Box 55267
Seattle, WA 98135
Green lacewings, ladybugs

Rincon Vitova Insectaries
P.O. Box 95
Oak View, CA 93022
Fly parasites, lacewing flies, ladybugs, trichogramma
wasps

Robert Robbins
424 N. Courtland St.
East Stroudsburg, PA 18301
Praying mantids

Unique Insect Controls
P.O. Box 15376
Sacramento, CA 95851
Green lacewings, ladybugs, mealybug destroyers,
parasitic wasps, predatory mites, whitefly parasites

CATALOG SOURCES OF GARDEN SUPPLIES

Numbers correspond to companies listed under Seed Catalogs, p. 241.

Animal controls, netting
7, 11, 13, 26, 36, 54, 55, 57

Cloches, hotcaps
7, 5, 11, 12, 17, 20, 25, 35, 47, 54, 57

Coldframes
7, 17, 26, 36

Compost bins
7, 13, 35

Compost makers
6, 11, 17, 36, 48

Containers
6, 11, 17, 33, 48, 55

Garden tools
33, 35, 48, 54, 55

Organic insect controls
6, 17, 13, 20, 25, 26, 35, 50, 55, 57

Organic nutrients
2, 13, 20, 35, 50, 54, 55, 57

pH testers
6, 11, 12, 13, 36, 40, 54

Planting cubes, trays
2, 5, 8, 11, 13, 17, 25, 26, 32, 33,
35, 36, 40, 48, 54, 57

Plant lights
11, 36

Plant supports, cages
7, 11, 13, 26, 36, 54, 55, 57

Plastic mulches
7, 13, 26, 33, 55

Protective nets
5, 11, 13, 17

Shredders
7

Soil heating cables
11, 13, 17, 55

Soil thermometers
7, 5, 13

Watering accessories
7, 17, 25, 26, 32, 33, 36, 40, 47, 48,
50, 55

SUPPLIERS OF TILLERS

AMCA International
Consumer Products Div.
2701 Industrial Dr.
Bowling Green, KY 42101

Allis-Chalmers Corp.
Lawn & Garden Equipment
P.O. Box 512
Milwaukee WI 53201

American Honda Motor Co.
P.O. Box 50
Gardena, CA 90247

Ariens Co.
655 W. Ryan St.
Brillion, WI 54110

Atlas Power Equipment Co.
201 E. Brink St.
Harvard, IL 60033

BCS Mosa
P.O. Box 7628
Charlotte NC 28217

Baird-Poulan
Weed Eater Div.
Emerson Electric Co.
5020 Flourny-Lucas Rd.
Shreveport, LA 71129

Banton Industries
Merry Tiller
P.O. Box 11406
Birmingham, AL 36202

C. S. Bell Co.
170 W. Davis St.
Tiffon, OH 44883

Bolens Corp.
215 S. Park
Port Washington, WI 53074

Borg-Warner Acceptance Corp.
225 N. Michigan Ave.
Chicago, IL 60601

Burns Outdoor Power Equipment Div.
Gilson Brothers
P.O. Box 152
Plymouth, WI 53073

Canadian Outdoor Products
155 Orenda Rd.
Brampton, Ontario
L6W 1W3

Carter Bros. Mfg. Co.
Hwy. 231 S
Brundidge, AL 36010

Central States
Mainline
Rotary Tiller
Distributors
P.O. Box 348
London, OH 43140

Clark Mfg. Co.
1718 Hwy. 138 E
Conyers, GA 30208

Clinton Engineering Corp.
Clark & Maple Sts.
Maquoketa, IA 52060

The Coleman Garden
Plow Mfg. Co.
1044 McCarly St.
Dunedin, FL 33528

Dynamark Corp.
165 W. Chicago Ave.
Chicago, IL 60610

Feldmann Engineering &
Manufacturing Co.
639 Monroe St.
Sheboygan Falls, WI 53085

Ferrari Maschio
116 Paoli St.
Verona, WI 53593

Flymo
P.O. Box 1980
Mansfield, OH 44901

Fuerst Brother
P.O. Box 356
Oregon, IL 61061

Gilson Bros.
P.O. Box 152
Plymouth, WI 53073

The Green Machine
2206 Montgomery St.
Silver Springs, MD 20910

Haban Mfg. Co.
2100 Northwestern Ave.
Racine, WI 53404

Heald
P.O. Box 1148
Benton Harbor, MI 49022

Howard Rotavator Co.
P.O. Box 7
Muscoda, WI 53573

Impex International
1824 E. Main St.
Spartanburg, SC 29302

Kaaz American Corp.
10035 S. Pioneer Blvd.
Santa Fe Springs, CA 90670

Kemp Co.
160 Koser Rd.
Lititz, PA 17543

The Kinsman Co.
River Rd.
Point Pleasant, PA 18950

Lely Corp.
P.O. Box 1060
Wilson, NC 27893

Little Wonder Div.
Schiller-Pfeiffer
1028 Street Rd.
Southampton, PA 18966

MTD Products
P.O. Box 36900
Cleveland, OH 44136

Maxium Mfg. Corp.
P.O. Drawer A
Sebastopol, MS 39359

Mobility Unlimited
P.O. Box 100
Raymond, MS 39154

Mono Manufacturing Co.
P.O. Box 2787
Springfield, MO 65803

Parmi Tool Co.
P.O. Box 326
Lynn, IN 47355

Roper Outdoor Power Equipment
P.O. 867
Kankakee, IL 60901

Simplicity Mfg. Co.
500 N. Spring St.
Port Washington, WI 53074

Solo
5100 Chestnut Ave.
Newport News, VA 23605

Trans Sphere Corp.
P.O. Box 1564
Mobile, AL 36633

Tru-Cut
3221 San Fernando Rd.
Los Angeles, CA 90065

United Farm Tools
4540 W. Washington St.
Charleston, WV 25313

Utility Tool & Body Co.
P.O. Box 360
Clintonville, WI 54229

W. W. Grainger
2011 C Ave.
Bethlehem, PA 18017

White Outdoor Products
White Farm Equipment
2625 Butterfield Rd.
Oak Brook, IL 60521

SUPPLIERS OF SHREDDERS

Amerind-MacKissic
P.O. Box 111
Parker Ford, PA 19457

Barclay Rothschild Mfg.
949 Wilson Ave.
Downsview, Toronto
M3K 1G2

The Bell C.S. Co.
170 W. Davis St.
Tiffin, OH 44883

Flowtron Div.
Armstrong International
2 Main St.
Melrose, MA 02176

Lindig Mfg. Corp.
1875 W. Country Rd.
St. Paul, MN 55113

MTD Products
P.O. Box 36900
Cleveland, OH 44136

National Greenhouse Co.
400 E. Main St.
Pana, IL 62557

Piqua Engineering
P.O. Box 605
Piqua, OH 45356

Promark Products
306 9th
Industry, CA 91746

The Roto-Hoe Co.
100 Auburn Rd.
Newbury, OH 44065

Rover-Scott Bonner
P.O. Box 292
Allendale, NJ 07401

Rover Founder & Machine Co.
158 Pringle St.
Kingston, PA 18704

SGK
2 Davis Ave.
Fraizer, PA 19355

Sterling Associates
687 Seville Rd.
Wadsworth, OH 44281

Trans-Sphere Corp.
P.O. Box 1564
Mobile, AL 36633

W-W Grinder
P.O. Box 4029
Wichita, KS 67204

Wheel Horse Products
515 W. Ireland Rd.
South Bend, IN 46614

White Outdoor Products
White Farm Equipment
2625 Butterfield Rd.
Oak Brook, IL 60521

Winona Attrition Mill Co.
1009 W. 5th St.
Winona, MN 55987

Yard Man Co.
P.O. Box 36940
Cleveland, OH 44136

BIBLIOGRAPHY

Bartholomew, Mel. *Square Foot Gardening*. Emmaus. Pa.: Rodale Press, 1981.

Crockett, James Underwood. *Crockett's Victory Garden*. Boston: Little, Brown, 1977.

Halpin, Anne M., ed. *Unusual Vegetables*. Emmaus, Pa.: Rodale Press, 1978.

Hardigree, Peggy. *The Edible Indoor Garden*. New York: St. Martin's Press, 1980.

Jeavons, John. *How to Grow More Vegetables Than You Ever Thought Possible on Less Land Than You Can Imagine*. Rev. ed. Berkeley, Calif.: Ten Speed Press, 1982.

Moment, Barbara Chipman. *The Salad-Green Gardener*. Boston: Houghton Mifflin, 1977.

Newcomb, Duane. *The Complete Vegetable Gardener's Sourcebook*. New York: Avon Books, 1980.

Philbrick, Helen, and Gregg, Richard. *Companion Plants*. New York: Devin Adair, 1966.

Wallace, Dan, ed. *Getting the Most from Your Garden*. Emmaus, Pa.: Rodale Press, 1980.

Yepsen, Roger B., Jr., ed. *The Encyclopedia of Natural Insect & Disease Control*. Emmaus, Pa.: Rodale Press, 1984.

INDEX

Page references in *italics* indicate charts and tables. Page references in **boldface** indicate illustrations.

More Great Books from Prima:

The Natural Food Garden by Patrick Lima and John Scanlan $19.95

Learn how to make the most of the wonderful natural alternatives that
work just as well, and in most cases better, than chemical pesticides, fertilizers, or herbicides. A complete guide to growing your own nutritious and
delicious vegetables, legumes, herbs, and fruits. Step-by-step instructions
on all aspects of the natural food garden: soil supplements, composting,
cold frames, and space design.

*Pay Dirt: How to Raise and Sell Specialty Herbs and Vegetables
for Serious Cash* by Mimi Luebbermann $19.95

If you have a backyard or a porch, you can cash in on the growing need for
specialty produce. Pro Mimi Luebbermann explains everything the small-
time farmer needs to know: what to grow, how to grow it, and where to sell
it. Includes a complete bibliography.

The Best 125 Meatless Main Dishes $12.95
The Best 125 Meatless Pasta Dishes $12.95
by Mindy Toomay and Susann Geiskopf-Hadler

Tantalizing and healthy, these recipes use fresh ingredients in an innovative
way. The results are meatless dishes the whole family will enjoy.

Lean and Luscious and Meatless by Bobbie Hinman
and Millie Snyder $15.95

Over 400 recipes designed for today's low-fat, low cholesterol, high-fiber
lifestyle. Each recipe comes with an at-a-glance nutritional breakdown.
Spiral comb-bound for easy reading.

FILL IN AND MAIL TODAY

PRIMA PUBLISHING
P.O. BOX 1260BK
ROCKLIN, CA 95677

USE YOUR VISA/MC AND ORDER BY PHONE:
(916) 786-0426 (M-F 9-4 PST)

Dear People at Prima,
I'd like to order the following titles:

QUANTITY	TITLE	AMOUNT
_____	_____	_____
_____	_____	_____
_____	_____	_____
_____	_____	_____
_____	_____	_____

	Subtotal	_____
	Postage & Handling	4.00
	Sales Tax	_____
	TOTAL (U.S. funds only)	_____

☐ Check enclosed for $_____ (payable to Prima Publishing)

Charge my   ☐ Mastercard   ☐ Visa

Account No. _____ Exp. Date_____

Signature _____

Your Name _____

Address _____

City/State/Zip _____

Daytime Telephone _____

YOU MUST BE SATISFIED, OR YOUR MONEY BACK!!!
Thank You for Your Order

How did you hear about this book?   ☐ Bookstore   ☐ Other_____